Nov 27 1985

Dear Mommy,

Happy Thanksgiving! Here's what the
otters write about!

I love you,
Pat

The Great Cat Massacre

And Other Episodes in French Cultural History

THE GREAT
CAT MASSACRE
AND OTHER EPISODES
IN FRENCH
CULTURAL HISTORY

Robert Darnton

Vintage Books
A Division of Random House
New York

First Vintage Books Edition, February 1985
Copyright © 1984 by Basic Books, Inc.
All rights reserved under International and Pan-American
Copyright Conventions. Published in the United States by
Random House, Inc., New York, and simultaneously in Canada
by Random House of Canada Limited, Toronto. Originally
published by Basic Books, Inc., in 1984.

Library of Congress Cataloging in Publication Data
Darnton, Robert.
The great cat massacre and other episodes in
French cultural history.
Includes bibliographical references and index.
1. France—Civilization—17th-18th centuries—
Addresses, essays, lectures.
2. National characteristics, French—Addresses, essays, lectures.
3. Folklore—France—Addresses, essays, lectures.
I. Title. [DC33.4.D37 1984]   944′.034   84-40515
ISBN 0-394-72927-7 (pbk.)

Manufactured in the United States of America

for Nicholas

CONTENTS

LIST OF
ILLUSTRATIONS

ACKNOWLEDGMENTS

THIS BOOK grew out of a course, History 406, that I have offered at Princeton University since 1972. Originally an introduction to the history of *mentalités,* the course developed into a seminar on history and anthropology, thanks to the influence of Clifford Geertz, who has taught the course with me for the last six years and in doing so has taught me most of what I know about anthropology. I should like to express my gratitude to him and to our students. I also owe a great deal to the Institute for Advanced Study at Princeton, where I began writing this book as a member of a program on self-perception and historical change financed by the Andrew W. Mellon Foundation. And finally, I would like to thank the John D. and Catherine T. MacArthur Foundation whose award of a prize fellowship made it possible for me to suspend my normal work in order to follow up and finish what must have appeared to be a risky enterprise.

The Great Cat Massacre

And Other Episodes in French Cultural History

INTRODUCTION

THIS BOOK investigates ways of thinking in eighteenth-century France. It attempts to show not merely what people thought but how they thought—how they construed the world, invested it with meaning, and infused it with emotion. Instead of following the high road of intellectual history, the inquiry leads into the unmapped territory known in France as *l'histoire des mentalités.* This genre has not yet received a name in English, but it might simply be called cultural history; for it treats our own civilization in the same way that anthropologists study alien cultures. It is history in the ethnographic grain.

Most people tend to think that cultural history concerns high culture, culture with a capital *c*. The history of culture in the lower case goes back as far as Burckhardt, if not Herodotus; but it is still unfamiliar and full of surprises. So the reader may want a word of explanation. Where the historian of ideas traces the filiation of formal thought from philosopher to philosopher, the ethnographic historian studies the way ordinary people made sense of the world. He attempts to uncover their cosmology, to show how they organized reality in their minds and expressed it in their behavior. He does not try to make a philosopher out of the man in the street but to see how street life called for a strategy. Operating at ground level, ordinary people learn to be "street smart"—and they can be as intelligent in their fashion as philosophers. But instead of deriving logical propositions, they think with things, or with anything else that their culture makes available to them, such as stories or ceremonies.

What things are good to think with? Claude Lévi-Strauss applied that question to the totems and tatoos of Amazonia twenty-five years ago. Why not try it out on eighteenth-century France? Because eighteenth-century Frenchmen cannot be interviewed, the skeptic will reply; and to drive the point home, he will add that archives can never serve as a substitute for field work. True, but the archives from the Old Regime are exceptionally rich, and one can always put new questions to old material. Furthermore, one should not imagine that the anthropologist has an easy time with his native informant. He, too, runs into areas of opacity and silence, and he must interpret the native's interpretation of what the other natives think. Mental undergrowth can be as impenetrable in the bush as in the library.

But one thing seems clear to everyone who returns from field work: other people are other. They do not think the way we do. And if we want to understand their way of thinking, we should set out with the idea of capturing otherness. Translated into the terms of the historian's craft, that may merely sound like the familiar injunction against anachronism. It is worth repeating, nonetheless; for nothing is easier than to slip into the comfortable assumption that Europeans thought and felt two centuries ago just as we do today—allowing for the wigs and wooden shoes. We constantly need to be shaken out of a false sense of familiarity with the past, to be administered doses of culture shock.

There is no better way, I believe, than to wander through the archives. One can hardly read a letter from the Old Regime without coming up against surprises—anything from the constant dread of toothaches, which existed everywhere, to the obsession with braiding dung for display on manure heaps, which remained confined to certain villages. What was proverbial wisdom to our ancestors is completely opaque to us. Open any eighteenth-century book of proverbs, and you will find entries such as: "He who is snotty, let him blow his nose." When we cannot get a proverb, or a joke, or a ritual, or a poem, we know we are on to something. By picking at the document where it is most opaque, we may be able to unravel an alien system of meaning. The thread might even lead into a strange and wonderful world view.

This book attempts to explore such unfamiliar views of the world. It proceeds by following up the surprises provided by an unlikely assortment of texts: a primitive version of "Little Red Riding Hood," an account of a massacre of cats, a bizarre description of a city, a curious file kept by a police inspector—documents that cannot be taken to typify eighteenth-century thought but that provide ways of entering into it. The discussion begins with the most vague and general expressions of world view and becomes increasingly precise. Chapter 1 provides an exegesis of the folklore that was familiar to nearly everyone in France but was especially pertinent to the peasantry. Chapter 2 interprets the lore of a group of urban artisans. Moving up the social scale, chapter 3 shows what urban life meant to a provincial bourgeois. The scene then shifts to Paris and the world of the intellectuals—first as it was seen by the police, who had their own way of framing reality (chapter 4), then as it was sorted out epistemologically in the key text of the Enlightenment, the *Discours préliminaire* of the *Encyclopédie* (chapter 5). The last chapter then shows how Rousseau's break with the Encyclopedists opened up a new way of thinking and feeling, one that can be appreciated by rereading Rousseau from the perspective of his readers.

The notion of reading runs through all the chapters, for one can read a ritual or a city just as one can read a folktale or a philosophic text. The mode of exegesis may vary, but in each case one reads for meaning—the meaning inscribed by contemporaries in whatever survives of their vision of the world. I have therefore tried to read my way through the eighteenth century, and I have appended texts to my interpretations so that my own reader can interpret these texts and disagree with me. I do not expect to have the last word and do not pretend to completeness. This book does not provide an inventory of ideas and attitudes in all the social groups and geographical regions of the Old Regime. Nor does it offer typical case studies, for I do not believe there is such a thing as a typical peasant or a representative bourgeois. Instead of chasing after them, I have pursued what seemed to be the richest run of documents, following leads wherever they went and quickening my pace as soon as I stumbled on a surprise. Straying from the beaten path may not be much of a methodology, but it creates the possibility of enjoying some unusual views, and they can be the most revealing. I do not see why cultural history should avoid the eccentric or embrace the average, for one cannot calculate the mean of meanings or reduce symbols to their lowest common denominator.

This confession of nonsystematism does not imply that anything goes in cultural history because anything can pass as anthropology. The anthropological mode of history has a rigor of its own, even if it may look suspiciously like literature to a hard-boiled social scientist. It begins from the premise that individual expression takes place within a general idiom, that we learn to classify sensations and make sense of things by thinking within a framework provided by our culture. It therefore should be possible for the historian to discover the social dimension of thought and to tease meaning from documents by relating them to the surrounding world of significance, passing from text to context and back again until he has cleared a way through a foreign mental world.

This kind of cultural history belongs to the interpretive sciences. It may seem too literary to be classified under the *appellation contrôlée* of "science" in the English-speaking world, but it fits in nicely with the *sciences humaines* in France. It is not an easy genre, and it is bound to be imperfect, but it should not be impossible, even in English. All of us, French and "Anglo-Saxons," pedants as well as peasants, operate within cultural constraints, just as we all share conventions of speech. So historians should be able to see how cultures shape ways of thinking, even for the greatest thinkers. A poet or philosopher may push a language to its limits, but at some point he will hit against the outer frame of meaning. Beyond it, madness lies—the fate of Hölderlin and Nietzsche. But within it, great men can test and shift the boundaries of meaning. Thus there should be room for Diderot and Rousseau in a book about *mentalités* in eighteenth-century France. By including them along with the peasant tellers of tales and the plebeian killers of cats, I have abandoned the usual distinction between elite and popular culture, and have tried to show how intellectuals and common people coped with the same sort of problems.

I realize there are risks in departing from the established modes of history. Some will object that the evidence is too vague for one ever to penetrate into the minds of peasants who disappeared two centuries ago. Others will take offense at the idea of interpreting a massacre of cats in the same vein as the *Discours préliminaire* of the *Encyclopédie,* or interpreting it at all. And still more readers will recoil at the arbitrariness of selecting a few strange documents as points of entry into eighteenth-century thought rather than proceeding in a systematic manner through the canon of classic texts. I think there are valid replies to those objections, but I do not want to turn this introduction into a discourse on method. Instead, I would like to invite the reader into my own text. He may not be convinced, but I hope he will enjoy the journey.

Mother Goose tales, from the original illustration
to Perrault's *Contes de ma mère l'oye*

PEASANTS TELL TALES: THE MEANING OF MOTHER GOOSE

THE MENTAL WORLD of the unenlightened during the Enlightenment seems to be irretrievably lost. It is so difficult, if not impossible, to locate the common man in the eighteenth century that it seems foolish to search for his cosmology. But before abandoning the attempt, it might be useful to suspend one's disbelief and to consider a story—a story everyone knows, though not in the following version, which is the tale more or less as it was told around firesides in peasant cottages during long winter evenings in eighteenth-century France.[1]

> Once a little girl was told by her mother to bring some bread and milk to her grandmother. As the girl was walking through the forest, a wolf came up to her and asked where she was going.
>
> "To grandmother's house," she replied.
>
> "Which path are you taking, the path of the pins or the path of the needles?"

"The path of the needles."

So the wolf took the path of the pins and arrived first at the house. He killed grandmother, poured her blood into a bottle, and sliced her flesh onto a platter. Then he got into her nightclothes and waited in bed.

"Knock, knock."

"Come in, my dear."

"Hello, grandmother. I've brought you some bread and milk."

"Have something yourself, my dear. There is meat and wine in the pantry."

So the little girl ate what was offered; and as she did, a little cat said, "Slut! To eat the flesh and drink the blood of your grandmother!"

Then the wolf said, "Undress and get into bed with me."

"Where shall I put my apron?"

"Throw it on the fire; you won't need it any more."

For each garment—bodice, skirt, petticoat, and stockings—the girl asked the same question; and each time the wolf answered, "Throw it on the fire; you won't need it any more."

When the girl got in bed, she said, "Oh, grandmother! How hairy you are!"

"It's to keep me warmer, my dear."

"Oh, grandmother! What big shoulders you have!"

"It's for better carrying firewood, my dear."

"Oh, grandmother! What long nails you have!"

"It's for scratching myself better, my dear."

"Oh, grandmother! What big teeth you have!"

"It's for eating you better, my dear."

And he ate her.

What is the moral of this story? For little girls, clearly: stay away from wolves. For historians, it seems to be saying something about the mental world of the early modern peasantry. But what? How can one begin to interpret such a text? One way leads through psychoanalysis. The analysts have given folktales a thorough going-over, picking out hidden symbols, unconscious motifs, and psychic mechanisms. Consider, for example, the exegesis of "Little Red Riding Hood" by two of the best known psychoanalysts, Erich Fromm and Bruno Bettelheim.

Fromm interpreted the tale as a riddle about the collective unconscious in primitive society, and he solved it "without difficulty" by decoding its "symbolic language." The story concerns an adolescent's confrontation with adult sexuality, he explained. Its hidden meaning shows through its symbolism—but the symbols he saw in his version of the text were based on details that did not exist in the versions known to peasants in the seventeenth and eighteenth centuries. Thus he makes a great deal of the (nonexistent) red riding hood as a symbol of menstruation and of the (nonexistent) bottle carried by the girl as a symbol of virginity: hence the mother's (nonexistent) admonition not to stray from the path into wild terrain where she might break it. The wolf is the ravishing male. And the two (nonexistent) stones that are placed in the wolf's belly after the (nonexistent) hunter extricates the girl and her grandmother, stand for sterility, the punishment for breaking a sexual taboo. So, with an uncanny sensitivity to detail that did not occur in the original folktale, the psychoanalyst takes us into a mental universe that never existed, at least not before the advent of psychoanalysis.[2]

How could anyone get a text so wrong? The difficulty does not derive from professional dogmatism—for psychoanalysts need not be more rigid than poets in their manipulation of symbols—but rather from blindness to the historical dimension of folktales.

Fromm did not bother to mention his source, but apparently he took his text from the brothers Grimm. The Grimms got it, along with "Puss 'n Boots," "Bluebeard," and a few other stories, from Jeannette Hassenpflug, a neighbor and close friend of theirs in Cassel; and she learned it from her mother, who came from a French Huguenot family. The Huguenots brought their own repertory of tales into Germany when they fled from the persecution of Louis XIV. But they did not draw them directly from popular oral tradition. They read them in books written by Charles Perrault, Marie Cathérine d'Aulnoy, and others during the vogue for fairy tales in fashionable Parisian circles at the end of the seventeenth century. Perrault, the master of the genre, did indeed take his material from the oral tradition of the common people (his principal source probably was his son's nurse). But he touched it up so that it would suit the taste of the salon sophisticates, *précieuses*, and courtiers to whom he directed the first printed version of Mother Goose, his *Contes de ma mère l'oye* of 1697. Thus the tales that reached the Grimms through the Hassenpflugs were neither very German nor very representative of folk tradition. Indeed, the Grimms recognized their literary and Frenchified character and therefore eliminated them from the second edition of the *Kinder- und Hausmärchen*—all but "Little Red Riding Hood." It remained in the collection, evidently, because Jeannette Hassenpflug had grafted on to it a happy ending derived from "The Wolf and the Kids" (tale type 123 according to the standard classification scheme developed by Antti Aarne and Stith Thompson), which was one of the most popular in Germany. So Little Red Riding Hood slipped into the German and later the English literary tradition with her French origins undetected. She changed character considerably as she passed from the French peasantry to Perrault's nursery, into print, across the Rhine, back into an oral tradition but this time as part of the Huguenot diaspora, and back into book form but now as a product of the Teutonic forest rather than the village hearths of the Old Regime in France.[3]

Fromm and a host of other psychoanalytical exegetes did not worry about the transformations of the text—indeed, they did not know about them—because they got the tale they wanted. It begins with pubertal sex (the red hood, which does not exist in the French oral tradition) and ends with the triumph of the ego (the rescued girl, who is usually eaten in the French tales) over the id (the wolf, who is never killed in the traditional versions). All's well that ends well.

The ending is particularly important for Bruno Bettelheim, the latest in the line of psychoanalysts who have had a go at "Little Red Riding Hood." For him, the key to the story, and to all such stories, is the affirmative message of its denouement. By ending happily, he maintains, folktales permit children to confront their unconscious desires and fears and to emerge unscathed, id subdued and ego triumphant. The id is the villain of "Little Red Riding Hood" in Bettelheim's version. It is the pleasure principle, which leads the girl astray when she is too old for oral fixation (the stage represented by "Hansel and Gretel") and too young for adult sex. The id is also the wolf, who is also the father, who is also the hunter, who is also the ego and, somehow, the superego as well. By directing the wolf to her grandmother, Little Red Riding Hood manages in oedipal fashion to do away with her mother, because mothers can also be grandmothers in the moral economy of the soul and the houses on either side of the woods are actually the same house, as in "Hansel and Gretel," where they are also the mother's body. This adroit mixing of symbols gives Little Red Riding Hood an opportunity to get into bed with her father, the wolf, thereby giving vent to her oedipal fantasies. She survives in the end because she is reborn on a higher level of existence when her father reappears as ego-superego-hunter and cuts her out of the belly of her father as wolf-id, so that everyone lives happily ever after.[4]

Bettelheim's generous view of symbolism makes for a less mechanistic interpretation of the tale than does Fromm's notion of a secret code, but it, too, proceeds from some unquestioned assumptions about the text. Although he cites enough commentators on Grimm and Perrault to indicate some awareness of folklore as an academic discipline, Bettelheim reads "Little Red Riding Hood" and the other tales as if they had no history. He treats them, so to speak, flattened out, like patients on a couch, in a timeless contemporaneity. He does not question their origins or worry over other meanings that they might have had in other contexts because he knows how the soul works and how it has always worked. In fact, however, folktales are historical documents. They have evolved over many centuries and have taken different turns in different cultural traditions. Far from expressing the unchanging operations of man's inner being, they suggest that *mentalités* themselves have changed. We can appreciate the distance between our mental world and that of our ancestors if we imagine lulling a child of our own to sleep with the primitive peasant version of "Little Red Riding Hood." Perhaps, then, the moral of the story should be: beware of psychoanalysts—and be careful in your use of sources. We seem to be back at historicism.[5]

Not quite, however, for "Little Red Riding Hood" has a terrifying irrationality that seems out of place in the Age of Reason. In fact, the peasants' version outdoes the psychoanalysts' in violence and sex. (Following the Grimms and Perrault, Fromm and Bettelheim do not mention the cannibalizing of grandmother and the strip-tease prelude to the devouring of the girl.) Evidently the peasants did not need a secret code to talk about taboos.

Little Red Riding Hood, by Gustave Doré

The other stories in the French peasant Mother Goose have the same nightmare quality. In one early version of "Sleeping Beauty" (tale type 410), for example, Prince Charming, who is already married, ravishes the princess, and she bears him several children, without waking up. The infants finally break the spell by biting her while nursing, and the tale then takes up its second theme: the attempts of the prince's mother-in-law, an ogress, to eat his illicit offspring. The original "Bluebeard" (tale type 312) is the story of a bride who cannot resist the temptation to open a forbidden door in the house of her husband, a strange man who has already gone through six wives. She enters a dark room and discovers the corpses of the previous wives, hanging on the wall. Horrified, she lets the forbidden key drop from her hand into a pool of blood on the floor. She cannot wipe it clean; so Bluebeard discovers her disobedience, when he inspects the keys. As he sharpens his knife in preparation for making her his seventh victim, she withdraws to her bedroom and puts on her wedding costume. But she delays her toilette long enough to be saved by her brothers, who gallop to the rescue after receiving a warning from her pet dove. In one early tale from the Cinderella cycle (tale type 510B), the heroine becomes a domestic servant in order to prevent her father from forcing her to marry him. In another, the wicked stepmother tries to push her in an oven but incinerates one of the mean stepsisters by mistake. In the French peasant's "Hansel and Gretel" (tale type 327), the hero tricks an ogre into slitting the throats of his own children. A husband eats a succession of brides in the wedding bed in "La Belle et le monstre" (tale type 433), one of the hundreds of tales that never made it into the printed versions of Mother Goose. In a nastier tale, "Les Trois Chiens" (tale type 315), a sister kills her brother by hiding spikes in the mattress of his wedding bed. In the nastiest of all, "Ma mère m'a tué, mon père m'a mangé" (tale type 720), a mother chops her son up into a Lyonnais-style casserole, which her daughter serves to the father. And so it goes, from rape and sodomy to incest and cannibalism. Far from veiling their message with symbols, the storytellers of eighteenth-century France portrayed a world of raw and naked brutality.

How can the historian make sense of this world? One way for him to keep his footing in the psychic undertow of early Mother Goose is to hold fast to two disciplines: anthropology and folklore. When they discuss theory, anthropologists disagree about the fundamentals of their science. But when they go into the bush, they use techniques for understanding oral traditions that can, with discretion, be applied to Western folklore. Except for some structuralists, they relate tales to the art of tale telling and to the context in which it takes place. They look for the way a raconteur adapts an inherited theme to his audience so that the specificity of time and place shows through the universality of the topos. They do not expect to find direct social comment or metaphysical allegories so much as a tone of discourse or a cultural style, which communicates a particular ethos and world view.[6] "Scientific" folklore, as the French call it (American specialists often distinguish between folklore and "fakelore"), involves the compilation and comparison of tales according to the standardized schemata of tale types developed by Antti Aarne and Stith Thompson. It does not necessarily exclude formalistic analysis such as that of Vladimir Propp, but it stresses rigorous documentation—the occasion of the telling, the background of the teller, and the degree of contamination from written sources.[7]

French folklorists have recorded about ten thousand tales, in many different dialects and in every corner of France and of French-speaking territories. For example, while on an expedition in Berry for the Musée des arts et traditions populaires in 1945, Ariane de Félice recorded a version of "Le Petit Poucet" ("Tom Thumb" or "Thumbling," tale type 327) by a peasant woman, Euphrasie Pichon, who had been born in 1862 in the village of Eguzon (Indre). In 1879 Jean Drouillet wrote down another version as he listened to his mother Eugénie, who had learned it from her mother, Octavie Riffet, in the village of Teillay (Cher). The two versions are nearly identical and owe nothing to the first printed account of the tale, which Charles Perrault published in 1697. They and eighty other "Petits Poucets," which folklorists have compiled and compared, motif by motif, belong to an oral tradition that survived with remarkably little contamination from print culture until late in the nineteenth century. Most of the tales in the French repertory were recorded between 1870 and 1914 during "the Golden Age of folktale research in France," and they were recounted by peasants who had learned them as children, long before literacy had spread throughout the countryside. Thus in 1874 Nannette Levesque, an illiterate peasant woman born in 1794, dictated a version of "Little Red Riding Hood" that went back to the eighteenth century; and in 1865 Louis Grolleau, a domestic servant born in 1803, dictated a rendition of "Le Pou" (tale type 621) that he had first heard under the Empire. Like all tellers of tales, the peasant raconteurs adjusted the setting of their stories to their own milieux; but they kept the main elements intact, using repetitions, rhymes, and other mnemonic devices. Although the "performance" element, which is central to the study of contemporary folklore, does not show through the old texts, folklorists argue that the recordings of the Third Republic provide enough evidence for them to reconstruct the rough outlines of an oral tradition that existed two centuries ago.[8]

That claim may seem extravagant, but comparative studies have revealed striking similarities in different recordings of the same tale, even though they were made in remote villages, far removed from one another and from the circulation of books. In a study of "Little Red Riding Hood," for example, Paul Delarue compared thirty-five versions recorded throughout a vast zone of the *langue d'oïl*. Twenty versions correspond exactly to the primitive "Conte de la mère grand" quoted above, except for a few details (sometimes the girl is eaten, sometimes she escapes by a ruse). Two versions follow Perrault's tale (the first to mention the red hood). And the rest contain a mixture of the oral and written accounts, whose elements stand out as distinctly as the garlic and mustard in a French salad dressing.[9]

Written evidence proves that the tales existed long before anyone conceived of "folklore," a nineteenth-century neologism.[10] Medieval preachers drew on the oral tradition in order to illustrate moral arguments. Their sermons, transcribed in collections of "Exempla" from the twelfth to the fifteenth century, refer to the same stories as those taken down in peasant cottages by folklorists in the nineteenth century. Despite the obscurity surrounding the origins of chivalric romances, *chansons de geste*, and *fabliaux*, it seems that a good deal of medieval literature drew on popular oral tradition, rather than vice versa. "Sleeping Beauty" appeared in an Arthurian romance of the fourteenth century, and "Cinderella" surfaced in Noel du Fail's *Propos rustiques* of 1547, a book that traced the tales to peasant lore and that showed how they were transmitted; for du Fail wrote the first account of an important French institution, the *veillée*, an evening fireside gathering, where men repaired tools and women sewed while listening to stories that would be recorded by folklorists three hundred years later and that were already centuries old.[11] Whether they were meant to amuse adults or to frighten children, as in the case of cautionary tales like "Little Red Riding Hood," the stories belonged to a fund of popular culture, which peasants hoarded over the centuries with remarkably little loss.

The great collections of folktales made in the late nineteenth and early twentieth centuries therefore provide a rare opportunity to make contact with the illiterate masses who have disappeared into the past without leaving a trace. To reject folktales because they cannot be dated and situated with precision like other historical documents is to turn one's back on one of the few points of entry into the mental world of peasants under the Old Regime. But to attempt to penetrate that world is to face a set of obstacles as daunting as those confronted by Jean de l'Ours (tale type 301) when he tried to rescue the three Spanish princesses from the underworld or by little Parle (tale type 328) when he set out to capture the ogre's treasure.

The greatest obstacle is the impossibility of listening in on the story tellers. No matter how accurate they may be, the recorded versions of the tales cannot convey the effects that must have brought the stories to life in the eighteenth century: the dramatic pauses, the sly glances, the use of gestures to set scenes—a Snow White at a spinning wheel, a Cinderella delousing a stepsister—and the use of sounds to punctuate actions—a knock on the door (often done by rapping on a listener's forehead) or a cudgeling or a fart. All of those devices shaped the meaning of the tales, and all of them elude the historian. He cannot be sure that the limp and lifeless text that he holds between the covers of a book provides an accurate account of the performance that took place in the eighteenth century. He cannot even be certain that the text corresponds to the unrecorded versions that existed a century earlier. Although he may turn up plenty of evidence to prove that the tale itself existed, he cannot quiet his suspicions that it could have changed a great deal before it reached the folklorists of the Third Republic.

Given those uncertainties, it seems unwise to build an interpretation on a single version of a single tale, and more hazardous still to base symbolic analysis on details—riding hoods and hunters—that may not have occurred in the peasant versions. But there are enough recordings of those versions—35 "Little Red Riding Hoods," 90 "Tom Thumbs," 105 "Cinderellas"—for one to picture the general outline of a tale as it existed in the oral tradition. One can study it on the level of structure, noting the way the narrative is framed and the motifs are combined, instead of concentrating on fine points of detail. Then one can compare it with other stories. And finally, by working through the entire body of French folktales, one can distinguish general characteristics, overarching themes, and pervasive elements of style and tone.[12]

One can also seek aid and comfort from specialists in the study of oral literature. Milman Parry and Albert Lord have shown how folk epics as long as *The Iliad* are passed on faithfully from bard to bard among the illiterate peasants of Yugoslavia. These "singers of tales" do not possess the fabulous powers of memorization sometimes attributed to "primitive" peoples. They do not memorize very much at all. Instead, they combine stock phrases, formulas, and narrative segments in patterns improvised according to the response of their audience. Recordings of the same epic by the same singer demonstrate that each performance is unique. Yet recordings made in 1950 do not differ in essentials from those made in 1934. In each case, the singer proceeds as if he were walking down a well-known path. He may branch off here to take a shortcut or pause there to enjoy a panorama, but he always remains on familiar ground—so familiar, in fact, that he will say that he repeated every step exactly as he has done before. He does not conceive of repetition in the same way as a literate person, for he has no notion of words, lines, and verses. Texts are not rigidly fixed for him as they are for readers of the printed page. He creates his text as he goes, picking new routes through old themes. He can even work in material derived from printed sources, for the epic as a whole is so much greater than the sum of its parts that modifications of detail barely disturb the general configuration.[13]

Lord's investigation confirms conclusions that Vladimir Propp reached by a different mode of analysis, one that showed how variations of detail remain subordinate to stable structures in Russian folktales.[14] Field workers among illiterate peoples in Polynesia, Africa, and North and South America have also found that oral traditions have enormous staying power. Opinions divide on the separate question of whether or not oral sources can provide a reliable account of past events. Robert Lowie, who collected narratives from the Crow Indians in the early twentieth century, took up a position of extreme skepticism: "I cannot attach to oral traditions any historical value whatsoever under any conditions whatsoever."[15] By historical value, however, Lowie meant factual accuracy. (In 1910 he recorded a Crow account of a battle against the Dakota; in 1931 the same informant described the battle to him, but claimed that it had taken place against the Cheyenne.) Lowie conceded that the stories, taken as stories, remained quite consistent; they forked and branched in the standard patterns of Crow narrative. So his findings actually support the view that in traditional story telling continuities in form and style outweigh variations in detail, among North American Indians as well as Yugoslav peasants.[16] Frank Hamilton Cushing noted a spectacular example of this tendency among the Zuni almost a century ago. In 1886 he served as interpreter to a Zuni delegation in the eastern United States. During a round robin of story telling one evening, he recounted as his contribution the tale of "The Cock and the Mouse," which he had picked up from a book of Italian folktales. About a year later, he was astonished to hear the same tale from one of the Indians back at Zuni. The Italian motifs remained recognizable enough for one to be able to classify the tale in the Aarne-Thompson scheme (it is tale type 2032). But everything else about the story—its frame, figures of speech, allusions, style, and general feel—had become intensely Zuni. Instead of Italianizing the native lore, the story had been Zunified.[17]

No doubt the transmission process affects stories differently in different cultures. Some bodies of folklore can resist "contamination" while absorbing new material more effectively than can others. But oral traditions seem to be tenacious and long-lived nearly everywhere among illiterate peoples. Nor do they collapse at their first exposure to the printed word. Despite Jack Goody's contention that a literacy line cuts through all history, dividing oral from "written" or "print" cultures, it seems that traditional tale telling can flourish long after the onset of literacy. To anthropologists and folklorists who have tracked tales through the bush, there is nothing extravagant about the idea that peasant raconteurs in late nineteenth-century France told stories to one another pretty much as their ancestors had done a century or more earlier.[18]

Comforting as this expert testimony may be, it does not clear all the difficulties in the way of interpreting the French tales. The texts are accessible enough, for they lie unexploited in treasure houses like the Musée des arts et traditions populaires in Paris and

in scholarly collections like *Le Conte populaire français* by Paul Delarue and Marie-Louise Tenèze. But one cannot lift them from
such sources and hold them up to inspection as if they were so
many photographs of the Old Regime, taken with the innocent
eye of an extinct peasantry. They are stories.

As in most kinds of narration, they develop standardized plots
from conventional motifs, picked up here, there, and everywhere.
They have a distressing lack of specificity for anyone who wants to
pin them down to precise points in time and place. Raymond
Jameson has studied the case of a Chinese Cinderella from the
ninth century. She gets her slippers from a magic fish instead of a
fairy godmother and loses one of them at a village fête instead of a
royal ball, but she bears an unmistakable resemblance to Perrault's
heroine.[19] Folklorists have recognized their tales in Herodotus and
Homer, on ancient Egyptian papyruses and Chaldean stone tablets;
and they have recorded them all over the world, in Scandinavia
and Africa, among Indians on the banks of the Bengal and Indians
along the Missouri. The dispersion is so striking that some have
come to believe in Ur-stories and a basic Indo-European repertory
of myths, legends, and tales. This tendency feeds into the cosmic
theories of Frazer and Jung and Lévi-Strauss, but it does not help
anyone attempting to penetrate the peasant mentalities of early
modern France.

Fortunately, a more down-to-earth tendency in folklore makes it
possible to isolate the peculiar characteristics of traditional French
tales. *Le Conte populaire français* arranges them according to the
Aarne-Thompson classification scheme, which covers all varieties
of Indo-European folktales. It therefore provides the basis for comparative study, and the comparisons suggest the way general
themes took root and grew in French soil. "Tom Thumb" ("Le
Petit Poucet," tale type 327), for example, has a strong French
flavor, in Perrault as well as the peasant versions, if one compares it
with its German cousin, "Hansel and Gretel." The Grimms' tale
emphasizes the mysterious forest and the naïveté of the children in
the face of inscrutable evil, and it has more fanciful and poetic
touches, as in the details about the bread-and-cake house and the
magic birds. The French children confront an ogre, but in a very
real house. Monsieur and Madame Ogre discuss their plans for a

dinner party as if they were any married couple, and they carp at each other just as Tom Thumb's parents did. In fact, it is hard to tell the two couples apart. Both simple-minded wives throw away their family's fortunes; and their husbands berate them in the same manner, except that the ogre tells his wife that she deserves to be eaten and that he would do the job himself if she were not such an unappetizing *vieille bête* (old beast).[20] Unlike their German relatives, the French ogres appear in the role of *le bourgeois de la maison* (burgher head of household),[21] as if they were rich local landowners. They play fiddles, visit friends, snore contentedly in bed beside fat ogress wives;[22] and for all their boorishness, they never fail to be good family men and good providers. Hence the joy of the ogre in "Pitchin-Pitchot" as he bounds into the house, a sack on his back: "Catherine, put on the big kettle. I've caught Pitchin-Pitchot."[23]

Where the German tales maintain a tone of terror and fantasy, the French strike a note of humor and domesticity. Firebirds settle down into hen yards. Elves, genii, forest spirits, the whole Indo-European panoply of magical beings become reduced in France to two species, ogres and fairies. And those vestigial creatures acquire human foibles and generally let humans solve their problems by their own devices, that is, by cunning and "Cartesianism"—a term that the French apply vulgarly to their propensity for craftiness and intrigue. The Gallic touch is clear in many of the tales that Perrault did not rework for his own Gallicized Mother Goose of 1697: the *panache* of the young blacksmith in "Le Petit Forgeron" (tale type 317), for example, who kills giants on a classic *tour de France;* or the provincialism of the Breton peasant in "Jean Bête" (tale type 675), who is given anything he wishes and asks for *un bon pêché de piquette et une écuelle de patates du lait* ("crude wine and a bowl of potatoes in milk"); or the professional jealousy of the master gardener, who fails to prune vines as well as his apprentice in "Jean le Teigneux" (tale type 314); or the cleverness of the devil's daughter in "La Belle Eulalie" (tale type 313), who escapes with her lover by leaving two talking pâtés in their beds. Just as one cannot attach the French tales to specific events, one should not dilute them in a timeless universal mythology. They really belong to a middle ground: *la France moderne* or the France that existed from the fifteenth through the eighteenth century.

That time span may look distressingly vague to anyone who expects history to be precise. But precision may be inappropriate as well as impossible in the history of *mentalités,* a genre that requires different methods from those used in conventional genres, like political history. World views can not be chronicled in the manner of political events, but they are no less "real." Politics could not take place without the preliminary mental ordering that goes into the common-sense notion of the real world. Common sense itself is a social construction of reality, which varies from culture to culture. Far from being the arbitrary figment of some collective imagination, it expresses the common basis of experience in a given social order. To reconstruct the way peasants saw the world under the Old Regime, therefore, one should begin by asking what they had in common, what experiences they shared in the everyday life of their villages.

Thanks to several generations of research by social historians, that question can be answered. The answer must be hedged with qualifications and restricted to a high level of generalization because conditions varied so much in the kingdom, which remained a patchwork of regions rather than a unified nation until the Revolution and perhaps even well into the nineteenth century. Pierre Goubert, Emmanuel Le Roy Ladurie, Pierre Saint-Jacob, Paul Bois, and many others have uncovered the particularities of peasant life region by region and have explicated them monograph by monograph. The density of monographs can make French social history look like a conspiracy of exceptions trying to disprove rules. Yet here, too, there exists a danger of misplaced professionalism; for if one stands at a safe enough distance from the details, a general picture begins to emerge. In fact, it has already reached the stage of assimilation in textbooks like *Histoire économique et sociale de la France* (Paris, 1970) and syntheses like *Histoire de la France rurale* (Paris, 1975/76). It goes roughly as follows.[24]

Despite war, plague, and famine, the social order that existed at village level remained remarkably stable during the early modern period in France. The peasants were relatively free—less so than the yeomen who were turning into landless laborers in England, more so than the serfs who were sinking into a kind of slavery east of the Elbe. But they could not escape from a seigneurial system that denied them sufficient land to achieve economic independence and that siphoned off whatever surplus they produced. Men labored from dawn to dusk, scratching the soil on scattered strips of land with plows like those of the Romans and hacking at their grain with primitive sickles, in order to leave enough stubble for communal grazing. Women married late—at age twenty-five to twenty-seven—and gave birth to only five or six children, of whom only two or three survived to adulthood. Great masses of people lived in a state of chronic malnutrition, subsisting mainly on porridge made of bread and water with some occasional, home-grown vegetables thrown in. They ate meat only a few times a year, on feast days or after autumn slaughtering if they did not have enough silage to feed the livestock over the winter. They often failed to get the two pounds of bread (2,000 calories) a day that they needed to keep up their health, and so they had little protection against the combined effects of grain shortage and disease. The population fluctuated between fifteen and twenty million, expanding to the limits of its productive capacity (an average density of forty souls per square kilometer, an average annual rate of forty births per thousand inhabitants), only to be devastated by demographic crises. For four centuries—from the first ravages of the Black Death in 1347 to the first great leap in population and productivity in the 1730s—French society remained trapped in rigid institutions and Malthusian conditions. It went through a period of stagnation, which Fernand Braudel and Emmanuel Le Roy Ladurie have described as *l'histoire immobile* (unmoving history).[25]

That phrase now seems exaggerated, for it hardly does justice to the religious conflict, grain riots, and rebellions against the extension of state power that disrupted the late medieval pattern of village life. But when first used in the 1950s, the notion of immobile history—a history of structural continuity over a long time span, *la longue durée*—served as a corrective to the tendency to see history as a succession of political events. Event history, *histoire événementielle*, generally took place over the heads of the peasantry, in the remote world of Paris and Versailles. While ministers came and went and battles raged, life in the village continued unperturbed, much as it had always been since times beyond the reach of memory.

History looked "immobile" at the village level, because sei-
gneurialism and the subsistence economy kept villagers bent over
the soil, and primitive techniques of farming gave them no
opportunity to unbend. Grain yields remained at a ratio of about 5-
to-1, a primitive return in contrast to modern farming, which produces fifteen or even thirty grains for every seed planted. Farmers
could not raise enough grain to feed large numbers of animals, and
they did not have enough livestock to produce the manure to fer-
tilize the fields to increase the yield. This vicious circle kept them
enclosed within a system of triennial or biennial crop rotation,
which left a huge proportion of their land lying fallow. They
could not convert the fallow to the cultivation of crops like clover,
which return nitrogen to the soil, because they lived too close to
penury to risk the experiment, aside from the fact that no one had
any notion of nitrogen. Collective methods of cultivation also reduced the margin for experimentation. Except in a few regions
with enclosures, like the *bocage* district of the west, peasants farmed
scattered strips in open fields. They sowed and harvested collec-
tively, so that common gleaning and common grazing could take
place. They depended on common lands and forests beyond the
fields for pasture, firewood, and chestnuts or berries. The only area
where they could attempt to get ahead by individual initiative was
the *basse-cour* or backyard attached to their household plots, or
manses. Here they struggled to build up manure heaps, to raise flax
for spinning, to produce vegetables and chickens for their home
brews and local markets.

The backyard garden often provided the margin of survival for
families that lacked the twenty, thirty, or forty acres that were
necessary for economic independence. They needed so much land
because so much of their harvest was drained from them by seigneurial dues, tithes, ground rents, and taxes. In most of central
and northern France, the wealthier peasants rigged the collection
of the main royal tax, the *taille,* in accordance with an old French
principle: soak the poor. So tax collecting opened up fissures within the village, and indebtedness compounded the damage. The
poorer peasants frequently borrowed from the rich—that is, the
few relatively wealthy *coqs du village* (cocks of the walk), who
owned enough land to sell surplus grain on the market, to build up

herds, and to hire the poor as laborers. Debt peonage may have made the wealthy peasants hated as much as the seigneur and the ecclesiastical *décimateur* (tithe collector). Hatred, jealousy, and conflicts of interest ran through peasant society. The village was no happy and harmonious *Gemeinschaft.*

For most peasants village life was a struggle for survival, and survival meant keeping above the line that divided the poor from the indigent. The poverty line varied from place to place, according to the amount of land necessary to pay taxes, tithes, and seigneurial dues; to put aside enough grain for planting next year; and to feed the family. In times of scarcity, poor families had to buy their food. They suffered as consumers, while prices shot up and the wealthier peasants made a killing. So a succession of bad harvests could polarize the village, driving the marginal families into indigence as the rich got richer. In the face of such difficulties, the "little people" (*petites gens*) survived by their wits. They hired themselves out as farm hands, spun and wove cloth in their cottages, did odd jobs, and took to the road, picking up work wherever they could find it.

Many of them went under. Then they took to the road for good, drifting about with the flotsam and jetsam of France's *population flottante* ("floating population"), which included several million desperate souls by the 1780s. Except for the happy few on an artisanal *tour de France* and the occasional troupes of actors and mountebanks, life on the road meant ceaseless scavenging for food. The drifters raided chicken coops, milked untended cows, stole laundry drying on hedges, snipped off horses' tails (good for selling to upholsterers), and lacerated and disguised their bodies in order to pass as invalids wherever alms were being given out. They joined and deserted regiment after regiment and served as false recruits. They became smugglers, highwaymen, pickpockets, prostitutes. And in the end they surrendered in *hôpitaux,* pestilential poor houses, or else crawled under a bush or a hay loft and died— *croquants* who had "croaked."[26]

Death came just as inexorably to families that remained in their villages and kept above the poverty line. As Pierre Goubert, Louis Henry, Jacques Dupâquier, and other historical demographers have shown, life was an inexorable struggle against death everywhere in early modern France. In Crulai, Normandy, 236 of every 1,000 babies died before their first birthdays during the seventeenth century, as opposed to twenty today. About 45 per cent of the Frenchmen born in the eighteenth century died before the age of ten. Few of the survivors reached adulthood before the death of at least one of their parents. And few parents reached the end of their procreative years, because death interrupted them. Terminated by death, not divorce, marriages lasted an average of fifteen years, half as long as they do in France today. In Crulai, one in five husbands lost his wife and then remarried. Stepmothers proliferated everywhere—far more so than stepfathers, as the remarriage rate among widows was one in ten. Stepchildren may not have been treated like Cinderella, but relations between siblings probably were harsh. A new child often meant the difference between poverty and indigence. Even if it did not overtax the family's larder, it could bring penury down upon the next generation by swelling the number of claimants when the parents' land was divided among their heirs.[27]

Whenever the population expanded, landholding fragmented and pauperization set in. Primogeniture slowed the process in some areas, but the best defense everywhere was delayed marriage, a tendency that must have taken its toll in the emotional life of the family. The peasants of the Old Regime, unlike those in contemporary India, generally did not marry until they could occupy a cottage, and they rarely had children out of wedlock or after they reached their forties. In Port-en-Bessin, for example, women married at twenty-seven and stopped bearing children at forty on the average. Demographers have found no evidence of birth control or widespread illegitimacy before the late eighteenth century. Early modern man did not understand life in a way that enabled him to control it. Early modern woman could not conceive of mastering nature, so she conceived as God willed it—and as Thumbkin's mother did in "Le Petit Poucet." But late marriage, a short period of fertility, and long stretches of breast-feeding, which reduces the likelihood of conception, limited the size of her family. The harshest and most effective limit was imposed by death, her own and those of her babies during childbirth and infancy. Stillborn children, called *chrissons,* were sometimes buried casually, in anonymous collective graves. Infants were sometimes smothered by their

Puss 'n Boots, by Gustave Doré

parents in bed—a rather common accident, judging by episcopal edicts forbidding parents to sleep with children who had not reached their first birthdays. Whole families crowded into one or two beds and surrounded themselves with livestock in order to keep warm. So children became participant observers of their parents' sexual activities. No one thought of them as innocent creatures or of childhood itself as a distinct phase of life, clearly distinguishable from adolescence, youth, and adulthood by special styles of dress and behavior. Children labored alongside their parents almost as soon as they could walk, and they joined the adult labor force as farm hands, servants, and apprentices as soon as they reached their teens.

The peasants of early modern France inhabited a world of stepmothers and orphans, of inexorable, unending toil, and of brutal emotions, both raw and repressed. The human condition has changed so much since then that we can hardly imagine the way it appeared to people whose lives really were nasty, brutish, and short. That is why we need to reread Mother Goose.

Consider four of the best-known stories from Perrault's Mother Goose—"Puss 'n Boots," "Tom Thumb," "Cinderella," and "The Ridiculous Wishes"—in comparison with some of the peasant tales that treat the same themes.

In "Puss 'n Boots," a poor miller dies, leaving the mill to his eldest son, an ass to the second, and only a cat to the third. "Neither a notary nor a lawyer were called in," Perrault observes "They would have eaten up the poor patrimony." We are clearly in France, although other versions of this theme exist in Asia, Africa, and South America. The inheritance customs of French peasants, as well as noblemen, often prevented the fragmentation of the patrimony by favoring the eldest son. The youngest son of the miller, however, inherits a cat who has a genius for domestic intrigue. Everywhere around him, this Cartesian cat sees vanity, stupidity, and unsatisfied appetite; and he exploits it all by a series of tricks, which lead to a rich marriage for his master and a fine estate for himself, although in some of the pre-Perrault versions the master ultimately dupes the cat, who is actually a fox and does not wear boots.

A tale from the oral tradition, "La Renarde" (tale type 460), begins in a similar way: "Once there were two brothers, who took up the inheritances left to them by their father. The older, Joseph, kept the farm. The younger, Baptiste, received only a handful of coins; and as he had five children and very little to feed them with, he fell into destitution."[28] In desperation, Baptiste begs for grain from his brother. Joseph tells him to strip off his rags, stand naked in the rain, and roll in the granary. He can keep as much grain as adheres to his body. Baptiste submits to this exercise in brotherly love, but he fails to pick up enough food to keep his family alive, so he takes to the road. Eventually he meets a good fairy, La Renarde, who helps him solve a string of riddles, which lead to a pot of buried gold and the fulfillment of a peasant's dream: a house, fields, pasture, woodland, "and his children had a cake apiece every day."[29]

"Tom Thumb" ("Le Petit Poucet," tale type 327) is a French version of "Hansel and Gretel," although Perrault took his title from a tale that belongs to type 700. It provides a glimpse of the Malthusian world, even in Perrault's watered-down version: "Once upon a time there was a woodsman and his wife, who had seven children, all boys. . . . They were very poor, and their seven children were a great inconvenience, because none was old enough to support himself. . . . A very difficult year came, and the famine was so great that these poor folk resolved to get rid of their children." The matter-of-fact tone suggests how commonplace the death of children had become in early modern France. Perrault wrote his tale in the mid-1690s, at the height of the worst demographic crisis in the seventeenth century—a time when plague and famine decimated the population of northern France, when the poor ate offal thrown in the street by tanners, when corpses were found with grass in their mouths and mothers "exposed" the infants they could not feed so that they got sick and died. By abandoning their children in the forest, Tom Thumb's parents were trying to cope with a problem that overwhelmed the peasantry many times in the seventeenth and eighteenth centuries—the problem of survival during a period of demographic disaster.

The same motif exists in the peasant versions of the tale and in other tales, along with other forms of infanticide and child abuse.

Sometimes the parents turn their children out on the road as beggars and thieves. Sometimes they run away themselves, leaving the children to beg at home. And sometimes they sell the children to the devil. In the French version of "The Sorcerer's Apprentice" ("La Pomme d'orange," tale type 325), a father is overwhelmed by "as many children as there are holes in a sieve,"[30] a phrase that occurs in several tales and that should be taken as hyperbole about Malthusian pressure rather than as evidence about family size. When a new baby arrives, the father sells it to the devil (a sorcerer in some versions) in exchange for receiving a full larder for twelve years. At the end of that time, he gets the boy back, thanks to a ruse that the boy devises, for the little rogue has picked up a repertory of tricks, including the power to transform himself into animals, during his apprenticeship. Before long, the cupboard is bare and the family is facing starvation again. The boy then changes himself into a hunting dog, so that his father can sell him once more to the devil, who reappears as a hunter. After the father has collected the money, the dog runs away and returns home as a boy. They try the same trick again, with the boy transformed into a horse. This time the devil keeps hold of a magic collar, which prevents the horse from changing back into a boy. But a farm hand leads the horse to drink at a pond, thereby, giving it a chance to escape in the form of a frog. The devil turns into a fish and is about to devour it, when the frog changes into a bird. The devil becomes a hawk and pursues the bird, which flies into the bedroom of a dying king and takes the form of an orange. Then the devil appears as a doctor and demands the orange in exchange for curing the king. The orange spills onto the floor, transformed into grains of millet. The devil turns into a chicken and starts to gobble up the grains. But the last grain turns into a fox, which finally wins the transformation contest by devouring the hen. The tale did not merely provide amusement. It dramatized the struggle over scarce resources, which pitted the poor against the rich, the "little people" (*menu peuple, petites gens*) against "the big" (*les gros, les grands*). Some versions make the social comment explicit by casting the devil in the role of a "seigneur" and concluding at the end: "And thus did the servant eat the master."[31]

To eat or not to eat, that was the question peasants confronted in their folklore as well as in their daily lives. It appears in a great many of the tales, often in connection with the theme of the wicked stepmother, which must have had special resonance around Old Regime hearths because Old Regime demography made stepmothers such important figures in village society. Perrault did justice to the theme in "Cinderella," but he neglected the related motif of malnutrition, which stands out in the peasant versions of the tale. In one common version ("La Petite Annette," tale type 511), the wicked stepmother gives poor Annette only a crust of bread a day and makes her keep the sheep, while her fat and indolent stepsisters lounge around the house and dine on mutton, leaving their dishes for Annette to wash upon her return from the fields. Annette is about to die of starvation, when the Virgin Mary appears and gives her a magic wand, which produces a magnificent feast whenever Annette touches it to a black sheep. Before long the girl is plumper than her stepsisters. But her new beauty—and fatness made for beauty under the Old Regime as in many primitive societies—arouses the stepmother's suspicions. By a ruse, the stepmother discovers the magic sheep, kills it, and serves its liver to Annette. Annette manages to bury the liver secretly and it grows into a tree, which is so high that no one can pick its fruit, except Annette; for it bends its branches down to her whenever she approaches. A passing prince (who is as gluttonous as everyone else in the country) wants the fruit so badly that he promises to marry the maiden who can pick some for him. Hoping to make a match for one of her daughters, the stepmother builds a huge ladder. But when she tries it out, she falls and breaks her neck. Annette then gathers the fruit, marries the prince, and lives happily ever after.

Malnutrition and parental neglect go together in several tales, notably "La Sirène et l'épervier" (tale type 316) and "Brigitte, la maman qui m'a pas fait, mais m'a nourri" (tale type 713). The quest for food can be found in nearly all of them, even in Perrault, where it appears in burlesque form in "The Ridiculous Wishes." A poor woodsman is promised the fulfillment of any three wishes as a reward for a good deed. While he ruminates, his appetite overcomes him; and he wishes for a sausage. After it appears on his plate, his wife, an insufferable scold, quarrels so violently over the wasting of the wish that he wishes the sausage would grow on her nose. Then, confronted with a disfigured spouse, he wishes her back to her normal state; and they return to their former miserable existence.

Wishing usually takes the form of food in peasant tales, and it is never ridiculous. The discharged, down-and-out soldier, La Ramée, a stock character like the abused stepdaughter, is reduced to beggary in "Le Diable et le maréchal ferrant" (tale type 330). He shares his last pennies with other beggars, one of whom turns out to be Saint Peter in disguise, and as a reward he is granted any wish he wants. Instead of taking paradise, he asks for "a square meal"—or, in other versions, "white bread and a chicken," "a bun, a sausage, and as much wine as he can drink," "tobacco and the food he saw in the inn," or "to always have a crust of bread."[32] Once supplied with magic wands, rings, or supernatural helpers, the first thought of the peasant hero is always for food. He never shows any imagination in his ordering. He merely takes the *plat du jour,* and it is always the same: solid peasant fare, though it may vary with the region, as in the case of the "cakes, fried bread, and pieces of cheese" *(canistrelli e fritelli, pezzi di broccio)* served up in a Corsican feast.[33] Usually the peasant raconteur does not describe the food in detail. Lacking any notion of gastronomy, he simply loads up his hero's plate; and if he wants to supply an extravagant touch, he adds, "There were even napkins."[34]

One extravagance clearly stands out: meat. In a society of de facto vegetarians, the luxury of luxuries was to sink one's teeth into a side of mutton, pork, or beef. The wedding feast in "Royaume des Valdars" (tale type 400) includes roast pigs who run around with forks sticking out of their flanks so that the guests can help themselves to ready-carved mouthfuls. The French version of a common ghost story, "La Goulue" (tale type 366), concerns a peasant girl who insists on eating meat every day. Unable to satisfy this extraordinary craving, her parents serve her a leg they have cut off a newly buried corpse. On the next day, the corpse appears before the girl in the kitchen. It orders her to wash its right leg, then its left leg. When she sees that the left leg is missing, it screams, "You ate it." Then it carries her back to the grave and devours her. The later, English versions of the tale, notably "The Golden Arm" made famous by Mark Twain, have the same plot without the carnivorousness—the very element that seems to have made the story fascinating for the peasants of the Old Regime. But whether they filled up on meat or porridge, the full belly came first among the wishes of the French peasant heroes. It was all the peasant Cinderella aspired to, even though she got a prince. "She touched the black sheep with the magic wand. Immediately a fully decked table appeared before her. She could eat what she wanted, and she ate a bellyful."[35] To eat one's fill, eat until the exhaustion of the appetite (*manger à sa faim*),[36] was the principal pleasure that the peasants dangled before their imaginations, and one that they rarely realized in their lives.

They also imagined other dreams coming true, including the standard run of castles and princesses. But their wishes usually remained fixed on common objects in the everyday world. One hero gets "a cow and some chickens"; another, an armoire full of linens. A third settles for light work, regular meals, and a pipe full of tobacco. And when gold rains into the fireplace of a fourth, he uses it to buy "food, clothes, a horse, land."[37] In most of the tales, wish fulfillment turns into a program for survival, not a fantasy of escape.

Despite the occasional touches of fantasy, then, the tales remain rooted in the real world. They almost always take place within two basic frameworks, which correspond to the dual setting of peasant life under the Old Regime: on the one hand, the household and village; on the other, the open road. The opposition between the village and the road runs through the tales, just as it ran through the lives of peasants everywhere in eighteenth-century France.[38]

Peasant families could not survive under the Old Regime unless everyone worked, and worked together as an economic unit. The folktales constantly show parents laboring in the fields while the children gather wood, guard sheep, fetch water, spin wool, or beg. Far from condemning the exploitation of child labor, they sound indignant when it does not occur. In "Les Trois Fileuses" (tale type 501), a father resolves to get rid of his daughter, because "she ate but did not work."[39] He persuades the king that she can spin seven *fusées* (100,800 yards) of flax a night, whereas in fact she eats seven crêpes (we are in Angoumois). The king orders her to do prodigious feats of spinning, promising to marry her if she succeeds. Three magic spinning women, one more deformed than the other, accomplish the tasks for her and in return ask only to be invited to the wedding. When they appear, the king inquires about the cause of their deformities. Overwork, they reply; and they warn him that his bride will look every bit as hideous if he permits her to continue spinning. So the girl escapes from slavery, the father gets rid of a glutton, and the poor turn the tables on the rich (in some versions the local seigneur takes the place of the king).

The French versions of "Rumpelstilzchen" (tale type 500 and some related versions of tale type 425) follow the same scenario. A mother beats her daughter for not working. When a passing king or the local seigneur asks what the matter is, the mother devises a ruse to get rid of an unproductive member of the family. She protests that the girl works too much, so obsessively, in fact, that she would spin the very straw in their mattresses. Sensing a good thing, the king carries off the girl and orders her to perform super-human tasks: she must spin whole haystacks into rooms full of linen, load and unload fifty carts of manure a day, separate mountains of wheat from chaff. Although the tasks always get done in the end, thanks to supernatural intervention, they express a basic fact of peasant life in hyperbolic form. Everyone faced endless, limitless labor, from early childhood until the day of death.

Marriage offered no escape; rather, it imposed an additional burden because it subjected women to work within the "putting-out" system (cottage industry) as well as work for the family and for the farm. The tales invariably place peasant wives at the spinning wheel after a day of tending livestock, hauling wood, or mowing hay. Some stories provide hyperbolic pictures of their work, showing them yoked to ploughs or hauling water up a well with their hair or cleaning ovens with their bare breasts.[40] And even though marriage meant accepting a new load of labor and the new danger of childbearing, a poor girl needed a dowry to enter into it—unless she would settle for a frog, a crow, or some hideous beast. The animals did not always turn into princes, although that was a common form of escapism. In one burlesque version of peasant marriage strategy ("Les Filles mariées à des animaux," tale type 552), the parents marry their daughters off to a wolf, a fox, a hare, and a pig. According to the Irish and North European versions of the tale, the couples set off on a series of adventures, which are necessary to metamorphose the animals back into men. The French versions simply recount what the young couples serve when the mother comes calling—mutton procured by the wolf, turkey fetched by the fox, cabbage filched by the hare, and filth from the pig. Having found good providers, each after his own fashion, the daughters must accept their lot in life; and everyone gets on with the basic business of foraging for a living.

Sons have more room to maneuver in the tales. They explore the second dimension of peasant experience, life on the road. The boys set out in search of their fortune, and often find it, thanks to the help of old crones, who beg for a crust of bread and turn out to be beneficent fairies in disguise. Despite the supernatural intervention, the heroes walk off into a real world, usually in order to escape poverty at home and to find employment in greener pastures. They do not always get princesses. In "Le Langage des bêtes" (tale type 670), a poor lad who has found work as a shepherd comes to the aid of a magic snake. In return, he finds some buried gold: "He filled his pockets with it and the next morning he led his flock back to the farm and asked to marry his master's daughter. She was the prettiest girl in the village, and he had loved her for a long time. Seeing that the shepherd was rich, the father gave him the girl. Eight days later they were married; and as the farmer and his wife were old, they made their son-in-law sole master of the farm."[41] Such was the stuff that dreams were made of in the peasant tales.

Other boys take to the road because there is no land, no work, no food at home.[42] They become farm hands or domestic servants or, in the best of cases, apprentices—to blacksmiths, tailors, carpenters, sorcerers, and the devil. The hero of "Jean de l'Ours" (tale type 301B) serves five years with a blacksmith, then sets off with an iron staff, which he takes as payment for his labor. Once en route he picks up strange fellow travelers (Twist-Oak and Slice-Mountain), braves haunted houses, fells giants, slays monsters, and marries a Spanish princess. Standard adventures, but they fall within the framework of a typical *tour de France*. "Jean-sans-Peur" (tale type 326) and many of the other favorite heroes of the French tales follow the same scenario.[43] Their exploits take place in a setting that would have been familiar to an audience of artisans who had spent their youth on the road and to peasants who regularly left their families after the summer harvest and covered hundreds of miles as shepherds, peddlers, and migratory laborers.

They confronted danger everywhere on their travels, for France had no effective police force, and bandits and wolves still roamed through the wild lands separating villages in vast stretches of the Massif Central, the Jura, Vosges, Landes, and *bocage.* Men had to make their way through this treacherous territory by foot, sleeping at night under haystacks and bushes when they could not beg hospitality in farms or pay for a bed in an inn—where they still stood a good chance of having their purses stolen or their throats cut. When the French versions of Tom Thumb and Hansel and Gretel knock at the doors of mysterious houses deep in the forest, the wolves baying at their backs add a touch of realism, not fantasy. True, the doors are opened by ogres and witches. But in many tales ("Le Garçon de chez la bucheronne," tale type 461, for example), the houses contain gangs of bandits like those of Mandrin and Cartouche, who really did make traveling hazardous in the eighteenth century. There was protection from traveling in groups, but you could never trust your fellow travelers. They might save you from disaster, as in "Moitié Poulet" (tale type 563) and "Le Navire sans pareil" (tale type 283); or they might turn on you when they caught the scent of booty, as in "Jean de l'Ours" (tale type 301B). Petit Louis' father was right when he advised the boy never to travel with a hunchback, a lame man, or a *Cacous* (a pariah-like ropemaker) (tale type 531). Anything out of the ordinary represented a threat. But no formula was adequate to the task of decoding danger on the road.

For most of the population flooding France's roads, fortune seeking was a euphemism for beggary. Beggars swarm through the tales, real beggars, not merely fairies in disguise. When poverty overwhelms a widow and her son in "Le Bracelet" (tale type 590), they abandon their hut at the edge of the village and take to the road, carrying all their goods in a single sack. Their way leads through a menacing forest to a gang of robbers and the poor house before rescue finally comes from a magic bracelet. In "Les Deux

Voyageurs" (tale type 613), two discharged soldiers draw lots to see which shall have his eyes put out. Desperate for food, they can think of no way to survive except by operating as a team of beggars, the blind man and his keeper. In "Norouâs" (tale type 563), a single crop of flax means the difference between survival and destitution for a peasant family living on a tiny plot of land. The crop is good, but the bad wind Norouâs blows the flax away while it is drying in the field. The peasant sets out with a club to beat Norouâs to death. But he runs out of provisions and soon is begging for crusts and a corner in the stable, like any vagabond. Finally he finds Norouâs on top of a mountain. "Give me back my flax! Give me back my flax!" he screams. Taking pity on him, the wind gives him a magic tablecloth, which produces a meal whenever it is unfolded. The peasant "eats his fill" and spends the next night in an inn, only to be robbed by the hostess. After two more rounds with Norouâs, he receives a magic staff, which thrashes the hostess, forcing her to surrender the cloth. The peasant lives happily—that is, with a full larder—ever after, but his tale illustrates the desperation of those tottering on the line between poverty in the village and destitution on the road.[44]

Thus, whenever one looks behind Perrault to the peasant versions of Mother Goose, one finds elements of realism—not photographic accounts of life in the barnyard (peasants did not actually have as many children as there are holes in a sieve, and they did not eat them) but a picture that corresponds to everything that social historians have been able to piece together from the archives. The picture fits, and the fit was a matter of consequence. By showing how life was lived, *terre à terre,* in the village and on the road, the tales helped orient the peasants. They mapped the ways of the world and demonstrated the folly of expecting anything more than cruelty from a cruel social order.

To show that a substratum of social realism underlay the fantasies and escapist entertainment of folktales is not to take the argument very far, however.[45] The peasants could have learned that life was cruel without the help of "Little Red Riding Hood." Cruelty can be found in folktales as well as in social history everywhere from India to Ireland and from Africa to Alaska. If we are to get beyond vague generalizations in interpreting the French tales, we need to know whether something set them off from other varieties. We need to make at least a brief attempt at comparative analysis.

Consider, first, the Mother Goose that is most familiar to English speakers. Admittedly, the disparate collection of lullabies, counting rhymes, and bawdy songs that became attached to the name of Mother Goose in eighteenth-century England bears little resemblance to the stock of tales that Perrault drew on for his *Contes de ma mère l'oye* in seventeenth-century France. But the English Mother Goose is as revealing in its way as the French; and fortunately a good deal of it can be dated, because the verses proclaim their character as period pieces. "At the Siege of Belle Isle" belongs to the Seven Years' War, "Yankee Doodle" to the American Revolution, and "The Grand Old Duke of York" to the French revolutionary wars. Most of the rhymes, however, appear to be relatively modern (post-1700), despite persistent attempts to link them with names and events in the remoter past. Experts like Iona and Peter Opie have found little evidence for the assertions that Humpty Dumpty was Richard III, that Curly Locks was Charles II, that Wee Willie Winkie was William III, that Little Miss Muffet was Mary Queen of Scots, and that the spider was John Knox.[46]

In any case, the historical significance of the rhymes lies more in their tone than in their allusions. They have more gaiety and whimsy than the French and German tales, perhaps because so many of them belong to the period after the seventeenth century when England freed itself from the grip of Malthusianism. But there is a note of demographic agony in some of the older verses. Thus the English counterpart to the mother of Le Petit Poucet:

> *There was an old woman who lived in a shoe;*
> *She had so many children she didn't know what to do.*

Like peasants everywhere, she fed them on broth, though she could not provide any bread; and she vented her despair by whipping them. The diet of other children in Mother Goose was not much better:

> *Pease porridge hot,*
> *Pease porridge cold,*
> *Pease porridge in the pot*
> *Nine days old.*

Nor was their clothing:

> *When I was a little girl,*
> *About seven years old,*
> *I hadn't got a petticoat,*
> *To keep me from the cold.*

And they sometimes disappeared down the road, as in the Tudor-Stuart rhyme:

> *There was an old woman had three sons*
> *Jerry and James and John.*
> *Jerry was hung and James was drowned,*
> *John was lost and never was found,*
> *So there was an end of her three sons,*
> *Jerry and James and John.*

Life was hard in the old Mother Goose. Many characters sank into destitution:

> *See-saw, Margery Daw,*
> *Sold her bed and lay upon straw.*

Others, it is true, enjoyed a life of indolence, as in the case of the Georgian barmaid, Elsie Marley (alias Nancy Dawson):

> *She won't get up to feed the swine,*
> *But lies in bed till eight or nine.*

Curly Locks luxuriated in a diet of strawberries, sugar, and cream; but she seems to have been a late eighteenth-century girl. Old Mother Hubbard, an Elizabethan character, had to cope with a bare cupboard, while her contemporary, Little Tommy Tucker, was forced to sing for his supper. Simple Simon, who probably belongs to the seventeenth century, did not have a penny. And he was a harmless village idiot, unlike the threatening poor of drifters and deviants, who appear in the older rhymes:

> *Hark, hark,*
> *The dogs do bark,*
> *The beggars are coming to town;*
> *Some in rags,*
> *And some in jags,*
> *And one in a velvet gown.*

Poverty drove many Mother Goose characters into beggary and theft:

> *Christmas is a-comin;*
> *The geese are gettin fat.*
> *Please to put a penny*
> *In an old man's hat.*

They preyed on defenseless children:

> *Then came a proud beggar*
> *And said he would have her,*
> *And stole my little moppet [doll] away.*

And on their fellow paupers:

> *There was a man and he had nought,*
> *And robbers came to rob him;*
> *He crept up to the chimney top,*
> *And then they thought they had him.*

The old rhymes contain plenty of nonsense and good-humored fantasy; but from time to time a note of despair can be heard through the merriment. It summons up lives that were brutally brief, as in the case of Solomon Grundy, or that were overwhelmed with misery, as in the case of another anonymous old woman:

> *There was an old woman*
> *And nothing she had,*
> *And so this old woman*
> *Was said to be mad.*
> *She'd nothing to eat,*
> *She'd nothing to wear,*
> *She'd nothing to lose,*
> *She'd nothing to fear,*

She'd nothing to ask,
And nothing to give,
And when she did die
She'd nothing to leave.

All is not jollity in Mother Goose. The older rhymes belong to an older world of poverty, despair, and death.

In general, then, the rhymes of England have some affinity with the tales of France. The two are not really comparable, however, because they belong to different genres. Although the French sang some *contines* (counting rhymes) and lullabies to their children, they never developed anything like the English nursery rhymes; and the English never developed as rich a repertory of folktales as the French. Nevertheless, the folktale flourished enough in England for one to venture a few comparative remarks and then to extend the comparisons to Italy and Germany, where they can be pursued more systematically.

English folktales have much of the whimsy, humor, and fanciful details that appear in the nursery rhymes. They concern many of the same characters: Simple Simon, Dr. Fell, the Wise Men of Gotham, Jack of "The House That Jack Built," and especially Tom Thumb, the hero of the folktale, who loaned his name to the first important collection of nursery rhymes to be published in England, *Tommy Thumb's Pretty Song Book* (1744).[47] But Tom Thumb bears little resemblance to his French cousin, Le Petit Poucet. The English tale dwells on his pranks and the Lilliputian quaintness of his dress: "The fairies dressed him in a hat made of an oak-leaf, a shirt of spiders' web, jacket of thistle-down, and trousers of feathers. His stockings were of apple-rind, tied with one of his mother's eyelashes, and his shoes of mouse-skin, with the hair inside."[48] No such details brightened the life of Poucet. The French tale (tale type 700) does not mention his clothing and does not provide him with help from fairies or any other supernatural beings. Instead, it places him in a harsh, peasant world and shows how he fends off bandits, wolves, and the village priest by using his wits, the only defense of the "little people" against the rapacity of the big.

Despite a considerable population of ghosts and goblins, the world of the English tales seems far more genial. Even giant killing takes place in a land of nod; thus the beginning of "Jack the Giant-Killer" in one oral version:

> Once upon a time—a very good time it was—when pigs were swine and dogs ate lime and monkeys chewed tobacco, when houses were thatched with pancakes, streets paved with plum puddings, and roasted pigs ran up and down the streets with knives and forks in their backs, crying "Come and eat me!" That was a good time for travellers.[49]

In numbskull fashion, Jack trades the family cow for a few beans and then climbs his way to riches with the help of magic props—a fantastic beanstalk, a hen that lays golden eggs, and a talking harp. He is a kind of Simple Simon, like the Jacks and Jocks of a great many British tales. Brave but lazy, good-natured but thick-headed, he blunders into a happy ending in a happy-go-lucky world. His initial poverty and the ominous chorus of fee-fi-fo-fums from above the beanstalk do not spoil the atmosphere. Having overcome adversity, Jack earns his reward and emerges in the end looking like Little Jack Horner: "Oh what a good boy am I!"

The French giant killer belongs to another species: Petit Jean, Parle, or Le Petit Fûteux, according to different versions of the same story (tale type 328). A pint-sized younger son, "extraordinarily sharp witted . . . always lively and alert," he joins the army with his nasty older brothers, who persuade the king to send him on the suicidal mission of stealing treasure from a giant. Like most French giants, this "bonhomme" does not live in a never-never land somewhere over the beanstalk. He is a local landlord, who plays the fiddle, quarrels with his wife, and invites the neighbors in for feasts of roasted little boys. Petit Jean does not merely run away with the treasure; he bamboozles the giant, torments him in his sleep, oversalts his soup, and tricks his wife and daughter into baking themselves to death in an oven. Finally, the king assigns Petit Jean the seemingly impossible task of capturing the giant himself. The little hero sets off disguised as a monarch and driving a coach loaded with a huge iron cage.

> "Monsieur le roi, what are you doing with that iron cage?" the giant asks. "I'm trying to catch Petit Jean, who has played all kinds of tricks on me," Petit Jean replies. "He can't have been worse to you than to

me. I'm looking for him, too." "But, Giant, do you think you are strong enough to catch him all alone? He is supposed to be terrifically powerful. I'm not sure that I can keep him locked up in this iron cage." "Don't worry, Monsieur le roi, I can handle him without a cage; and if you like, I'll test yours."

So the giant gets in the cage. Petit Jean locks it. And after the giant exhausts himself trying to break the bars, Petit Jean announces his true identity and delivers his victim, helpless with rage, to the true king, who rewards him with a princess.[50]

If one blends an Italian variety into the different versions of the same tale type, one can observe the flavor changing from English fantasy to French cunning and Italian burlesque. In the case of tale type 301, which concerns the rescue of princesses from an enchanted underworld, the English hero is another Jack, the French another Jean. Jack frees his princesses by following the instructions of a dwarf. He descends into a pit, runs after a magic ball, and slays a succession of giants in copper, gold, and silver palaces. The French Jean has to contend with more treacherous surroundings. His fellow travelers abandon him to the devil in a haunted house and then cut the rope when he tries to haul himself out of the pit after delivering the princesses. The Italian hero, a palace baker who is run out of town for flirting with the king's daughter, follows the same path through the same dangers, but he does so in a spirit of buffoonery as well as bravura. The devil comes down the chimney of the haunted house in a magic ball and tries to trip him by bouncing between his feet. Unperturbed, the baker stands on a chair, then on a table, and finally on a chair mounted on the table while plucking a chicken as the diabolical ball pounds helplessly around him. Unable to overcome this circus act, the devil steps out of the ball and offers to help prepare the meal. The baker asks him to hold the firewood and then deftly chops off his head. He uses a similar trick in the underground pit to behead a sorcerer, who meanwhile has abducted the princess. Thus piling trick on trick, he finally wins his true love. The plot, identical to those in the English and French versions, seems to lead through the Commedia dell' Arte rather than into any kind of fairy land.[51]

The buffa-Machiavellianism of the Italian tales comes through even more strongly, if they are compared with the German. The Italian version of "The Youth Who Wanted to Know What Fear Was" (Grimm 4) contains an Alphonse-Gaston routine, in which the hero out-tricks the devil by making him go first through a succession of traps.[52] The Italian Little Red Riding Hood bamboozles the wolf by tossing him a cake full of nails, although later, as in the French tales, he tricks her into eating grandmother and then eats her himself.[53] The Italian Puss 'n Boots, like the French but unlike the German (tale type 545, Grimm 106), is a fox who plays on the vanity and gullibility of everyone around him to win a castle and a princess for his master. And the Italian "Bluebeard" shows how completely a tale can change in tone while remaining the same in structure.

In Italy, Bluebeard is a devil, who lures a succession of peasant girls into hell by hiring them to do his laundry and then tempting them with the usual device of the key to the forbidden door. The door leads to hell; so when they try it, flames leap out, singeing a flower that he places in their hair. After the devil returns from his travels, the singed flower shows him that the girls have broken the taboo; and he tosses them into the flames, one after the other—until he comes to Lucia. She agrees to work for him after her older sisters have disappeared. And she, too, opens the forbidden door, but just enough to glimpse her sisters in the flames. Because she has had the foresight to leave her flower in a safe place, the devil cannot condemn her for disobedience. On the contrary, she acquires power over him—enough, at least, to be granted one wish. She asks him to carry some laundry bags back to her mama so that she can have help in coping with the gigantic backlog of filthy washing that he has accumulated. The devil accepts the task and boasts that he is strong enough to make the entire trip without laying the bags down for a rest. Lucia replies that she will hold him to his word, for she has the power to see great distances. Then she frees her sisters from the hellfire and sneaks them into the laundry bags. Soon the devil is lugging them back to safety. Every time he begins to stop for a rest they call out, "I see you! I see you!" In the end, Lucia frees herself by the same ruse. So all the girls reach safety, using the devil himself to do the job and making a fool of him while they are at it.[54]

The German version of the tale (Grimm 46) follows the same story line, but it adds macabre touches where the Italian version uses humor. The villain is a mysterious wizard, who carries the girls off to a castle in the midst of a gloomy forest. The forbidden room is a chamber of horrors, and the narrative dwells on the murdering itself: "He threw her down, dragged her along by her hair, cut her head off on the block, and hewed her in pieces so that her blood ran on the ground. Then he threw her into the basin with the rest."[55] The heroine escapes this fate and acquires some magic power over the wizard by holding on to her key. She brings her sisters back to life by reassembling their mutilated corpses. Then she hides them in a basket, covers it with gold, and orders the wizard to carry it to her parents, while she prepares for the wedding that is to unite her with the wizard. She dresses a skull in bridal ornaments and flowers and sets it in a window. Then she disguises herself as a giant bird by rolling in honey and feathers. Coming upon her on her way back, the wizard asks her about the wedding preparations. She answers in verse that his bride has cleaned the house and is waiting for him at the window. The wizard hurries on; and when he and his accomplices have gathered for the ceremony, the girl's kinsmen sneak up, lock the doors, and burn the house to the ground with everyone in it.

As already mentioned, the French versions (tale types 311 and 312), including Perrault's, contain some gruesome details but nothing approaching the horror of the Grimms. Some of them emphasize the escape ruse, and most depend for their dramatic effect on the delaying tactics of the heroine, who slowly dons her wedding dress, while the villain (a devil, a giant, a "Monsieur" with a blue or green beard) sharpens his knife and her brothers rush to the rescue. The English versions seem almost jolly in comparison. "Peerifool" begins in Peter Rabbit fashion, with some robbing of a cabbage patch. It meanders through episodes involving riddles and elves but no hacked-up corpses, and it ends with some good, clean giant killing (by boiling water).[56] Although each story adheres to the same structure, the versions in the different traditions produce entirely different effects—comic in the Italian versions, horrific in the German, dramatic in the French, and droll in the English.

Of course, a storyteller could produce almost any effect from a tale, depending on how he told it. There is no way of knowing what effects the different versions of "Bluebeard" actually produced on listeners in different parts of Europe two centuries ago. And even if that could be known, it would be absurd to draw conclusions about national character by comparing variations of a single tale. But systematic comparisons of several tales should help one to isolate the qualities that gave the French oral tradition its peculiar character. The comparing works best where the tales are most comparable, in the French and German versions. If done thoroughly, it could extend to many volumes filled with statistics and structural diagrams. But one should be able to do enough within the bounds of a single essay to advance a few general propositions.

Consider "Godfather Death" (tale type 332). The French and German versions have exactly the same structure: (a) A poor man chooses Death as a godfather for his son. (b) Death makes the son prosper as a doctor. (c) The son tries to cheat Death and dies. In both versions the father refuses to accept God as godfather because he observes that God favors the rich and powerful, whereas Death treats everyone equally. This impiety is rejected in the Grimms' transcription of the German tale: "Thus spoke the man, for he did not know how wisely God apportions riches and poverty."[57] The French version leaves the question open and goes on to suggest that cheating works very well as a way of life. The doctor makes a fortune, because Death provides him with an infallible prognostic technique. When he sees Death standing at the foot of a sick person's bed, he knows the person will die. When Death appears at the head of the bed, the patient will recover and can be given any kind of fake medicine. In one instance, the doctor successfully predicts the death of a lord and in return receives two farms from the delighted heirs. In another, he sees Death at the foot of a princess's bed and pivots her body around so that Death is duped. The princess survives, he marries her, and they live to a ripe and happy old age. When the German doctor tries the same stratagem, Death seizes him by the throat and hauls him off to a cave full of candles, each of which stands for a life. Seeing that his own candle has almost expired, the doctor begs to have it lengthened. But Death snuffs it out, and the doctor falls dead at his feet. The French doctor eventually comes to the same end, but he postpones it quite successfully. In one version, he asks to say a *Pater* before the extinction of the candle, and by leaving the prayer unfinished tricks Death into allowing him a still longer life. Death finally gets him by pretending to be a cadaver at the side of the road—a common sight in early modern Europe and one that evoked a common response: the saying of a *Pater*, which brings the tale to a rather unedifying end. True, the story demonstrates that no one can cheat death, at least not in the long run. But cheating gives the Frenchman an excellent short run for his money.

"Le Chauffeur du diable" (tale type 475, Grimm 100) conveys a similar message. It, too, has the same organization in the French and German versions: (a) A poor, discharged soldier agrees to work for the devil, stoking fires under cauldrons in hell. (b) He disobeys the devil's order not to look inside the cauldrons and finds his former commanding officer(s). (c) He escapes from hell with a magic object, which, though nasty looking, produces all the gold he needs to live happily for the rest of his life. In the German version the plot unwinds in a straightforward manner but with fanciful details that do not exist in the French. As a condition for hiring the soldier, the devil demands that he not trim his nails, cut his hair, or bathe during the seven-year term of his service. After finding his former commanding officers in the cauldrons, the soldier stokes the fire higher; so the devil forgives him for his disobedience, and the soldier serves his seven years without further incident, growing more and more hideous in appearance. He emerges from hell looking like *Struwelpeter* and calling himself "the devil's sooty brother" as the devil had commanded. His obedience is rewarded, for the sack of sweepings which the devil had given him as wages turns into gold. When an innkeeper steals it, the devil intervenes to get it restored. And in the end, well-heeled and well-scrubbed, the soldier marries a princess and inherits a kingdom.

The French version turns on trickery. The devil lures the soldier into hell by pretending to be a gentleman in search of a servant for his kitchen. When the soldier discovers his former captain cooking in the cauldron, his first impulse is to pile new logs on the fire. But the captain stops him by revealing that they are in hell and offering advice on how to escape. The soldier should feign ignorance of his true situation and demand to be released on the grounds that he does not like the work. The devil will tempt him by offering gold—a ruse to get him to reach into a chest so that he can be beheaded when its cover slams down. Instead of gold, the soldier should demand an old pair of the devil's breeches as payment. This strategy works; and the next evening, as he arrives at an inn, the soldier finds the pockets full of gold. While he sleeps, however, the innkeeper's wife grabs the magic breeches and screams that he is trying to rape and murder her—another ruse, this time aimed at capturing the gold and sending the soldier to the gallows. But the devil intervenes in time to save him and to claim the breeches. And meanwhile the soldier has siphoned enough gold out of the pockets to retire happily and even, in some versions, to marry a princess. By out-tricking the tricksters, he arrives at the same point that his German counterpart reached by hard work, obedience, and self-degradation.

"Le Panier de figues" (tale type 570, Grimm 165) provides another example of how different messages can be construed from the same structure. It goes as follows: (a) A king promises his daughter to whoever can produce the finest fruit. (b) A peasant boy wins the contest after being kind to a magic helper whom his elder brothers had treated discourteously. (c) The king refuses to give the princess up and sets the hero a round of impossible tasks. (d) Aided by the helper, the hero performs the tasks and marries the princess after a final confrontation with the king. The hero of the German version is a good-natured numbskull, Hans Dumm. He carries out the tasks in a setting charged with supernatural forces and crowded by fanciful props—a boat that flies over land, a magic whistle, a hideous griffin, dwarfs, castles, and damsels in distress. Although he sometimes shows glimmers of intelligence, Hans overcomes disaster and wins his princess by taking orders from his magic helper and by following his nose.

His French counterpart, Benoît, lives by his wits in a rough-and-ready world of dupe or be duped. The king defends his daughter like a peasant battling for his barnyard, using one ruse after another. As in the German tale, he refuses to surrender the princess unless the hero can guard a flock of rabbits without letting any of them stray, and Benoît succeeds with the help of the magic whistle, which makes the rabbits come when they are called, no matter how hopelessly they seem to be dispersed. But instead of sending Benoît, like Hans, on a chase after a man-eating griffin, the king tries to separate rabbits from the pack by a series of stratagems. Disguised as a peasant, he offers to buy one for a high price. Benoît sees through the maneuver and uses it as an opportunity to turn the tables on the king. He will only surrender the rabbit to someone who can succeed in an ordeal, he announces. The king must drop his breeches and submit to a flogging. The king agrees but loses the rabbit as soon as it hears the magic whistle. The queen tries the same ruse and gets the same treatment, although in some versions she has to turn cartwheels, exposing her bare bottom. Then the princess has to kiss the hero—or, in some cases, to lift his donkey's tail and kiss its anus. No one can pry a rabbit from the pack. Still the king holds out. He will not give up his daughter until Benoît produces three bags of truth. As the court gathers round, Benoît lets loose his first truth, *sotto voce*: "Is it not true, Sire, that I switched you on the bare behind?" The king is trapped. He cannot bear to hear the next two truths and surrenders the princess. The magic props have fallen by the side. Battle has been joined *terre à terre*, in a real world of power, pride, and deviousness. And the weak win with the only weapon they possess: cunning. The tale pits the clever against the clever by half: "A rusé, rusé et demi," as one of the peasant raconteurs observes.[58]

That formula hardly does justice to the variety of themes that would emerge from a more thorough comparison of the French and German tales. One can certainly find clever underdogs in Grimm and magic in *Le Conte populaire français,* especially in the tales from Brittany and Alsace-Lorraine. A few of the French tales hardly differ at all from their counterparts in the Grimms' collection.[59] But allowing for exceptions and complications, the differences between the two traditions fall into consistent patterns. The peasant raconteurs took the same themes and gave them characteristic twists, the French in one way, the German in another. Where the French tales tend to be realistic, earthy, bawdy, and comical, the German veer off toward the supernatural, the poetic, the exotic, and the violent. Of course, cultural differences cannot be reduced to a formula—French craftiness versus German cruelty—but the comparisons make it possible to identify the peculiar inflection that the French gave to their stories, and their way of telling stories provides clues about their way of viewing the world.

Consider a final set of comparisons. In "La Belle Eulalie" (tale type 313), as already mentioned, the devil's daughter makes some talking pâtés and hides them under her pillow and the pillow of her lover, a discharged soldier who has sought shelter in the devil's house, in order to cover their escape. Suspecting foul play, the devil's wife nags at him to check on the youngsters. But he merely calls out from his bed and then snores off again, while the pâtés return reassuring replies and the lovers dash to safety. In the corresponding tale from the Grimms ("Der liebste Roland," number 56), a witch mistakenly decapitates her own daughter while trying to dispatch her stepdaughter one night. The stepdaughter drips blood on the stairs from the severed head and then runs away with her lover while the drops answer the witch's questions.

The good daughter who obligingly delouses the strange woman at the well in "Les Fées" (tale type 480) finds gold louis in the hair and becomes beautiful, while the bad daughter finds only lice and turns ugly. In "Frau Holle" (Grimm 24), the good daughter descends into a magic land beneath the well and serves the strange woman as a housekeeper. When she shakes a feather quilt, she makes it snow on earth. And when she receives a reward for her good work, a shower of golden rain clings to her and she becomes beautiful. The bad daughter performs the tasks begrudgingly and is showered with black pitch.

Persinette, the French Rapunzel (tale type 310), lets down her hair so that she can make love with the prince in her tower. She hides him from the fairy who keeps her captive and devises a variety of burlesque stratagems to impugn the testimony of the pet parrot who keeps betraying them. (In one version Persinette and the prince sew up the parrot's rear end, so it can only cry, "Ass stitched, ass stitched.")[60] The lovers finally escape, but the fairy changes Persinette's nose into the nose of an ass, which ruins their standing in court, until at last the fairy relents and restores her beauty. In Grimm's "Rapunzel" (number 12), the enchantress separates the lovers by banishing Rapunzel, with her hair shorn, to a desert and by forcing the prince to leap from the tower into some thorns, which blind him. He wanders in the wilderness for years, until at last he stumbles upon Rapunzel, and her tears falling on his eyes restore his sight.

After sharing his food with a fairy disguised as a beggar, the poor shepherd boy in "Les Trois Dons" (tale type 592) gets three wishes: that he can hit any bird with his bow and arrow, that he can make anyone dance with his flute, and that he can make his wicked stepmother fart whenever he says "atchoo." Soon he has the old woman farting all over the house, at the *veillée,* and at mass on Sundays. The priest has to turn her out of church in order to get through his sermon. Later, when she explains her problem, he tries to trick the boy into revealing his secret. But the little shepherd, who is trickier still, shoots a bird and asks him to fetch it. When the priest tries to grab it in a thorn bush, the boy plays the flute, forcing him to dance until his robe is torn to shreds and he is ready to drop. After he has recovered, the priest seeks vengeance by an accusation of witchcraft, but the boy sets the courtroom to dancing so uncontrollably with his flute that they let him free. In "Der Jude im Dorn" (Grimm 110), the hero is an underpaid servant, who gives his poor wages to a dwarf and in return receives a gun that can hit anything, a fiddle that can make anyone dance, and the power to make one unrefusable request. He meets a Jew listening to a bird singing in a tree. He shoots the bird, tells the Jew to retrieve it from a thorn bush, and then fiddles so implacably that the Jew nearly kills himself on the thorns and buys his release with a purse of gold. The Jew retaliates by getting the servant condemned for highway robbery. But as he is about to be hanged, the servant makes a last request for his fiddle. Soon everyone is dancing wildly around the gallows. The exhausted judge sets the servant free and hangs the Jew in his place.

It would be abusive to take this tale as evidence that anticlericalism functioned in France as the equivalent of anti-Semitism in Germany.[61] The comparison of folktales will not yield such specific conclusions. But it helps one to identify the peculiar flavor of the French tales. Unlike their German counterparts, they taste of salt. They smell of the earth. They take place in an intensely human world, where farting, delousing, rolling in the hay, and tossing on the dung heap express the passions, values, interests, and attitudes of a peasant society that is now extinct. If that is the case, can one be more precise in construing what the tales might have meant to the tellers and their audiences? I would like to advance two propositions: the tales told peasants how the world was put together, and they provided a strategy for coping with it.

Without preaching or drawing morals, French folktales demonstrate that the world is harsh and dangerous. Although most were not directed toward children, they tend to be cautionary. They erect warning signs around the seeking of fortune: "Danger!" "Road out!" "Go slow!" "Stop!" True, some have a positive message. They show that generosity, honesty, and courage win rewards. But they do not inspire much confidence in the effectiveness of loving enemies and turning the other cheek. Instead, they demonstrate that laudable as it may be to share your bread with beggars, you cannot trust everyone you meet along the road. Some strangers may turn into princes and good fairies; but others may be wolves and witches, and there is no sure way to tell them apart. The magic helpers whom Jean de l'Ours (tale type 301) picks up while seeking his fortune have the same Gargantuan powers as those in "Le Sorcier aux trois ceintures" (tale type 329) and "Le Navire sans pareil" (tale type 513). But they try to murder the hero at the point in the plot where the others save him.

However edifying some folktale characters may be in their behavior, they inhabit a world that seems arbitrary and amoral. In "Les Deux Bossus" (tale type 503), a hunchback comes upon a band of witches dancing and singing, "Monday, Tuesday, and Wednesday. Monday, Tuesday, and Wednesday." He joins the group and adds "and Thursday" to their song. Delighted with the innovation, they reward him by removing his deformity. A second hunchback tries the same device, adding, "and Friday." "That doesn't go," says one of the witches. "Not at all," says another. They punish him by inflicting him with the first hunchback. Doubly deformed, he cannot bear the taunts of the village and dies within the year. There is neither rhyme nor reason in such a universe. Disaster strikes fortuitously. Like the Black Death, it cannot be predicted or explained. it must simply be endured. More than half of the thirty-five recorded versions of "Little Red Riding Hood" end like the version recounted earlier, with the wolf devouring the girl. She had done nothing to deserve such a fate; for in the peasant tales, unlike those of Perrault and the Grimms, she did not disobey her mother or fail to read the signs of an implicit moral order written in the world around her. She simply walked into the jaws of death. It is the inscrutable, inexorable character of calamity that makes the tales so moving, not the happy endings that they frequently acquired after the eighteenth century.

As no discernible morality governs the world in general, good behavior does not determine success in the village or on the road, at least not in the French tales, where cunning takes the place of the pietism in the German. True, the hero often wins a magic helper by a good deed, but he gets the princess by using his wits. And sometimes he cannot get her without performing unethical acts. The hero in "Le Fidèle Serviteur" (tale type 516) escapes with the princess only because he refuses to help a beggar drowning in a lake. Similarly, in "L'Homme qui ne voulait pas mourir" (tale type 470B), he is finally caught by Death because he stops to help a poor wagon driver who is stuck in the mud. And in some versions of "Le Chauffeur du diable" (tale type 475) the hero wards off danger only as long as he or she (the protagonist can be a servant girl as well as a discharged soldier) can maintain a string of lies. As soon as he tells the truth, he is undone. The tales do not advocate immorality, but they undercut the notion that virtue will be rewarded or that life can be conducted according to any principle other than basic mistrust.

Those assumptions underlie the nastiness of village life as it appears in the tales. Neighbors are presumed to be hostile (tale type 162) and may be witches (tale type 709). They spy on you and rob your garden, no matter how poor you may be (tale type 330). You should never discuss your affairs in front of them or let them know in case you acquire sudden wealth by some stroke of magic, for they will denounce you as a thief if they fail to steal it themselves (tale type 563). In "La Poupée" (tale type 571C), a simple-minded orphan girl fails to observe these basic rules after receiving a magic doll, which excretes gold whenever she says, "Crap, crap, my little rag doll." Before long she has bought several chickens and a cow and invites the neighbors in. One of them pretends to fall asleep by the fire and runs off with the doll as soon as the girl goes to bed. But when he says the magic words, it craps real crap all over him. So he throws it on the dung heap. Then, one day when he is doing some crapping of his own, it reaches up and bites him. He cannot pry it loose from his *derrière* until the girl arrives, reclaims her property, and lives mistrustfully ever after.

If the world is cruel, the village nasty, and mankind infested with rogues, what is one to do? The tales do not give an explicit answer, but they illustrate the aptness of the ancient French proverb, "One must howl with the wolves."[62] Roguery runs through the whole corpus of French tales, though it often takes the milder and more agreeable form of tricksterism. Of course, tricksters exist in folklore everywhere, notably in the tales of the Plains Indians and in the Brer' Rabbit stories of American slaves.[63] But they seem especially prevalent in the French tradition. As shown above, whenever a French and a German tale follow the same pattern, the German veers off in the direction of the mysterious, the supernatural, and the violent, while the French steers straight for the village, where the hero can give full play to his talent for intrigue. True, the hero belongs to the same species of underdog that one meets in all European folktales. He or she will be a younger son, a stepdaughter, an abandoned child, a poor shepherd, an underpaid farm hand, an oppressed servant, a sorcerer's apprentice, or a Tom Thumb. But this common cloth has a French cut to it, particularly when the raconteur drapes it over favorite characters like Petit Jean, the feisty blacksmith's apprentice; Cadiou, the quick-witted tailor; and La Ramée, the tough and disillusioned soldier, who bluffs and braves his way through many tales, along with Pipette, the clever young recruit, and a host of others—Petit-Louis, Jean le Teigneux, Fench Coz, Belle Eulalie, Pitchin-Pitchot, Parle, Bonhomme Misère. Sometimes the names themselves suggest the qualities of wit and duplicity that carry the hero through his trials; thus Le Petit Fûteux, Finon-Finette, Parlafine, and Le Rusé Voleur. When passed in review, they seem to constitute an ideal type, the little guy who gets ahead by outwitting the big.

The trickster heroes stand out against a negative ideal, the numbskull. In the English tales, Simple Simon provides a good deal of innocent amusement. In the German, Hans Dumm is a likeable lout, who comes out on top by good-natured bumbling and help from magic auxiliaries. The French tales show no sympathy for village idiots or for stupidity in any form, including that of the wolves and ogres who fail to eat their victims on the spot (tale types 112D and 162). Numbskulls represent the antithesis of trick-sterism; they epitomize the sin of simplicity, a deadly sin, because naïveté in a world of confidence men is an invitation to disaster. The numbskull heroes of the French tales are therefore false numbskulls, like Petit Poucet and Crampoûes (tale types 327 and 569), who pretend to be dumb, all the better to succeed in manipulating a cruel but credulous world. Little Red Riding Hood—without the riding hood—uses the same strategy in the versions of the French tale where she escapes alive. "I have to relieve myself, Grandmother," she says as the wolf clutches her. "Do it here in bed, my dear," the wolf replies. But the girl insists, so the wolf permits her to go outside, tied to a rope. The girl attaches the rope to a tree and runs away, as the wolf tugs on it and calls out, having lost patience with waiting, "What are you doing, shitting coils of rope?"[64] In true, Gaulois fashion, the tale recounts the education of a trickster. Graduating from a state of innocence to one of fake naïveté, Little Red Riding Hood joins the company of Tom Thumb and Puss 'n Boots.

These characters have in common not merely cunning but weakness, and their adversaries are distinguished by strength as well as stupidity. Tricksterism always pits the little against the big, the poor against the rich, the underprivileged against the powerful. By structuring stories in this way, and without making explicit social comment, the oral tradition provided the peasants with a strategy for coping with their enemies under the Old Regime. Again, it should be stressed that there was nothing new or unusual about the theme of the weak outwitting the strong. It goes back to Ulysses's struggle against Cyclops and David's felling of Goliath, and it stands out strongly in the "clever maiden" motif of the German tales.[65] What matters is not the novelty of the theme but its significance—the way it fits into a narrative framework and takes shape in the telling of a tale. When the French underdogs turn the tables on the high and mighty, they do so in an earthy manner and a down-to-earth setting. They do not slay giants in a never-never land, even if they have to climb beanstalks to reach them. The giant in "Jean de l'Ours" (tale type 301) is *le bourgeois de la maison*,[66] living in an ordinary house like that of any wealthy farmer. The giant in "Le Conte de Parle" (tale type 328) is an overgrown *coq du village* "having supper with his wife and daughter"[67] when the hero arrives to bamboozle him. The giant in "La Soeur infidèle" (tale type 315) is a nasty miller; those in "Le Chasseur adroit" (tale type 304) are common bandits; those in "L'Homme sauvage" (tale type 502) and "Le Petit Forgeron" (tale type 317) are tyrannical landlords, whom the hero fells after a dispute over grazing rights. It required no great leap of the imagination to see them as the actual tyrants—the bandits, millers, estate stewards, and lords of the manor—who made the peasants' lives miserable within their own villages.

Some of the tales make the connection explicit. "Le Capricorne" (tale type 571) takes the theme of "The Golden Goose" as it is found in the Grimms (number 64) and transforms it into a burlesque indictment of the rich and the powerful in village society. A poor blacksmith is being cuckolded by his priest and tyrannized by the local seigneur. At the priest's instigation, the seigneur orders the smith to execute impossible tasks, which will keep him out of the way while the priest is occupied with his wife. The smith succeeds in the tasks twice, thanks to the help of a fairy. But on the third time, the seigneur orders a "capricorn," and the smith does not even know what it is. The fairy directs him to bore a hole in his attic floor and to call out "hold tight!" at whatever he sees. First he sees the servant girl with her nightdress between her teeth picking fleas from her private parts. The "hold tight!" freezes her in that position, just as her mistress calls for the chamber pot so that the priest can relieve himself. Walking in backward in order to hide her nudity, the girl presents the pot to the mistress, and both hold it for the priest just as another "hold tight!" sticks all three of them together. In the morning, the smith drives the trio out of the house with a whip and, by a series of well-timed "hold tights!," attaches a whole parade of village characters to them. When the procession arrives at the seigneur's residence, the smith calls out, "Here is your capricorn, Monsieur." The seigneur pays him off and everyone is released.

A Jacobin might be able to tell that story in such a way as to make it smell of gunpowder. But however little respect it shows for the privileged orders, it does not go beyond the bounds of nose thumbing and table turning. The hero is satisfied with exacting humiliation; he does not dream of revolution. Having ridiculed the local authorities, he leaves them to resume their places while he resumes his, unhappy as it is. Defiance does not take the heroes any farther in the other tales that venture close to social comment. When Jean le Teigneux (tale type 314) gets the upper hand on a king and two haughty princes, he makes them eat a peasant's meal of boiled potatoes and black bread; then, having won the princess, he takes his rightful place as heir to the throne. La Ramée wins his princess by using a kind of flea circus in a contest to make her laugh (tale type 559). Unable to bear the idea of a beggar for a son-in-law, the king goes back on his word and tries to force a courtier on her instead. Finally, it is decided that she will go to bed with both pretenders and choose the one she prefers. La Ramée wins this second contest by dispatching a flea into his rival's anus.

The bawdiness may have produced some belly laughs around eighteenth-century hearths, but did it knot the peasant viscera into a gutlike determination to overthrow the social order? I doubt it. A considerable distance separates ribaldry from revolution, *gauloiserie* from *jacquerie*. In another variation on the eternal theme of under-dog boy meets overprivileged girl, "Comment Kiot-Jean épousa Jacqueline" (tale type 593), the poor peasant, Kiot-Jean, is thrown out of the house when he submits his proposal to his true love's father, a prototypical *fermier* or wealthy peasant, who lorded it over the poor in the villages of the Old Regime and especially in Picardy, where this story was collected in 1881. Kiot-Jean consults a local witch and receives a handful of magic goat dung, which he hides under the ashes of the wealthy peasant's hearth. Trying to revive the fire, the daughter blows on it, and "Poop!" she lets out an enormous fart. The same thing happens to the mother, the father, and finally the priest, who emits a spectacular string of farts while sprinkling holy water and mumbling Latin exorcisms. The farting continues at such a rate—and one should imagine the peasant raconteur punctuating every few words of his improvised dialogue with a kind of Bronx cheer—that life becomes impossible in the household. Kiot-Jean promises to deliver them if they will give up the girl; and so he wins his Jacqueline after surreptitiously removing the goat dung.

No doubt the peasants derived some satisfaction from outwitting the rich and powerful in their fantasies as they tried to outwit them in everyday life, by lawsuits, cheating on manorial dues, and poaching. They probably laughed approvingly when the underdog dumped his worthless daughter on the king in "Les Trois Fileuses" (tale type 501), when he whipped the king in "Le Panier de figues" (tale type 570), tricked him into rowing the boat as a servant of the devil in "Le Garçon de chez la bucheronne" (tale type 461), and made him sit on the peak of his castle roof until he surrendered the princess in "La Grande Dent" (tale type 562). But it would be vain to search in such fantasies for the germ of republicanism. To dream of confounding a king by marrying a princess was hardly to challenge the moral basis of the Old Regime.

Taken as fantasies of table turning, the tales seem to dwell on the theme of humiliation. The clever weakling makes a fool of the strong oppressor by raising a chorus of laughter at his expense, preferably by some bawdy stratagem. He forces the king to lose face by exposing his backside. But laughter, even Rabelaisian laughter, has limits. Once it subsides, the tables turn back again; and as in the succession of Lent to Carnival in the unfolding of the calendar year, the old order regains its hold on the revelers. Tricksterism is a kind of holding operation. It permits the underdog to grasp some marginal advantage by playing on the vanity and stupidity of his superiors. But the trickster works within the system, turning its weak points to his advantage and therefore ultimately confirming it. Moreover, he may always meet someone trickier than himself, even in the ranks of the rich and powerful. The outtricked trickster demonstrates the vanity of expecting a final victory.

Ultimately then, tricksterism expressed an orientation to the world rather than a latent strain of radicalism. It provided a way of coping with a harsh society instead of a formula for overthrowing it. Consider a final tale, "Le Diable et le maréchal ferrant" (tale type 330), one of the trickiest in the repertory. A blacksmith cannot resist giving food and shelter to every beggar who knocks at the door, although he "has no more religion than a dog."[68] Soon he is reduced to beggary himself, but he escapes from it by selling his soul to the devil in return for seven years of freedom from poverty back at the smithy. After he has resumed his old habit of careless generosity, Jesus and Saint Peter call on him, disguised as beggars. The smith gives them a good meal, clean clothes, and a fresh bed. In return Jesus grants him three wishes. Saint Peter advises him to wish for paradise, but instead he asks for unedifying things, which vary according to different versions of the tale: that he can have a good meal (the usual fare: biscuits, sausage, and plenty of wine), that his pack of cards will always win for him, that his fiddle will make anyone dance, that his sack will be filled with anything he wishes, and in most cases that anyone who sits on his bench will remain stuck. When the devil's messenger comes to claim him at the end of the seven years, the smith offers hospitality as usual and then keeps him stuck to the bench until he grants a reprieve of seven years. Once they have elapsed, he wishes the next emissary from the devil into the sack and then pounds him on the anvil until he gives up another seven years. Finally, the smith agrees to go to hell, but the terrified devils refuse to take him in, or alternatively he wins his way out by playing at cards. Leading a troop of the damned—souls that he has won at the devil's gambling table—he presents himself at the gates to heaven. Saint Peter will not have him because of his impiety. But the smith takes out his fiddle and makes Peter dance until he relents, or else tosses his sack over the gate and wishes himself inside. Then, in some versions, he plays cards with the angels and wins his way up the celestial hierarchy: from a corner, to a place by the fire, to a seat on a chair, and finally a position close to God the Father. It goes without saying that heaven will be as stratified as the court of Louis XIV and that you can cheat your way into it. Cheating serves very well as a strategy for living. Indeed, it is the only strategy available to the "little people," who must take things as they are and make the most of them. Better to live like the smith, and to keep the belly full, than to worry about salvation and the equity of the social order. Unlike the German version (Grimm 81), which is full of piety and nearly empty of tricks, the French tale celebrates the trickster as a social type and suggests that tricksterism will work quite well as a way of life—or as well as anything in a cruel and capricious world.

The moral of these stories has passed into proverbial wisdom in France—a very French kind of proverbializing to the Anglo-Saxon ear:[69]

A rusé, rusé et demi: Against the clever, the clever by half.

A bon chat, bon rat: Against a good cat, a good rat.

Au pauvre, la besace: To the poor man, the beggar's bag.

On ne fait pas d'omelette sans casser les oeufs: You don't make an omelette without cracking eggs.

Ventre affamé n'a point d'oreilles: A famished stomach has no ears.

Là où la chèvre est attachée, il faut qu'elle broute: Where the goat is tied it must graze.

Ce n'est pas de sa faute, si les grenouilles n'ont pas de queue: It's not his fault if frogs don't have tails.

Il faut que tout le monde vive, larrons et autres: Everyone has to make a living, thieves and the rest.

The peasant raconteurs did not moralize explicitly in this fashion. They simply told tales. But the tales became absorbed into the general stock of images, sayings, and stylizations that constitute Frenchness. Now, "Frenchness" may seem to be an intolerably vague idea, and it smells of related notions like *Volksgeist* that have acquired a bad odor since ethnography became polluted with racism in the 1930s. Nonetheless, an idea may be valid even if it is vague and has been abused in the past. Frenchness exists. As the awkwardness of the proverbs' translations suggests, it is a distinct cultural style; and it conveys a particular view of the world—a sense that life is hard, that you had better not have any illusions about selflessness in your fellow men, that clear-headedness and quick wit are necessary to protect what little you can extract from your surroundings, and that moral nicety will get you nowhere. Frenchness makes for ironic detachment. It tends to be negative and disabused. Unlike its Anglo-Saxon opposite, the Protestant ethic, it offers no formula for conquering the world. It is a defense strategy, well suited to an oppressed peasantry or an occupied country. It still speaks today in colloquial exchanges like: *Comment vas-tu?* ("How are you?") *Je me défends.* ("I defend myself.")

How was this common coinage minted? No one can say, but the case of Perrault demonstrates that it was a complex process.[70] On the face of it, Perrault would seem to be the last person likely to take an interest in folk tales. A courtier, self-conscious "moderne," and architect of the authoritarian cultural policies of Colbert and Louis XIV, he had no sympathy for peasants or their archaic culture. Yet he picked up stories from the oral tradition and adapted them to the salon, adjusting the tone to suit the taste of a sophisticated audience. Away went the nonsense about paths of pins and needles and the cannibalizing of grandmother in "Little Red Riding Hood." Nevertheless the tale retained much of its original power. Unlike Mme d'Aulnoy, Mme de Murat, and other leaders of the fad for fairy tales under Louis XIV, Perrault did not deviate from the original story line and did not spoil the earthiness and simplicity of the oral version with prettified details. He acted as a *conteur doué* for his own milieu, as if he were the Louisquatorzean equivalent of the storytellers who squat around fires in Amazonia and New Guinea. Homer probably had reworked his material in a similar way twenty-six centuries earlier; Gide and Camus would do so again two centuries later.

But much as he has in common with all storytellers who adapt standard themes to particular audiences, Perrault represents something unique in the history of French literature: the supreme point of contact between the seemingly separate worlds of elite and popular culture. How the contact took place cannot be determined, but it may have occurred in a scene like the one in the frontispiece to the original edition of his tales, the first printed version of Mother Goose, which shows three well-dressed children listening raptly to an old crone at work in what seems to be the servants' quarters. An inscription above her reads *Contes de ma mère l'oye,* an allusion, apparently, to the cackling sound of old wives' tales. Marc Soriano has argued that Perrault's son learned the stories in some such scene and that Perrault then reworked them. But Perrault himself probably heard them in a similar setting, and so did most persons of his class; for all gentle folk passed their early childhood with wet nurses and nannies, who lulled them to sleep with popular songs and amused them, after they had learned to talk, with *histoires ou contes du temps passé,* as Perrault put it on his title page—that is, old wives' tales. While the *veillée* perpetuated popular traditions within the village, servants and wet nurses provided the link between the culture of the people and the culture of the elite. The two cultures were connected, even at the height of the Grand Siècle, when they would seem to have least in common; for the audiences of Racine and Lully had imbibed folklore with their milk.

Furthermore, Perrault's version of the tales reentered the stream of popular culture through the *Bibliothèque bleue,* the primitive paperbacks that were read aloud at *veillées* in villages where someone was capable of reading. These little blue books featured Sleeping Beauty and Little Red Riding Hood as well as Gargantua, Fortunatus, Robert le Diable, Jean de Calais, les Quatre Fils Aymon, Maugis l'Enchanteur, and many other characters from the oral tradition that Perrault never picked up. It would be a mistake to identify his meager Mother Goose with the vast folklore of early modern France. But a comparison of the two points up the inadequacy of envisaging cultural change in linear fashion, as the downward seepage of great ideas. Cultural currents intermingled, moving up as well as down, while passing through different media and connecting groups as far apart as peasants and salon sophisticates.[71]

Those groups did not inhabit completely separate mental worlds. They had a great deal in common—first and foremost, a common stock of tales. Despite the distinctions of social rank and geographical particularity, which permeated the society of the Old Regime, the tales communicated traits, values, attitudes, and a way of construing the world that was peculiarly French. To insist upon their Frenchness is not to fall into romantic rhapsodizing about national spirit, but rather to recognize the existence of distinct cultural styles, which set off the French, or most of them (for one must make allowances for the peculiarities of Bretons, Basques, and other ethnic groups), from other peoples identified at the time as German, Italian, and English.[72]

The point might seem obvious or belabored, except that it flies in the face of conventional wisdom in the history profession, which is to cut the past into tiny segments and wall them up within monographs, where they can be analyzed in minute detail and rearranged in rational order. The peasants of the Old Regime did not think monographically. They tried to make sense of the world, in all its booming, buzzing confusion, with the materials they had at hand. Those materials included a vast repertory of stories derived from ancient Indo-European lore. The peasant tellers of tales did not merely find the stories amusing or frightening or functional. They found them "good to think with." They reworked them in their own manner, using them to piece together a picture of reality and to show what that picture meant for persons at the bottom of the social order. In the process, they infused the tales with many meanings, most of which are now lost because they were embedded in contexts and performances that cannot be recaptured. At a general level, however, some of the significance still shows through the texts. By studying the entire corpus of them and by comparing them with corresponding tales in other traditions, one can see this general dimension of meaning expressed in characteristic narrative devices—ways of framing stories, setting tone, combining motifs, and inflecting plots. The French tales have a common style, which communicates a common way of construing experience. Unlike the tales of Perrault, they do not provide morals; and unlike the philosophies of the Enlightenment, they do not deal in abstractions. But they show how the world is made and how one can cope with it. The world is made of fools and knaves, they say: better to be a knave than a fool.

In the course of time, the message spread beyond the limits of folktales and beyond the bounds of the peasantry. It became a master theme of French culture in general, at its most sophisticated as well as its most popular. Perhaps it reached its fullest development in Perrault's Puss 'n Boots, the embodiment of "Cartesian" cunning. Puss belongs to a long line of tricksters: on the one hand, the crafty younger sons, stepdaughters, apprentices, servants, and foxes of the folk tales; on the other, the artful dodgers and confidence men of French plays and novels—Scapin, Crispin, Scaramouche, Gil Blas, Figaro, Cyrano de Bergerac, Robert Macaire. The theme still lives in films like *Les Règles du jeu* and journals like *Le Canard enchaîné.* It survives in ordinary language, as in the approving way one Frenchman will call another *méchant* and *malin* (both "wicked" and "shrewd"—France is a country where it is good to be bad). It has passed from the ancient peasantry into everyone's everyday life.

Of course everyday life no longer resembles the Malthusian misery of the Old Regime. The modern trickster follows new scenarios: he cheats on his income tax and dodges an all-powerful state instead of trying to outwit a local *seigneur.* But every move he makes is a tribute to his ancestors—Puss 'n Boots and all the rest. As the old stories spread across social boundaries and over centuries, they developed enormous staying power. They changed without losing their flavor. Even after they had become absorbed in the main currents of modern culture, they testified to the tenacity of an old view of the world. Guided by proverbial wisdom, the French are still trying to outwit the system. *Plus ça change, plus c'est la même chose.*

APPENDIX: VARIATIONS OF A TALE

So that the reader can see how the same tale type is inflected in different ways in the oral traditions of Germany and France, I have transcribed the Grimms' version of "Der Jude im Dorn" (tale type 592, Grimm 110, reprinted with permission from *The Complete Grimm's Fairy Tales,* by Jakob Ludwig Karl Grimm and Wilhelm Karl Grimm, translated by Margaret Hunt and James Stern, copyright 1944 by Pantheon Books, Inc. and renewed 1972 by Random House, Inc. Reprinted by permission of Pantheon Books, a Division of Random House, Inc., pp. 503–08, followed by its French counterpart, "Les Trois Dons" (*Le Conte populaire français,* vol. 2 [Paris, 1976], pp. 492–95, my translation).

THE JEW AMONG THE THORNS

There was once a rich man, who had a servant who served him diligently and honestly: he was every morning the first out of bed, and the last to go to rest at night; and whenever there was a difficult job to be done, which nobody cared to undertake, he was always the first to set himself to it. Moreover, he never complained, but was contented with everything, and always merry.

When a year was ended, his master gave him no wages, for he said to himself: "That is the cleverest way; for I shall save something, and he will not go away, but stay quietly in my service." The servant said nothing, but did his work the second year as he had done it the first; and when at the end of this, likewise, he received no wages, he submitted and still stayed on.

When the third year also was past, the master considered, put his hand in his pocket, but pulled nothing out. Then at last the servant said: "Master, for three years I have served you honestly, be so good as to give me what I ought to have; for I wish to leave, and look about me a little more in the world."

"Yes, my good fellow," answered the old miser; "you have served me industriously, and therefore you shall be graciously rewarded"; and he put his hand into his pocket, but counted out only three farthings, saying: "There, you have a farthing for each year; that is large and liberal pay, such as you would have received from few masters."

The honest servant, who understood little about money, put his fortune into his pocket, and thought: "Ah! now that I have my purse full, why need I trouble and plague myself any longer with hard work!" So on he went, up hill and down dale; and sang and jumped to his heart's content. Now it came to pass that as he was going by a thicket a little man stepped out, and called to him: "Whither away, merry brother? I see you do not carry many cares." "Why should I be sad?" answered the servant; "I have enough; three years' wages are jingling in my pocket."

"How much is your treasure?" the dwarf asked him.

"How much? Three farthings sterling, all told."

"Look here," said the dwarf, "I am a poor needy man, give me your three farthings; I can work no longer, but you are young, and can easily earn your bread."

And as the servant had a good heart, and felt pity for the little man, he gave him the three farthings, saying: "Take them in the name of Heaven, I shall not be any the worse for it."

Then the little man said: "As I see you have a good heart, I grant you three wishes, one for each farthing. They shall all be fulfilled."

"Aha?" said the servant, "you are one of those who can work wonders! Well, then, if it is to be so, I wish, first, for a gun, which shall hit everything that I aim at; secondly, for a fiddle, which when I play on it, shall compel all who hear it to dance; thirdly, that if I ask a favor of any one he shall not be able to refuse it."

"All that shall you have," said the dwarf; and put his hand into the bush and just imagine, there lay a fiddle and gun, all ready, just as if they had been ordered. These he gave to the servant, and then said to him: "Whatever you may ask at any time, no man in the world shall be able to deny you."

"Heart alive! What more can one desire?" said the servant to himself, and went merrily onwards. Soon afterwards he met a Jew with a long goat's-beard, who was standing listening to the song of a bird which was sitting up at the top of a tree. "Good heavens," he was exclaiming, "that such a small creature should have such a fearfully loud voice! If it were but mine! If only some one would sprinkle some salt upon its tail!"

"If that is all," said the servant, "the bird shall soon be down here," and taking aim he shot, and down fell the bird into the thorn-bushes. "Go, you rogue," he said to the Jew, "and fetch the bird out for yourself!"

"Oh!" said the Jew, "leave out the rogue, my master, and I will do it at once. I will get the bird out for myself, now that you have hit it." Then he lay down on the ground, and began to crawl into the thicket.

When he was fast among the thorns, the good servant's humor so tempted him that he took up his fiddle and began to play. In a moment the Jew's legs began to move, and to jump into the air, and the more the servant fiddled the better went the dance. But the thorns tore his shabby coat from him, combed his beard, and pricked and plucked him all over the body. "Oh dear," cried the Jew, "what do I want with your fiddling? Leave the fiddle alone, master; I do not want to dance."

But the servant did not listen to him, and thought, "You have fleeced people often enough, now the thorn-bushes shall do the same to you"; and he began to play over again, so that the Jew had to jump higher than ever, and scraps of his coat were left hanging on the thorns. "Oh, woe's me!" cried the Jew; "I will give the gentleman whatsoever he asks if only he leaves off fiddling—a whole purse full of gold." "If you are so liberal," said the servant, "I will stop my music; but this I must say to your credit, that you dance to it so well that one must really admire it"; and having taken the purse, he went his way.

The Jew stood still and watched the servant quietly until he was far off and out of sight, and then he screamed out with all his might: "You miserable musician, you beer-house fiddler! Wait till I catch you alone, I will hunt you till the soles of your shoes fall off! You ragamuffin! Just put six farthings in your mouth, that you may be worth three halfpence!" and went on abusing him as fast as he could speak. As soon as he had refreshed himself a little in this way, and got his breath again, he ran into the town to the justice.

"My lord judge," he said, "I have come to make a complaint; see how a rascal has robbed and ill-treated me on the public highway! A stone on the ground might pity me; my clothes all torn, my body pricked and scratched, my little all gone with my purse— good ducats, each piece better than the last; for God's sake let the man be thrown into prison!"

"Was it a soldier," asked the judge, "who cut you thus with his sabre?" "Nothing of the sort!" said the Jew; "it was no sword that he had, but a gun hanging at his back, and a fiddle at his neck; the wretch may easily be recognized."

So the judge sent his people out after the man, and they found the good servant, who had been going quite slowly along, and they found, too, the purse with the money upon him. As soon as he was taken before the judge he said: "I did not touch the Jew, nor take his money; he gave it to me of his own free will, that I might leave off fiddling because he could not bear my music."

"Heaven defend us!" cried the Jew, "his lies are as thick as flies upon the wall."

But the judge also did not believe his tale, and said: "This is a bad defense, no Jew would do that." And because he had committed robbery on the public highway, he sentenced the good servant to be hanged. As he was being led away the Jew again screammed after him: "You vagabond! You dog of a fiddler! Now you are going to receive your well-earned reward!" The servant walked quietly with the hangman up the ladder, but upon the last step he turned round and said to the judge: "Grant me just one request before I die."

"Yes, if you do not ask your life," said the judge.

"I do not ask for life," answered the servant, "but as a last favor let me play once more upon my fiddle."

The Jew raised a great cry of "Murder! Murder! For goodness' sake do not allow it! Do not allow it!" But the judge said: "Why should I not let him have this short pleasure? It has been granted to him, and he shall have it." However, he could not have refused on account of the gift which had been bestowed on the servant.

Then the Jew cried: "Oh! woe's me! tie me fast!" while the good servant took his fiddle from his neck, and made ready. As he gave the first scrape, they all began to quiver and shake, the judge, his clerk, and the hangman and his men, and the cord fell out of the hand of the one who was going to tie the Jew fast. At the second scrape all raised their legs, and the hangman let go his hold of the good servant, and made himself ready to dance. At the third scrape they all leaped up and began to dance; the judge and the Jew being the best at jumping. Soon all who had gathered in the market-place out of curiosity were dancing with them; old and young, fat and lean, one with another. The dogs, likewise, which had run there, got up on their hind legs and capered about; and the longer he played, the higher sprang the dancers, so that they knocked against each other's heads, and began to shriek terribly.

At length the judge cried, quite out of breath: "I will give you your life if you will only stop fiddling." The good servant thereupon had compassion, took his fiddle and hung it round his neck again, and stepped down the ladder. Then he went up to the Jew, who was lying upon the ground panting for breath, and said: "You rascal, now confess, whence you got the money, or I will take my fiddle and begin to play again." "I stole it, I stole it!" cried he; "but you have honestly earned it." So the judge had the Jew taken to the gallows and hanged as a thief.

THE THREE GIFTS

Once upon a time there was a little boy, whose mother died soon after his birth. His father, who was still young, remarried soon afterward; but the second wife, instead of taking care of her stepson, detested him with all her heart and treated him harshly.

She sent him out to tend the sheep along the roadside. He had to stay outdoors all day, with only tattered and patched-up clothes to cover himself. For food, she gave him only a small slice of bread with so little butter that it hardly covered the surface, no matter how thinly he spread it.

One day as he was eating this meager meal while sitting on a bench and watching over his flock, he saw a ragged old woman come along the road leaning on a stick. She looked just like a beggar, but was really a fairy in disguise, such as existed in those times. She came up to the little boy and said to him, "I am very hungry. Will you give me some of your bread?"

"Alas! I hardly have enough for myself, for my stepmother is so stingy that every day she cuts me a smaller slice. Tomorrow it will be smaller still."

"Take pity on a poor old woman, my boy, and give me a bit of your dinner."

The child, who had a good heart, agreed to share his bread with the beggar, who returned the next day when he was about to eat and asked for pity once again. Although the piece was still smaller than the one from the previous day, he agreed to cut off part of it for her.

On the third day, the bread and butter was hardly as large as your hand, but still the old woman received her share.

When she had eaten it, she said, "You were good to an old woman who you thought was begging for bread. I am really a fairy, and I have the power to grant you three wishes as a recompense. Choose the three things that will give you the most pleasure."

The little shepherd had a crossbow in his hand. He wished that all of his arrows would fell small birds without a miss and that the tunes he played on his flute would have the power to make everyone dance, whether they wanted to or not. He had a little trouble deciding on the third wish; but in thinking back on all the cruel treatment he had received from his stepmother, he wanted to have vengeance and wished that every time he sneezed she would not be able to resist letting out a loud fart.

"Your desires will be accomplished, my little man," said the fairy, whose rags had become transformed into a beautiful dress and whose face appeared young and fresh.

In the evening, the little boy led his flock back; and as he entered the house, he sneezed. Immediately, his stepmother, who was busy making buckwheat cakes at the hearth, let out a loud, resounding fart. And every time he said "atchoo," the old woman answered with such an explosive sound that she was covered with shame. That night when the neighbors gathered together at the *veillée*, the little boy took to sneezing so often that everyone reproached the woman for her nastiness.

The next day was a Sunday. The stepmother took the little fellow to mass, and they sat underneath the pulpit. Nothing unusual happened during the first part of the service; but as soon as the priest began his sermon, the child began to sneeze and his stepmother, despite all her efforts to contain them, immediately let out a salvo of farts and turned so red in the face that everyone stared at her and she wished she were a hundred feet under the ground. As the improper noise continued without letting up, the priest could not go on with his sermon and ordered the beadle to usher out this woman who showed so little respect for the holy place.

The next day the priest came to the farm and scolded the woman for behaving so badly in church. She had scandalized the entire parish. "It's not my fault," she said. "Every time my husband's son sneezes, I can't prevent myself from farting. It's driving me crazy." Just at that moment the little fellow, who was about to leave with his sheep, let out two or three sneezes and the woman responded immediately.

The priest left the house with the boy and walked along with him, trying to discover his secret and giving him a scolding all the while. But the crafty little rogue would not confess anything. When they passed near a bush where several small birds were perched, he shot one of them with his crossbow and asked the priest to fetch it. The priest agreed, but when he arrived at the spot where the bird had fallen, a thorny area overrun with brambles, the little boy played on his flute and the priest began to whirl and dance so fast, in spite of himself, that his cassock got caught in the thorns; and before long it was torn to shreds.

When at last the music died down, the priest was able to stop; but he was completely out of breath. He brought the little boy before the justice of the peace and accused him of destroying his cassock. "He is a wicked witch," the priest said. "He must be punished."

The boy took out his flute, which he had carefully slipped into his pocket, and as soon as he sounded the first note, the priest, who was standing, began to dance; the clerk began to whirl on his chair; the justice of the peace himself bounded up and down on his seat; and everyone present shook their legs so wildly that the courtroom looked like a dance hall.

Soon they became tired of this forced exercise, and they promised the little boy that they would leave him alone if he would stop playing.

The "First Stage of Cruelty" by William Hogarth

2

WORKERS REVOLT: THE GREAT CAT MASSACRE OF THE RUE SAINT-SÉVERIN

THE FUNNIEST THING that ever happened in the printing shop of Jacques Vincent, according to a worker who witnessed it, was a riotous massacre of cats. The worker, Nicolas Contat, told the story in an account of his apprenticeship in the shop, rue Saint-Séverin, Paris, during the late 1730s.[1] Life as an apprentice was hard, he explained. There were two of them: Jerome, the somewhat fictionalized version of Contat himself, and Léveillé. They slept in a filthy, freezing room, rose before dawn, ran errands all day while dodging insults from the journeymen and abuse from the master, and received nothing but slops to eat. They found the food especially galling. Instead of dining at the master's table, they had to eat scraps from his plate in the kitchen. Worse still, the cook secretly sold the leftovers and gave the boys cat food—old, rotten bits of meat that they could not stomach and so passed on to the cats, who refused it.

This last injustice brought Contat to the theme of cats. They occupied a special place in his narrative and in the household of the rue Saint-Séverin. The master's wife adored them, especially *la grise* (the gray), her favorite. A passion for cats seemed to have swept through the printing trade, at least at the level of the masters, or *bourgeois* as the workers called them. One bourgeois kept twenty-five cats. He had their portraits painted and fed them on roast fowl. Meanwhile, the apprentices were trying to cope with a profusion of alley cats who also thrived in the printing district and made the boys' lives miserable. The cats howled all night on the roof over the apprentices' dingy bedroom, making it impossible to get a full night's sleep. As Jerome and Léveillé had to stagger out of bed at four or five in the morning to open the gate for the earliest arrivals among the journeymen, they began the day in a state of exhaustion while the bourgeois slept late. The master did not even work with the men, just as he did not eat with them. He let the foreman run the shop and rarely appeared in it, except to vent his violent temper, usually at the expense of the apprentices.

One night the boys resolved to right this inequitable state of affairs. Léveillé, who had an extraordinary talent for mimickry, crawled along the roof until he reached a section near the master's bedroom, and then he took to howling and meowing so horribly that the bourgeois and his wife did not sleep a wink. After several nights of this treatment, they decided they were being bewitched. But instead of calling the curé—the master was exceptionally devout and the mistress exceptionally attached to her confessor—they commanded the apprentices to get rid of the cats. The mistress gave the order, enjoining the boys above all to avoid frightening her *grise*.

Gleefully Jerome and Léveillé set to work, aided by the journeymen. Armed with broom handles, bars of the press, and other tools of their trade, they went after every cat they could find, beginning with *la grise*. Léveillé smashed its spine with an iron bar and Jerome finished it off. Then they stashed it in a gutter while the journeymen drove the other cats across the rooftops, bludgeoning every one within reach and trapping those who tried to escape in strategically placed sacks. They dumped sackloads of half-dead cats in the courtyard. Then the entire workshop gathered round and staged a mock trial, complete with guards, a confessor, and a public executioner. After pronouncing the animals guilty and administering last rites, they strung them up on an improvised gallows. Roused by gales of laughter, the mistress arrived. She let out a shriek as soon as she saw a bloody cat dangling from a noose. Then she realized it might be *la grise*. Certainly not, the men assured her: they had too much respect for the house to do such a thing. At this point the master appeared. He flew into a rage at the general stoppage of work, though his wife tried to explain that they were threatened by a more serious kind of insubordination. Then master and mistress withdrew, leaving the men delirious with "joy," "disorder," and "laughter."[2]

The laughter did not end there. Léveillé reenacted the entire scene in mime at least twenty times during subsequent days when the printers wanted to knock off for some hilarity. Burlesque reenactments of incidents in the life of the shop, known as *copies* in printers' slang, provided a major form of entertainment for the men. The idea was to humiliate someone in the shop by satirizing his peculiarities. A successful *copie* would make the butt of the joke fume with rage—*prendre la chèvre* (take the goat) in the shop slang—while his mates razzed him with "rough music." They would run their composing sticks across the tops of the type cases, beat their mallets against the chases, pound on cupboards, and bleat like goats. The bleating (*bais* in the slang) stood for the humiliation heaped on the victims, as in English when someone "gets your goat." Contat emphasized that Léveillé produced the funniest *copies* anyone had ever known and elicited the greatest choruses of rough music. The whole episode, cat massacre compounded by *copies,* stood out as the most hilarious experience in Jerome's entire career.

Yet it strikes the modern reader as unfunny, if not downright repulsive. Where is the humor in a group of grown men bleating like goats and banging with their tools while an adolescent reenacts the ritual slaughter of a defenseless animal? Our own inability to get the joke is an indication of the distance that separates us from the workers of preindustrial Europe. The perception of that distance may serve as the starting point of an investigation, for anthropologists have found that the best points of entry in an attempt to penetrate an alien culture can be those where it seems to be most opaque. When you realize that you are not getting something—a joke, a proverb, a ceremony—that is particularly meaningful to the natives, you can see where to grasp a foreign system of meaning in order to unravel it. By getting the joke of the great cat massacre, it may be possible to "get" a basic ingredient of artisanal culture under the Old Regime.

It should be explained at the outset that we cannot observe the killing of the cats at firsthand. We can study it only through Contat's narrative, written about twenty years after the event. There can be no doubt about the authenticity of Contat's quasi-fictional autobiography, as Giles Barber has demonstrated in his masterful edition of the text. It belongs to the line of autobiographical writing by printers that stretches from Thomas Platter to Thomas Gent, Benjamin Franklin, Nicolas Restif de la Bretonne, and Charles Manby Smith. Because printers, or at least compositors, had to be reasonably literate in order to do their work, they were among the few artisans who could give their own accounts of life in the working classes two, three, and four centuries ago. With all its misspellings and grammatical flaws, Contat's is perhaps the richest of these accounts. But it cannot be regarded as a mirror-image of what actually happened. It should be read as Contat's version of a happening, as his attempt to tell a story. Like all story telling, it sets the action in a frame of reference; it assumes a certain repertory of associations and responses on the part of its audience; and it provides meaningful shape to the raw stuff of experience. But since we are attempting to get at its meaning in the first place, we should not be put off by its fabricated character. On the contrary, by treating the narrative as fiction or meaningful fabrication we can use it to develop an ethnological *explication de texte*.

The first explanation that probably would occur to most readers of Contat's story is that the cat massacre served as an oblique attack on the master and his wife. Contat set the event in the context of remarks about the disparity between the lot of workers and the bourgeois—a matter of the basic elements in life: work, food, and sleep. The injustice seemed especially flagrant in the case of the apprentices, who were treated like animals while the animals were promoted over their heads to the position the boys should have occupied, the place at the master's table. Although the apprentices seem most abused, the text makes it clear that the killing of the cats expressed a hatred for the bourgeois that had spread among all the workers: "The masters love cats; consequently [the workers] hate them." After masterminding the massacre, Léveillé became the hero of the shop, because "all the workers are in league against the masters. It is enough to speak badly of them [the masters] to be esteemed by the whole assembly of typographers."[3]

Historians have tended to treat the era of artisanal manufacturing as an idyllic period before the onset of industrialization. Some even portray the workshop as a kind of extended family in which master and journeymen labored at the same tasks, ate at the same table, and sometimes slept under the same roof.[4] Had anything happened to poison the atmosphere of the printing shops in Paris by 1740?

During the second half of the seventeenth century, the large printing houses, backed by the government, eliminated most of the smaller shops, and an oligarchy of masters seized control of the industry.[5] At the same time, the situation of the journeymen deteriorated. Although estimates vary and statistics cannot be trusted, it seems that their number remained stable: approximately 335 in 1666, 339 in 1701, and 340 in 1721. Meanwhile the number of masters declined by more than half, from eighty-three to thirty-six, the limit fixed by an edict of 1686. That meant fewer shops with larger work forces, as one can see from statistics on the density of presses: in 1644 Paris had seventy-five printing shops with a total of 180 presses; in 1701 it had fifty-one shops with 195 presses. This trend made it virtually impossible for journeymen to rise into the ranks of the masters. About the only way for a worker to get ahead in the craft was to marry a master's widow, for masterships had become hereditary privileges, passed on from husband to wife and from father to son.

The journeymen also felt threatened from below because the

masters tended increasingly to hire *alloués,* or underqualified printers, who had not undergone the apprenticeship that made a journeyman eligible, in principle, to advance to a mastership. The *alloués* were merely a source of cheap labor, excluded from the upper
ranks of the trade and fixed, in their inferior status, by an edict of
1723. Their degradation stood out in their name: they were *à louer*
(for hire), not *compagnons* (journeymen) of the master. They personified the tendency of labor to become a commodity instead of a
partnership. Thus Contat served his apprenticeship and wrote his
memoirs when times were hard for journeymen printers, when the
men in the shop in the rue Saint-Séverin stood in danger of being
cut off from the top of the trade and swamped from the bottom.

How this general tendency became manifest in an actual workshop may be seen from the papers of the Société typographique de
Neuchâtel (STN). To be sure, the STN was Swiss, and it did not
begin business until seven years after Contat wrote his memoirs
(1762). But printing practices were essentially the same way everywhere in the eighteenth century. The STN's archives conform in
dozens of details to Contat's account of his experience. (They even
mention the same shop foreman, Colas, who supervised Jerome for
a while at the Imprimerie Royale and took charge of the STN's
shop for a brief stint in 1779.) And they provide the only surviving
record of the way masters hired, managed, and fired printers in the
early modern era.

The STN's wage book shows that workers usually stayed in the
shop for only a few months.[6] They left because they quarreled
with the master, they got in fights, they wanted to pursue their
fortune in shops further down the road, or they ran out of work.
Compositors were hired by the job, *labeur* or *ouvrage* in printer's
slang. When they finished a job, they frequently were fired, and a
few pressmen had to be fired as well in order to maintain the
balance between the two halves of the shop, the *casse* or composing
sector and the *presse* or pressroom (two compositors usually set
enough type to occupy a team of two pressmen.) When the foreman took on new jobs, he hired new hands. The hiring and firing
went on at such a fierce pace that the work force was rarely the
same from one week to the next. Jerome's fellow workers in the
rue Saint-Séverin seem to have been equally volatile. They, too,

were hired for specific *labeurs,* and they sometimes walked off the job after quarrels with the bourgeois—a practice common enough to have its own entry in the glossary of their slang which Contat appended to his narrative: *emporter son Saint Jean* (to carry off your set of tools or quit). A man was known as an *ancien* if he remained in the shop for only a year. Other slang terms suggest the atmosphere in which the work took place: *une chèvre capitale* (a fit of rage), *se donner la gratte* (to get in a fight), *prendre la barbe* (to get drunk), *faire la déroute* (to go pub crawling), *promener sa chape* (to knock off work), *faire des loups* (to pile up debts).[7]

The violence, drunkenness, and absenteeism show up in the statistics of income and output one can compile from the STN's wage book. Printers worked in erratic spurts—twice as much in one week as in another, the weeks varying from four to six days and the days beginning anywhere from four in the morning until nearly noon. In order to keep the irregularity within bounds, the masters sought out men with two supreme traits: assiduousness and sobriety. If they also happened to be skilled, so much the better. A recruiting agent in Geneva recommended a compositor who was willing to set out for Neuchâtel in typical terms: "He is a good worker, capable of doing any job he gets, not at all a drunkard and assiduous at his labor."[8]

The STN relied on recruiters because it did not have an adequate labor pool in Neuchâtel and the streams of printers on the typographical *tours de France* sometimes ran dry. The recruiters and employers exchanged letters that reveal a common set of assumptions about eighteenth-century artisans: they were lazy, flighty, dissolute, and unreliable. They could not be trusted, so the recruiter should not loan them money for travel expenses and the employer could keep their belongings as a kind of security deposit in case they skipped off after collecting their pay. It followed that they could be discarded without compunction, whether or not they had worked diligently, had families to support, or fell sick. The STN ordered them in "assortments" just as it ordered paper and type. It complained that a recruiter in Lyon "sent us a couple in such a bad state that we were obliged to ship them off"[9] and lectured him about failing to inspect the goods: "Two of those whom you have sent to us have arrived all right, but so sick that they could infect all the rest; so we haven't been able to hire them. No one in town wanted to give them lodging. They have therefore left again and took the route for Besançon, in order to turn themselves in at the *hôpital.*"[10] A bookseller in Lyon advised them to fire most of their men during a slack period in their printing in order to flood the labor supply in eastern France and "give us more power over a wild and undisciplinable race, which we cannot control."[11] Journeymen and masters may have lived together as members of a happy family at some time somewhere in Europe, but not in the printing houses of eighteenth-century France and Switzerland.

Contat himself believed that such a state had once existed. He began his description of Jerome's apprenticeship by invoking a golden age when printing was first invented and printers lived as free and equal members of a "republic," governed by its own laws and traditions in a spirit of fraternal "union and friendship."[12] He claimed that the republic still survived in the form of the *chapelle* or workers' association in each shop. But the government had broken up general associations; the ranks had been thinned by *alloués;* the journeymen had been excluded from masterships; and the masters had withdrawn into a separate world of *haute cuisine* and *grasses matinées.* The master in the rue Saint-Séverin ate different food, kept different hours, and talked a different language. His wife and daughters dallied with worldly abbés. They kept pets. Clearly, the bourgeois belonged to a different subculture—one which meant above all that he did not work. In introducing his account of the cat massacre, Contat made explicit the contrast between the worlds of worker and master that ran throughout the narrative: "Workers, apprentices, everyone works. Only the masters and mistresses enjoy the sweetness of sleep. That makes Jerome and Léveillé resentful. They resolve not to be the only wretched ones. They want their master and mistress as associates (*associés*)."[13] That is, the boys wanted to restore a mythical past when masters and men worked in friendly association. They also may have had in mind the more recent extinction of the smaller printing shops. So they killed the cats.

But why cats? And why was the killing so funny? Those questions take us beyond the consideration of early modern labor relations and into the obscure subject of popular ceremonies and symbolism.

Folklorists have made historians familiar with the ceremonial cycles that marked off the calendar year for early modern man.[14] The most important of these was the cycle of carnival and Lent, a period of revelry followed by a period of abstinence. During carnival the common people suspended the normal rules of behavior and ceremoniously reversed the social order or turned it upside down in riotous procession. Carnival was a time for cutting up by youth groups, particularly apprentices, who organized themselves in "abbeys" ruled by a mock abbot or king and who staged charivaris or burlesque processions with rough music in order to humiliate cuckolds, husbands who had been beaten by their wives, brides who had married below their age group, or someone else who personified the infringement of traditional norms. Carnival was high season for hilarity, sexuality, and youth run riot—a time when young people tested social boundaries by limited outbursts of deviance, before being reassimilated in the world of order, submission, and Lentine seriousness. It came to an end on Shrove Tuesday or Mardi Gras, when a straw mannequin, King Carnival or Caramantran, was given a ritual trial and execution. Cats played an important part in some charivaris. In Burgundy, the crowd incorporated cat torture into its rough music. While mocking a cuckold or some other victim, the youths passed around a cat, tearing its fur to make it howl. *Faire le chat,* they called it. The Germans called charivaris *Katzenmusik,* a term that may have been derived from the howls of tortured cats.[15]

Cats also figured in the cycle of Saint John the Baptist, which took place on June 24, at the time of the summer solstice. Crowds made bonfires, jumped over them, danced around them, and threw into them objects with magical power, hoping to avoid disaster and obtain good fortune during the rest of the year. A favorite object was cats—cats tied up in bags, cats suspended from ropes, or cats burned at the stake. Parisians liked to incinerate cats by the sackful, while the Courimauds (*cour à miaud* or cat chasers) of Saint Chamond preferred to chase a flaming cat through the streets. In parts of Burgundy and Lorraine they danced around a kind of burning

The world turned upside down in a carnival procession

May pole with a cat tied to it. In the Metz region they burned a dozen cats at a time in a basket on top of a bonfire. The ceremony took place with great pomp in Metz itself, until it was abolished in 1765. The town dignitaries arrived in procession at the Place du Grand-Saulcy, lit the pyre, and a ring of riflemen from the garrison fired off volleys while the cats disappeared screaming in the flames. Although the practice varied from place to place, the ingredients were everywhere the same: a *feu de joie* (bonfire), cats, and an aura of hilarious witch-hunting.[16]

In addition to these general ceremonies, which involved entire communities, artisans celebrated ceremonies peculiar to their craft. Printers processed and feasted in honor of their patron, Saint John the Evangelist, both on his saint's day, December 27, and on the anniversary of his martyrdom, May 6, the festival of Saint Jean Porte Latine. By the eighteenth century, the masters had excluded the journeymen from the confraternity devoted to the saint, but the journeymen continued to hold ceremonies in their chapels.[17] On Saint Martin's day, November 11, they held a mock trial followed by a feast. Contat explained that the chapel was a tiny "republic," which governed itself according to its own code of conduct. When a worker violated the code, the foreman, who was the head of the chapel and not part of the management, entered a fine in a register: leaving a candle lit, five sous; brawling, three livres; insulting the good name of the chapel, three livres; and so on. On Saint Martin's, the foreman read out the fines and collected them. The workers sometimes appealed their cases before a burlesque tribunal composed of the chapel's "ancients," but in the end they had to pay up amidst more bleating, banging of tools, and riotous laughter. The fines went for food and drink in the chapel's favorite tavern, where the hell-raising continued until late in the night.[18]

Taxation and commensality characterized all the other ceremonies of the chapel. Special dues and feasts marked a man's entry into the shop (*bienvenue*), his exit (*conduite*), and even his marriage (*droit de chevet*). Above all, they punctuated a youth's progress from apprentice to journeyman. Contat described four of these rites, the most important being the first, called the taking of the apron, and the last, Jerome's initiation as a full-fledged *compagnon*.

The taking of the apron (*la prise de tablier*) occurred soon after

Jerome joined the shop. He had to pay six livres (about three days' wages for an ordinary journeyman) into a kitty, which the journeymen supplemented by small payments of their own (*faire la reconnaissance*). Then the chapel repaired to its favorite tavern, Le Panier Fleury in the rue de la Huchette. Emissaries were dispatched to procure provisions and returned loaded down with bread and meat, having lectured the shopkeepers of the neighborhood on which cuts were worthy of typographers and which could be left for cobblers. Silent and glass in hand, the journeymen gathered around Jerome in a special room on the second floor of the tavern. The subforeman approached, carrying the apron and followed by two "ancients," one from each of the "estates" of the shop, the *casse* and the *presse*. He handed the apron, newly made from close-woven linen, to the foreman, who took Jerome by the hand and led him to the center of the room, the subforeman and "ancients" falling in behind. The foreman made a short speech, placed the apron over Jerome's head and tied the strings behind him, as everyone drank to the health of the initiate. Jerome was then given a seat with the chapel dignitaries at the head of the table. The rest rushed for the best places they could find and fell on the food. They gobbled and guzzled and called out for more. After several Gargantuan rounds, they settled down to shop talk—and Contat lets us listen in:

> "Isn't it true," says one of them, "that printers know how to shovel it in? I am sure that if someone presented us with a roast mutton, as big as you like, we would leave nothing but the bones behind. . . ." They don't talk about theology nor philosophy and still less of politics. Each speaks of his job: one will talk to you about the *casse*, another the *presse*, this one of the tympan, another of the ink ball leathers. They all speak at the same time, whether they can be heard or not.

At last, early in the morning after hours of swilling and shouting, the workers separated—sotted but ceremonial to the end: "Bonsoir, Monsieur notre prote [foreman]"; Bonsoir, Messieurs les compositeurs"; "Bonsoir, Messieurs les imprimeurs"; "Bonsoir Jerome." The text explains that Jerome will be called by his first name until he is received as a journeyman.[19]

That moment came four years later, after two intermediary cere-

Diversions of the common people in Ramponeau's tavern outside Paris

monies (the *admission à l'ouvrage* and the *admission à la banque*) and a vast amount of hazing. Not only did the men torment Jerome, mocking his ignorance, sending him on wild goose chases, making him the butt of practical jokes, and overwhelming him with nasty chores; they also refused to teach him anything. They did not want another journeyman in their over-flooded labor pool, so Jerome had to pick up the tricks of the trade by himself. The work, the food, the lodging, the lack of sleep, it was enough to drive a boy mad, or at least out of the shop. In fact, however, it was standard treatment and should not be taken too seriously. Contat recounted the catalogue of Jerome's troubles in a light-hearted manner, which suggested a stock comic genre, the *misère des apprentis*.[20] The *misères* provided farcical accounts, in doggerel verse or broadsides, of a stage in life that was familiar and funny to everyone in the artisanate. It was a transitional stage, which marked the passage from childhood to adulthood. A young man had to sweat his way through it so that he would have paid his dues—the printers demanded actual payments, called *bienvenues* or *quatre heures*, in addition to razzing the apprentices—when he reached full membership in a vocational group. Until he arrived at that point, he lived in a fluid or liminal state, trying out adult conventions by subjecting them to some hell-raising of his own. His elders tolerated his pranks, called *copies* and *joberies* in the printing trade, because they saw them as wild oats, which needed to be sewn before he could settle down. Once settled, he would have internalized the conventions of his craft and acquired a new identity, which was often symbolized by a change in his name.[21]

Jerome became a journeyman by passing through the final rite, *compagnonnage*. It took the same form as the other ceremonies, a celebration over food and drink after the candidate paid an initiation fee and the journeymen chipped in with *reconnaissance*. But this time Contat gave a summary of the foreman's speech:[22]

> The newcomer is indoctrinated. He is told never to betray his colleagues and to maintain the wage rate. If a worker doesn't accept a price [for a job] and leaves the shop, no one in the house should do the job for a smaller price. Those are the laws among the workers. Faithfulness and probity are recommended to him. Any worker who betrays the others, when something forbidden, called *marron* [chestnut], is be-

ing printed, must be expelled ignominiously from the shop. The workers blacklist him by circular letters sent around all the shops of Paris
and the provinces. . . . Aside from that, anything is permitted: excessive
drinking is considered a good quality, gallantry and debauchery as
youthful feats, indebtedness as a sign of wit, irreligion as sincerity. It's a
free and republican territory in which everything is permitted. Live as
you like but be an *honnête homme*, no hypocrisy.

Hypocrisy turned out in the rest of the narrative to be the main
characteristic of the bourgeois, a superstitious religious bigot. He
occupied a separate world of pharasaical bourgeois morality. The
workers defined their "republic" against that world and against
other journeymen's groups as well—the cobblers, who ate inferior
cuts of meat, and the masons or carpenters who were always good
for a brawl when the printers, divided into "estates" (the *casse* and
the *presse*) toured country taverns on Sundays. In entering an "estate," Jerome assimilated an ethos. He identified himself with a
craft; and as a full-fledged journeyman compositor, he received a
new name. Having gone through a rite of passage in the full,
anthropological sense of the term, he became a *Monsieur*.[23]

So much for ceremonies. What about cats? It should be said at
the outset that there is an indefinable *je ne sais quoi* about cats, a
mysterious something that has fascinated mankind since the time
of the ancient Egyptians. One can sense a quasi-human intelligence
behind a cat's eyes. One can mistake a cat's howl at night for a
human scream, torn from some deep, visceral part of man's animal
nature. Cats appealed to poets like Baudelaire and painters like
Manet, who wanted to express the humanity in animals along with
the animality of men—and especially of women.[24]

This ambiguous ontological position, a straddling of conceptual
categories, gives certain animals—pigs, dogs, and cassowaries as
well as cats—in certain cultures an occult power associated with
the taboo. That is why Jews do not eat pigs, according to Mary
Douglas, and why Englishmen can insult one another by saying
"son-of-a-bitch" rather than "son-of-a-cow," according to Ed-
mund Leach.[25] Certain animals are good for swearing, just as they
are "good for thinking" in Lévi-Strauss's famous formula. I would
add that others—cats in particular—are good for staging ceremo-

nies. They have ritual value. You cannot make a charivari with a cow. You do it with cats: you decide to *faire le chat,* to make *Katzenmusik.*

The torture of animals, especially cats, was a popular amusement throughout early modern Europe. You have only to look at Hogarth's *Stages of Cruelty* to see its importance, and once you start looking you see people torturing animals everywhere. Cat killings provided a common theme in literature, from *Don Quixote* in early seventeenth-century Spain to *Germinal* in late nineteenth-century France.[26] Far from being a sadistic fantasy on the part of a few half-crazed authors, the literary versions of cruelty to animals expressed a deep current of popular culture, as Mikhail Bakhtin has shown in his study of Rabelais.[27] All sorts of ethnographic reports confirm that view. On the *dimanche des brandons* in Semur, for example, children used to attach cats to poles and roast them over bonfires. In the *jeu du chat* at the Fete-Dieu in Aix-en-Provence, they threw

A nude with a cat, from a study for the "Olympia" by Edouard Manet

cats high in the air and smashed them on the ground. They used expressions like "patient as a cat whose claws are being pulled out" or "patient as a cat whose paws are being grilled." The English were just as cruel. During the Reformation in London, a Protestant crowd shaved a cat to look like a priest, dressed it in mock vestments, and hanged it on the gallows at Cheapside.[28] It would be possible to string out many other examples, but the point should be

Cruelty to animals as an everyday scene of domestic life

clear: there was nothing unusual about the ritual killing of cats. On the contrary, when Jerome and his fellow workers tried and hanged all the cats they could find in the rue Saint-Séverin, they drew on a common element in their culture. But what significance did that culture attribute to cats?

To get a grip on that question, one must rummage through collections of folktales, superstitions, proverbs, and popular medicine. The material is rich, varied, and vast but extremely hard to handle. Although much of it goes back to the Middle Ages, little can be dated. It was gathered for the most part by folklorists in the late nineteenth and early twentieth centuries, when sturdy strains of folklore still resisted the influence of the printed word. But the collections do not make it possible to claim that this or that practice existed in the printing houses of mid-eighteenth-century Paris. One can only assert that printers lived and breathed in an atmosphere of traditional customs and beliefs which permeated everything. It was not everywhere the same—France remained a patchwork of *pays* rather than a unified nation until late in the nineteenth century—but everywhere some common motifs could be found. The commonest were attached to cats. Early modern Frenchmen probably made more symbolic use of cats than of any other animal, and they used them in distinct ways, which can be grouped together for the purposes of discussion, despite the regional peculiarities.

First and foremost, cats suggested witchcraft. To cross one at night in virtually any corner of France was to risk running into the devil or one of his agents or a witch abroad on an evil errand. White cats could be as satanic as the black, in the daytime as well as at night. In a typical encounter, a peasant woman of Bigorre met a pretty white house cat who had strayed in the fields. She carried it back to the village in her apron, and just as they came to the house of a woman suspected of witchcraft, the cat jumped out, saying "Merci, Jeanne." [29] Witches transformed themselves into cats in order to cast spells on their victims. Sometimes, especially on Mardi Gras, they gathered for hideous sabbaths at night. They howled, fought, and copulated horribly under the direction of the devil himself in the form of a huge tomcat. To protect yourself from sorcery by cats there was one, classic remedy: maim it. Cut its

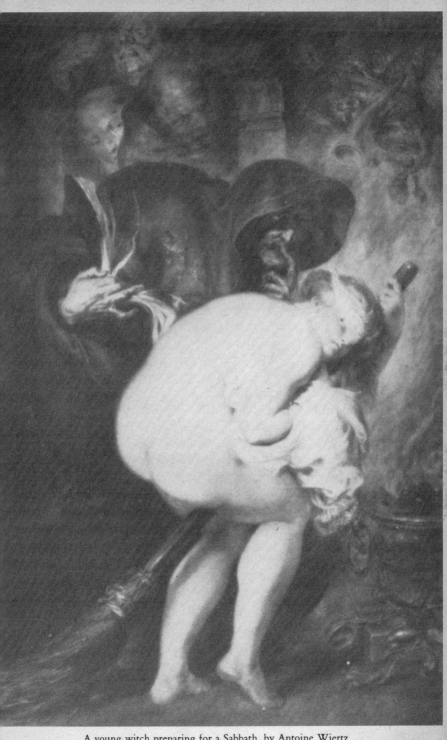

A young witch preparing for a Sabbath, by Antoine Wiertz

tail, clip its ears, smash one of its legs, tear or burn its fur, and you would break its malevolent power. A maimed cat could not attend a sabbath or wander abroad to cast spells. Peasants frequently cudgeled cats who crossed their paths at night and discovered the next day that bruises had appeared on women believed to be witches—or so it was said in the lore of their village. Villagers also told stories of farmers who found strange cats in barns and broke their limbs to save the cattle. Invariably a broken limb would appear on a suspicious woman the following morning.

Cats possessed occult power independently of their association with witchcraft and deviltry. They could prevent the bread from rising if they entered bakeries in Anjou. They could spoil the catch if they crossed the path of fishermen in Brittany. If buried alive in Béarn, they could clear a field of weeds. They figured as staple ingredients in all kinds of folk medicine aside from witches' brews. To recover from a bad fall, you sucked the blood out of a freshly amputated tail of a tomcat. To cure yourself from pneumonia, you drank blood from a cat's ear in red wine. To get over colic, you mixed your wine with cat excrement. You could even make yourself invisible, at least in Brittany, by eating the brain of a newly killed cat, provided it was still hot.

There was a specific field for the exercise of cat power: the household and particularly the person of the master or mistress of the house. Folktales like "Puss 'n Boots" emphasized the identification of master and cat, and so did superstitions such as the practice of tying a black ribbon around the neck of a cat whose mistress had died. To kill a cat was to bring misfortune upon its owner or its house. If a cat left a house or stopped jumping on the sickbed of its master or mistress, the person was likely to die. But a cat lying on the bed of a dying man might be the devil, waiting to carry his soul off to hell. According to a sixteenth-century tale, a girl from Quintin sold her soul to the devil in exchange for some pretty clothes. When she died, the pallbearers could not lift her coffin; they opened the lid, and a black cat jumped out. Cats could harm a house. They often smothered babies. They understood gossip and would repeat it out of doors. But their power could be contained or turned to your advantage if you followed the right procedures, such as greasing their paws with butter or maiming them when they first arrived. To protect a new house, Frenchmen enclosed live cats within its walls—a very old rite, judging from cat skeletons that have been exhumed from the walls of medieval buildings.

Finally, the power of cats was concentrated on the most intimate aspect of domestic life: sex. *Le chat, la chatte, le minet* mean the same thing in French slang as "pussy" does in English, and they have served as obscenities for centuries.[30] French folklore attaches special importance to the cat as a sexual metaphor or metonym. As far back as the fifteenth century, the petting of cats was recommended for success in courting women. Proverbial wisdom identified women with cats: "He who takes good care of cats will have a pretty wife." If a man loved cats, he would love women; and vice versa: "As he loves his cat, he loves his wife," went another proverb. If he did not care for his wife, you could say of him, "He has other cats to whip." A woman who wanted to get a man should avoid treading on a cat's tail. She might postpone marriage for a year—or for seven years in Quimper and for as many years as the cat meowed in parts of the Loire Valley. Cats connoted fertility and female sexuality everywhere. Girls were commonly said to be "in love like a cat"; and if they became pregnant, they had "let the cat go to the cheese." Eating cats could bring on pregnancy in itself. Girls who consumed them in stews gave birth to kittens in several folktales. Cats could even make diseased apple trees bear fruit, if buried in the correct manner in upper Brittany.

It was an easy jump from the sexuality of women to the cuckolding of men. Caterwauling could come from a satanic orgy, but it might just as well be toms howling defiance at each other when their mates were in heat. They did not call as cats, however. They issued challenges in their masters' names, along with sexual taunts about their mistresses: "Reno! Francois!" "Où allez-vous?—Voir la femme à vous.—Voir la femme à moi! Rouah!" (Where are you going?—To see your wife.—To see my wife! Ha!) Then the toms would fly at each other like the cats of Kilkenny, and their sabbath would end in a massacre. The dialogue differed according to the imaginations of the listeners and the onomatopoetic power of their dialect, but it usually emphasized predatory sexuality.[31] "At night all cats are gray," went the proverb, and the gloss in an eighteenth-century proverb collection made the sexual hint explicit: "That is to say that all women are beautiful enough at night."[32] Enough for what? Seduction, rape, and murder echoed in the air when the cats howled at night in early modern France. Cat calls summoned up *Katzenmusik,* for charivaris often took the form of howling under a cuckold's window on the eve of Mardi Gras, the favorite time for cat sabbaths.

Witchcraft, orgy, cuckoldry, charivari, and massacre, the men of the Old Regime could hear a great deal in the wail of a cat. What the men of the rue Saint-Séverin actually heard is impossible to say. One can only assert that cats bore enormous symbolic weight in the folklore of France and that the lore was rich, ancient, and widespread enough to have penetrated the printing shop. In order to determine whether the printers actually drew on the ceremonial and symbolic themes available to them, it is necessary to take another look at Contat's text.

The text made the theme of sorcery explicit from the beginning. Jerome and Léveillé could not sleep because "some bedeviled cats make a sabbath all night long."[33] After Léveillé added his cat calls to the general caterwauling, "the whole neighborhood is alarmed. It is decided that the cats must be agents of someone casting a spell." The master and mistress considered summoning the curé to exorcise the place. In deciding instead to commission the cat hunt, they fell back on the classic remedy for witchcraft: maiming. The bourgeois—a superstitious, priest-ridden fool—took the whole business seriously. To the apprentices it was a joke. Léveillé in particular functioned as a joker, a mock "sorcerer" staging a fake "sabbath," according to the terms chosen by Contat. Not only did the apprentices exploit their master's superstition in order to run riot at his expense, but they also turned their rioting against their mistress. By bludgeoning her familiar, *la grise,* they in effect accused her of being the witch. The double joke would not be lost on anyone who could read the traditional language of gesture.

The theme of charivari provided an additional dimension to the fun. Although it never says so explicitly, the text indicates that the mistress was having an affair with her priest, a "lascivious youth," who had memorized obscene passages from the classics of pornography—Aretino and *L'Academie des dames*—and quoted them to her, while her husband droned on about his favorite subjects, money and religion. During a lavish dinner with the family, the priest defended the thesis "that it is a feat of wit to cuckold one's husband and that cuckolding is not a vice." Later, he and the wife spent the night together in a country house. They fit perfectly into the typical triangle of printing shops: a doddering old master, a middle-aged mistress, and her youthful lover.[34] The intrigue cast the master in the role of a stock comic figure: the cuckold. So the revelry of the workers took the form of a charivari. The apprentices managed it, operating within the liminal area where novitiates traditionally mocked their superiors, and the journeymen responded to their antics in the traditional way, with rough music. A riotous, festival atmosphere runs through the whole episode, which Contat described as a *fête:* "Léveillé and his comrade Jerome preside over the *fête,*" he wrote, as if they were kings of a carnival and the cat bashing corresponded to the torturing of cats on Mardi Gras or the *fête* of Saint John the Baptist.

As in many Mardi Gras, the carnival ended in a mock trial and execution. The burlesque legalism came naturally to the printers because they staged their own mock trials every year at the *fête* of Saint Martin, when the chapel squared accounts with its boss and succeeded spectacularly in getting his goat. The chapel could not condemn him explicitly without moving into open insubordination and risking dismissal. (All the sources, including the papers of the STN, indicate that masters often fired workers for insolence and misbehavior. Indeed, Léveillé was later fired for a prank that attacked the bourgeois more openly.) So the workers tried the bourgeois in absentia, using a symbol that would let their meaning show through without being explicit enough to justify retaliation. They tried and hanged the cats. It would be going too far to hang *la grise* under the master's nose after being ordered to spare it; but they made the favorite pet of the house their first victim, and in doing so they knew they were attacking the house itself, in accordance with the traditions of cat lore. When the mistress accused them of killing *la grise,* they replied with mock deference that "nobody would be capable of such an outrage and that they have too much respect for that house." By executing the cats with such elaborate ceremony, they condemned the house and declared the bourgeois guilty—guilty of overworking and underfeeding his apprentices, guilty of living in luxury while his journeymen did all the work, guilty of withdrawing from the shop and swamping it with *alloués* instead of laboring and eating with the men, as masters were said to have done a generation or two earlier, or in the primitive "republic" that existed at the beginning of the printing industry. The guilt extended from the boss to the house to the whole system. Perhaps in trying, confessing, and hanging a collection of half-dead cats, the workers meant to ridicule the entire legal and social order.

They certainly felt debased and had accumulated enough resentment to explode in an orgy of killing. A half-century later, the artisans of Paris would run riot in a similar manner, combining indiscriminate slaughter with improvised popular tribunals.[35] It would be absurd to view the cat massacre as a dress rehearsal for the September Massacres of the French Revolution, but the earlier outburst of violence did suggest a popular rebellion, though it remained restricted to the level of symbolism.

Cats as symbols conjured up sex as well as violence, a combination perfectly suited for an attack on the mistress. The narrative identified her with *la grise,* her *chatte favorite.* In killing it, the boys struck at her: "It was a matter of consequence, a murder, which had to be hidden." The mistress reacted as if she had been assaulted: "They ravished from her a cat without an equal, a cat that she loved to madness." The text described her as lascivious and "impassioned for cats" as if she were a she-cat in heat during a wild cat's sabbath of howling, killing, and rape. An explicit reference to rape would violate the proprieties that were generally observed in eighteenth-century writing. Indeed, the symbolism would work only if it remained veiled—ambivalent enough to dupe the master and sharp enough to hit the mistress in the quick. But Contat used strong language. As soon as the mistress saw the cat execution she let out a scream. Then the scream was smothered in the realization that she had lost her *grise.* The workers assured her with feigned sincerity of their respect and the master arrived. "'Ah! the scoundrels,' he says. 'Instead of working they are killing cats.' Madame to Monsieur: 'These wicked men can't kill the masters; they have killed my cat.' . . . It seems to her that all the blood of the workers would not be sufficient to redeem the insult."

It was metonymic insult, the eighteenth-century equivalent of the modern schoolboy's taunt: "Ah, your mother's girdle!" But it was stronger, and more obscene. By assaulting her pet, the workers ravished the mistress symbolically. At the same time, they delivered the supreme insult to their master. His wife was his most precious possession, just as her *chatte* was hers. In killing the cat, the men violated the most intimate treasure of the bourgeois household and escaped unharmed. That was the beauty of it. The symbolism disguised the insult well enough for them to get away with it. While the bourgeois fumed over the loss of work, his wife, less obtuse, virtually told him that the workers had attacked her sexually and would like to murder him. Then both left the scene in humiliation and defeat. "Monsieur and Madame retire, leaving the workers in liberty. The printers, who love disorder, are in a state of great joy. Here is an ample subject for their laughter, a beautiful *copie,* which will keep them amused for a long time."

This was Rabelaisian laughter. The text insists upon its importance: "The printers know how to laugh, it is their sole occupation." Mikhail Bakhtin has shown how the laughter of Rabelais expressed a strain of popular culture in which the riotously funny could turn to riot, a carnival culture of sexuality and sedition in which the revolutionary element might be contained within symbols and metaphors or might explode in a general uprising, as in 1789. The question remains, however, what precisely was so funny about the cat massacre? There is no better way to ruin a joke than to analyze it or to overload it with social comment. But this joke cries out for commentary—not because one can use it to prove that artisans hated their bosses (a truism that may apply to all periods of labor history, although it has not been appreciated adequately by eighteenth-century historians), but because it can help one to see how workers made their experience meaningful by playing with themes of their culture.

The only version of the cat massacre available to us was put into writing, long after the fact, by Nicolas Contat. He selected details, ordered events, and framed the story in such a way as to bring out what was meaningful for him. But he derived his notions of meaning from his culture just as naturally as he drew in air from the atmosphere around him. And he wrote down what he had helped to enact with his mates. The subjective character of the writing does not vitiate its collective frame of reference, even though the written account must be thin compared with the action it describes. The workers' mode of expression was a kind of popular theater. It involved pantomime, rough music, and a dramatic "theater of violence" improvised in the work place, in the street, and on the rooftops. It included a play within a play, because Léveillé reenacted the whole farce several times as *copies* in the shop. In fact, the original massacre involved the burlesquing of other ceremonies, such as trials and charivaris. So Contat wrote about a burlesque of a burlesque, and in reading it one should make allowances for the refraction of cultural forms across genres and over time.

Those allowances made, it seems clear that the workers found the massacre funny because it gave them a way to turn the tables on the bourgeois. By goading him with cat calls, they provoked him to authorize the massacre of cats, then they used the massacre to put him symbolically on trial for unjust management of the shop. They also used it as a witch hunt, which provided an excuse to kill his wife's familiar and to insinuate that she herself was the witch. Finally, they transformed it into a charivari, which served as a means to insult her sexually while mocking him as a cuckold. The bourgeois made an excellent butt of the joke. Not only did he become the victim of a procedure he himself had set in motion, he did not understand how badly he had been had. The men had subjected his wife to symbolic aggression of the most intimate kind, but he did not get it. He was too thick-headed, a classic cuckold. The printers ridiculed him in splendid Boccaccian style and got off scot-free.

The joke worked so well because the workers played so skillfully with a repertory of ceremonies and symbols. Cats suited their purposes perfectly. By smashing the spine of *la grise* they called the master's wife a witch and a slut, while at the same time making the master into a cuckold and a fool. It was metonymic insult, delivered by actions, not words, and it struck home because cats occupied a soft spot in the bourgeois way of life. Keeping pets was as alien to the workers as torturing animals was to the bourgeois. Trapped between incompatible sensitivities, the cats had the worst of both worlds.

The workers also punned with ceremonies. They made a roundup of cats into a witch hunt, a festival, a charivari, a mock trial, and a dirty joke. Then they redid the whole thing in pantomime. Whenever they got tired of working, they transformed the shop into a theater and produced *copies*—their kind of copy, not the authors'. Shop theater and ritual punning suited the traditions of their craft. Although printers made books, they did not use written words to convey their meaning. They used gestures, drawing on the culture of their craft to inscribe statements in the air.

Insubstantial as it may seem today, this joking was a risky business in the eighteenth century. The risk was part of the joke, as in many forms of humor, which toy with violence and tease repressed passions. The workers pushed their symbolic horseplay to the brink of reification, the point at which the killing of cats would turn into an open rebellion. They played on ambiguities, using symbols that would hide their full meaning while letting enough of it show through to make a fool of the bourgeois without giving him a pretext to fire them. They tweaked his nose and prevented him from protesting against it. To pull off such a feat required great dexterity. It showed that workers could manipulate symbols in their idiom as effectively as poets did in print.

The boundaries within which this jesting had to be contained suggest the limits to working-class militancy under the Old Regime. The printers identified with their craft rather than their class. Although they organized in chapels, staged strikes, and sometimes forced up wages, they remained subordinate to the bourgeois. The master hired and fired men as casually as he ordered paper, and he turned them out into the road when he sniffed insubordination. So until the onset of proletarianization in the late nineteenth century, they generally kept their protests on a symbolic level. A *copie,* like a carnival, helped to let off steam; but it also produced laughter, a vital ingredient in early artisanal culture and one that has been lost in labor history. By seeing the way a joke worked in the horseplay of a printing shop two centuries ago, we may be able to recapture that missing element—laughter, sheer laughter, the thigh-slapping, rib-cracking Rabelaisian kind, rather than the Voltairian smirk with which we are familiar.

APPENDIX: CONTAT'S ACCOUNT
OF THE CAT MASSACRE

The following account comes from Nicolas Contat, *Anecdotes typographiques où l'on voit la description des coutumes, moeurs et usages singuliers des compagnons imprimeurs,* ed. Giles Barber (Oxford, 1980), pp. 51–53. After a day of exhausting work and disgusting food, the two apprentices retire to their bedroom, a damp and draughty lean-to in a corner of the courtyard. The episode is recounted in the third person, from the viewpoint of Jerome:

He is so tired and needs rest so desperately that the shack looks like a palace to him. At last the persecution and misery he has suffered throughout the day have come to an end, and he can relax. But no, some bedeviled cats celebrate a witches' sabbath all night long, making so much noise that they rob him of the brief period of rest allotted to the apprentices before the journeymen arrive for work early the next morning and demand admission by constant ringing of an infernal bell. Then the boys have to get up and cross the courtyard, shivering under their nightshirts, in order to open the door. Those journeymen never let up. No matter what you do, you always make them lose their time and they always treat you as a lazy good-for-nothing. They call for Léveillé. Light the fire under the cauldron! Fetch water for the dunking-troughs! True, those jobs are supposed to be done by the beginner apprentices, who live at home, but they don't arrive until six or seven. Thus everyone is soon at work—apprentices, journeymen, everyone but the master and the mistress: they alone enjoy the sweetness of sleep. That makes Jerome and Léveillé jealous. They resolve that they will not be the only ones to suffer; they want their master and mistress as associates. But how to turn the trick?

Léveillé has an extraordinary talent for imitating the voices and the smallest gestures of everyone around him. He is a perfect actor; that's the real profession that he has picked up in the printing shop. He also can produce perfect imitations of the cries of dogs and cats. He decides to climb from roof to roof until he reaches a gutter next to the bedroom of the bourgeois and the bourgeoise. From there he can ambush them with a volley of meows. It's an easy job for him:

he is the son of a roofer and can scramble across roofs like a cat.

Our sniper succeeds so well that the whole neighborhood is alarmed. The word spreads that there is witchcraft afoot and that the cats must be the agents of someone casting a spell. It is a case for the curé, who is an intimate of the household and the confessor of Madame. No one can sleep any more.

Léveillé stages a sabbath the next night and the night after that. If you didn't know him, you would be convinced he was a witch. Finally, the master and the mistress cannot stand it any longer. "We'd better tell the boys to get rid of those malevolent animals," they declare. Madame gives them the order, exhorting them to avoid frightening la grise. That is the name of her pet pussy.

This lady is impassioned for cats. Many master printers are also. One of them has twenty-five. He has had their portraits painted and feeds them on roast fowl.

The hunt is soon organized. The apprentices resolve to make a clean sweep of it, and they are joined by the journeymen. The masters love cats, so consequently they must hate them. This man arms himself with the bar of a press, that one with a stick from the drying-room, others with broom handles. They hang sacks at the windows of the attic and the storerooms to catch the cats who attempt to escape by leaping outdoors. The beaters are named, everything is organized. Léveillé and his comrade Jerome preside over the fête, each of them armed with an iron bar from the shop. The first thing they go for is la grise, Madame's pussy. Léveillé stuns it with a quick blow on the kidneys, and Jerome finishes it off. Then Léveillé stuffs the body in a gutter, for they don't want to get caught: it is a matter of consequence, a murder, which must be kept hidden. The men produce terror on the rooftops. Seized by panic, the cats throw themselves into the sacks. Some are killed on the spot. Others are condemned to be hanged for the amusement of the entire printing shop.

Printers know how to laugh; it is their sole occupation.

The execution is about to begin. They name a hangman, a troop of guards, even a confessor. Then they pronounce the sentence.

In the midst of it all, the mistress arrives. What is her surprise, when she sees the bloody execution! She lets out a scream; then her voice is cut, because she thinks she sees la grise, and she is certain that such a fate has been reserved for her favorite puss. The workers assure her that no one would be capable of such a crime: they have too much respect for the house.

The bourgeois arrives. "Ah! The scoundrels," he says. "Instead of working, they are killing cats." Madame to Monsieur: "These wicked men can't kill the masters, so they have killed my pussy. She can't be found. I have called la grise everywhere. They must have hanged her." It seems to her that all the workers' blood would not be sufficient to redeem the insult. The poor grise, a pussy without a peer!

Monsieur and Madame retire, leaving the workers in liberty. The printers delight in the disorder; they are beside themselves with joy.

What a splendid subject for their laughter, for a *belle copie!* They will amuse themselves with it for a long time. Léveillé will take the leading role and will stage the play at least twenty times. He will mime the master, the mistress, the whole house, heaping ridicule on them all. He will spare nothing in his satire. Among printers, those who excel in this entertainment are called *jobeurs:* they provide *joberie.*

Léveillé receives many rounds of applause.

It should be noted that all the workers are in league against the masters. It is enough to speak badly of them [the masters] to be esteemed by the whole assembly of typographers. Léveillé is one of those. In recognition of his merit, he will be pardoned for some previous satires against the workers.

A procession honoring the Spanish infanta in Paris, 1722

3

A BOURGEOIS PUTS HIS WORLD IN ORDER: THE CITY AS A TEXT

IF THE GRIM FOLKLORE of peasants and the violent rituals of artisans belong to a world that seems unthinkable today, we might expect to be able to think ourselves into the skin of an eighteenth-century bourgeois. The opportunity arises thanks to another document, as extraordinary in its way as Contat's account of the cat massacre: it is a description of Montpellier written in 1768 by an anonymous but solidly middle-class citizen of the city. To be sure, the casual nonfiction of the eighteenth century was full of "descriptions," guidebooks, almanacs, and amateur accounts of local monuments and celebrities. What set our bourgeois apart from others who dealt in the genre was his obsession with completeness. He wanted to capture his entire city, every bit of it, and so he wrote on and on—for 426 manuscript pages, covering every chapel, every wig maker, every stray dog in what to him was the center of the universe.[1]

Exactly why he undertook such a vast and exhausting project cannot be determined. He may have intended to publish a kind of guidebook, for he explained in an introduction to his *Etat et description de la ville de Montpellier fait en 1768* (referred to henceforth as *Description*) that he wanted to describe Montpellier in a way that would be helpful to visitors and that would "give the true idea of a city which, though not particularly large in size, nonetheless occupies a distinguished place in the kingdom."[2] He sounds proud of his city and eager to tell us about it, as if we were foreigners looking rather bewildered on an unfamiliar street corner and he were offering directions. Not an unusual situation, perhaps, but one that raises a question worth considering: What is it to describe a world? How would we reduce our own surroundings to writing, if we felt the urge and had the energy? Would we begin with a bird's-eye view and then narrow the focus as we descended to a key intersection, the local version of Main and Vine? Or would we enter the city like a stranger, passing from countryside to suburbs to some imposing cluster of buildings at the heart of the urban space—a town hall or church or department store? Perhaps we would organize our description sociologically, beginning with the municipal power elite or working upward from the workers. We could even strike a spiritual note, starting with a Fourth of July oration or a sermon. The possibilities seem infinite, or at least extensive enough to be paralyzing. For how can one put "the true idea of a city" on paper, especially if one cares about the city and the supply of paper is endless?

Consider a famous example, which will provide some perspective to the picture of eighteenth-century Montpellier:

> London. Michaelmas Term lately over, and the Lord Chancellor sitting in Lincoln's Inn Hall. Implacable November weather. As much mud in the streets as if the waters had but newly retired from the face of the earth, and it would not be wonderful to meet a Megalosaurus, forty feet long or so, waddling like an elephantine lizard up Holborn Hill. Smoke lowering down from chimney-pots, making a soft black drizzle, with flakes of soot in it as big as full-grown snowflakes—gone

into mourning, one might imagine, for the death of the sun. Dogs, undistinguishable in mire. Horses, scarcely better—splashed to their very blinkers. Foot passengers, jostling one another's umbrellas, in a general infection of ill-temper, and losing their foothold at street corners, where tens of thousands of other foot passengers have been slipping and sliding since the day broke (if this day ever broke), adding new deposits to the crust upon crust of mud, sticking at those points tenaciously to the pavement, and accumulating at compound interest.[3]

A great deal could be said about Dickens's descriptions of London. But these first sentences of *Bleak House* suffice to show how charged with emotion, values, and world view an urban view can be. The muck, the clutter, the pervasive sense of moral rot clinging to decrepit institutions gives the description the unmistakable mark of Dickensian London. Our Montpelliérain inhabited a different world. But it was to an equal degree a world that he constructed with his mind, that he fit within a mental framework and colored with emotion, even if he did not have Dickens's literary talent for conveying what he felt. Literary or not, the sense of place is fundamental to our general orientation in life. To find it spelled out in words, a whole flood of words, by a seemingly ordinary bourgeois from the Old Regime is to come up against a basic element in eighteenth-century world views. But how to make sense of it?

It is as problematic for us to read our author's description as it was for him to write it. Every phrase expresses a foreign consciousness trying to order a world that no longer exists. To penetrate that consciousness, we need to concentrate more on the modes of description than on the objects described. Did our author utilize standard schemes for ordering urban topography? Where did he draw lines in order to separate this phenomenon from that? And what categories did he choose for sorting out sensations when he put his pen to paper? Our task is not to discover what Montpellier really looked like in 1768 but to understand how our observer observed it.

But first a word about the tendentious term "bourgeois." It is abusive, aggravating, inexact, and unavoidable. Historians have argued over it for generations, and are arguing still. In France, it generally has Marxist connotations. The bourgeois is the owner of

A procession of dignitaries in Toulouse

the modes of production, a certain variety of Economic Man with his own way of life and his own ideology. He was the key figure of the eighteenth century, a time of enormous expansion, if not downright industrialization: "le take-off," according to the fractured-French view of "Anglo-Saxon" economics. Faced with the contradiction between his economic power and his political impotence—aggravated during the period of aristocratic resurgence on the eve of 1789—the bourgeois acquired class consciousness and revolted, leading a popular front of peasants and artisans into the French Revolution. Ideology was essential for the fusion of this striking force, because the bourgeoisie managed to saturate the common people with its own ideas of liberty (especially free trade) and equality (especially the destruction of aristocratic privilege). By 1789, the Enlightenment had done its work: as the most influential French textbooks by the most prestigious French historians assured a generation of readers, "The eighteenth century thought bourgeois."[4]

This version of the sempiternal theme, the rise of the middle classes, rests on a view of history as a process that operates on three levels, the economic, social, and cultural. The deeper the level, the

more powerful the force. Thus changes in the economy produce changes in the social structure and ultimately in values and ideas. To be sure, some historians developed very different views. Roland Mousnier and his students elaborated an idealistic picture of the Old Regime as a society of orders, based on juridical norms and social status. Among the Marxists, a Gramscian tendency attributed some autonomy to ideological forces in the formation of hegemonic sociopolitical "blocks." Nonetheless, the dominant trend in French historical writing from the 1950s through the 1970s was an attempt to create a "total" history based on a three-tiered model of causality.[5]

This view placed the bourgeois squarely at stage center. As possessor of the modes of production, rising element in the social structure, and champion of a modern ideology, he was destined to sweep everything before him—and did so in the French Revolution. But no one knew him very well. He appeared in the history books as a category without a face. So in 1955, Ernest Labrousse, the supreme spokesman of triple-layered, total history launched a campaign to track the bourgeois to his hiding places in the archives. Vast statistical surveys compiled according to a socio-occupational grid were to situate the bourgeoisie within social structures everywhere in the West, beginning with eighteenth-century Paris. Paris, however, proved intractable. Soundings in 2,597 marriage contracts from the year 1749 by François Furet and Adeline Daumard uncovered an urban society composed of artisans, shopkeepers, professionals, royal officials, and nobles, but no manufacturers and only a handful of merchants. A comparative study of Paris and Chartres by Daniel Roche and Michel Vovelle produced similar results. Each city had bourgeois all right, but they were "bourgeois d'Ancien Régime"—primarily *rentiers,* who lived from annuities and land rents and did not work, the very opposite of the industrial bourgeoisie of Marxist historiography. True, manufacturers could be found in textile centers like Amiens and Lyon, but they usually directed putting-out enterprises of a kind that had existed for centuries and bore no resemblance to the mechanized, factory production that was beginning to transform the urban landscape in England. Insofar as France had entrepreneurs, they tended to come from the nobility. Noblemen invested in all sorts of industry and commerce, not merely in the traditional sectors of mining and metallurgy, while merchants frequently got out of trade as soon as they had accumulated enough capital to live like gentlemen, on land and *rentes.*[6]

As the monographs continued to pour in, covering city after city and province after province, Old Regime France came to look more and more archaic. The best studies, such as those of Maurice Garden on Lyon and Jean-Claude Perrot on Caen, turned up a few genuine manufacturers and merchants; but this undeniably capitalist bourgeoisie seemed trivial in comparison with the vast population of artisans and shopkeepers that proliferated in all the cities of early modern France. Nowhere, except perhaps in Lille and one or two sectors of other cities, did the social historians find the dynamic, self-conscious, industrializing class imagined by the Marxists. Michel Morineau went so far as to argue that the economy remained stagnant throughout the eighteenth century and that the standard picture of economic expansion epitomized by the rising waves of grain prices on the graphs produced by Labrousse in the 1930s and 1940s was actually an illusion—the product of Malthusian pressure rather than of an increase in productivity. The economy may not have been quite that feeble, but it clearly did not go through an industrial or even an agricultural revolution. Seen from the French side of the Channel, "le take-off" began to look particularly "Anglo-Saxon."[7]

This tendency swept away most of the modernity in the bottom level of the three-tiered model of the Old Regime and eroded most of the population in the progressive forces located at level two. Where did it leave the notion of a century that "thought bourgeois"? A massive sociological analysis of the main centers of thought, the provincial academies, showed that the thinkers belonged to a traditional elite of nobles, priests, state officials, doctors, and lawyers. The audience for the books of the Enlightenment looked very much the same, while the theater audiences—even those who wept at the new genre of *drames bourgeois*—appeared to be even more aristocratic. And as we shall see in the next chapter, the writers themselves came from every segment of society, except the industrial. Of course Enlightenment literature could still be interpreted as "bourgeois" because one can always attach that term to a set of values and then find those values expressed in print. But that procedure has a way of spinning around in redundancies—bourgeois literature is literature that expresses the outlook of the bourgeoisie—without making contact with social history. Thus at all levels of research, scholars have responded to the call—*cherchez le bourgeois*—but they have failed to find him.[8]

In view of that experience, it may seem extravagant to present our Montpelliérain as a specimen of such a rare species—and all the more so as we cannot identify him precisely. But he can be located in a general way by the voice he assumes in his text. He disassociates himself from the nobility on the one hand and the common people on the other; and his sympathies, proclaimed on every page with a marvelously opinionated openness, place him somewhere in the middle range of urban society, among the doctors, lawyers, administrators, and *rentiers,* who formed the intelligentsia in most provincial cities. These men belonged to the "bourgeoisie d'Ancien Régime." They were bourgeois in the eighteenth-century sense of the term, which contemporary dictionaries defined simply as "citizen of a city," though the dictionaries also noted special usages of the adjective, such as "a bourgeois house," "a bourgeois soup," "a bourgeois wine," and their examples of the adverb evoked a certain way of life: "He lives, he speaks, he reasons *bourgeoisement*. At noon, he dines *bourgeoisement*, with his family, but well and with good appetite."[9]

Beginning with that modest, contemporary notion of the bourgeois, we should be able to enter into the *Description* in a sympathetic spirit; and then, working from the inside, we may be able to roam around in the world that our author constructed with his text.

Before taking the plunge, however, we should look briefly at the Montpellier that has been reconstructed by historians, if only to find some points of comparison with which to orient ourselves.[10]

Eighteenth-century Montpellier was essentially an administrative center and a marketplace, the third largest city after Toulouse and Nîmes in the vast province of Languedoc. Its population grew rapidly, from about twenty thousand in 1710 to about thirty-one thousand in 1789—not merely because of immigration from the countryside, as in many other cities, but because of a decline in mortality and, ultimately, an increase of wealth. Economic historians have now whittled down the "century of expansion," as the last phase of the Old Regime used to be known, to three decades, 1740 to 1770; but in Montpellier those years were enough to make life easier for almost everyone, even if they did not transform the economy. Harvests were good, prices healthy, and profits spilled over from the city's agricultural hinterland into its markets, then spread throughout its workshops and boutiques.

Montpellier was no Manchester, however. It produced the same articles that it had made since the late Middle Ages, working on the same small scale. The manufacture of verdigris, for example, occupied about eight hundred families and brought in as much as 800,000 livres a year. It was made in the cellars of ordinary homes, where copper plates were stacked in clay pots filled with distilled wine. The women of the household scraped the "verdet" (copper acetate) off the plates once a week. Agents collected it, going from house to house; and large merchant firms like François Durand et fils marketed it everywhere in Europe. Montpelliérains also produced other local specialties: playing cards, perfumes, and gloves. Up to two thousand of them wove and finished woolen blankets known as *flassadas,* working in their rooms according to the putting-out system. Woolens in general had gone into decline, but Montpellier served as an *entrepôt* (warehouse) for the cloth produced in the rest of the province. And in the 1760s, the cotton industry began to develop, some of it in factories (*fabriques*), which grew up on the outskirts of the city and employed hundreds of workers. Many of them made calicoes and handkerchiefs, which were greatly in demand thanks to the growing fashion for taking snuff. But snuff and verdigris were not the stuff of which an industrial revolution could be made, and the factories were but a small outgrowth on a huge body of workshops, where journeymen and masters—the local equivalents of Jerome and his "bourgeois"—went about their business pretty much as they had done two hundred years earlier. Despite the expansion of the mid-century years, the economy remained underdeveloped—an economy of tinkers banging on pots in doorways, of tailors sitting cross-legged in shop windows, and of merchants weighing coin in counting houses.

The coin accumulated to such an extent that Montpellier developed something of a commercial oligarchy. As in other French cities, the merchants tended to shift their capital from trade to land and offices. And when they bought positions in the upper ranks of the judiciary and the royal bureaucracy, they became ennobled. The wealthiest families—the Lajard, Durand, Périé, and Bazille—dominated the social and cultural life of Montpellier, all the more so as the town had virtually no ancient feudal nobility. Their ranks were swollen by a great many state officials because Montpellier was the most important administrative center of the province, the site of the intendancy, the provincial estates, the office of the governor, and of several royal courts, though not the provincial *parlement* (sovereign law court). But it was impossible for the upper crust to be very thick in a city that had only twenty-five thousand inhabitants, approximately, in 1768. Almost everyone in the elite knew everyone else. They met at concerts in the Académie de musique, at plays in the Salle de Spectacles, at lectures in the Académie Royale des Sciences, and at ceremonies in a dozen masonic lodges. They crossed one another's path every day in the Promenade du Peyrou, and dined together every week, especially on Sundays, when they sat down to elaborate meals after attending mass in the Cathédrale de Saint Pierre. Many of them also gathered in the bookstore of Rigaud et Pons and in the *cabinet littéraire* (reading club) of Abraham Fontanel, where they read the same books, including a large number of works by Voltaire, Diderot, and Rousseau.

It was this town—a fairly prosperous and progressive city of the second rank—that our author sat down to describe in 1768. But his description should not be set against our own in an attempt to compare the facts on the one hand (the historian's Montpellier) with the interpretation of the facts on the other (the Montpellier of the *Description*). For we can never disentangle interpretation and facts. Nor can we fight our way past the text to some hard and fast reality beyond it. Indeed, the previous three paragraphs describe the city in the very categories that I have been criticizing. They begin with demography and economics and move on to social structure and culture. That mode of description would have been unthinkable to the Montpelliérain of 1768. He began with the bishop and the clergy, then ran through the civil authorities, and ended with a survey of the different "estates" of society and their customs. Each segment of the text follows its predecessor as if it were on parade. In fact, the first half of the *Description* reads like an account of a procession—and understandably so, for processions were important events everywhere in early modern Europe. They displayed the *dignités, qualités, corps,* and *états* of which the social order was thought to be composed. Thus when he described his city, our author organized his thoughts in the same way as his countrymen arranged their processions. With minor deviations here and there, he translated onto paper what they acted out in the streets because the procession served as a traditional idiom for urban society.

What, then, was Montpellier on parade? As reconstructed from the first half of the *Description,* a typical *procession générale* conformed closely to what today would be called the city's superstructure. It opened with a burst of color and sound from the ceremonial guard who escorted the municipal officials on all important occasions: two commanders dressed entirely in red with silver lacing on their sleeves; six mace-bearers in robes, half-blue, half-red, carrying silver maces and plaques with the town's arms; eight halberdiers bearing spears; and a trumpeteer in a red costume with silver lace, who cleared the way for the dignitaries behind him with a blast of music.

The First Estate (clergy) came first, beginning with a succession of religious confraternities: the Pénitents Blancs, who carried candles and marched in long, white gowns, their heads hidden in hoods; then the lesser orders in different shades of sackcloth—La Vraie-Croix, Tous les Saints, and Saint Paul. After these filed by, perhaps a hundred strong, a line of orphans appeared, dressed in the coarse blue and grey uniforms of the Hôpital Général (poorhouse). The boys and girls marched separately, followed by six intendants, twelve rectors, and six syndics of the Hôpital—a statement of the city's commitment to care for its poor and at the same time an appeal for Divine favor because the poor were considered especially close to God and effective in obtaining His mercy. So they often marched in funerals, bearing candles and ceremonial gifts of cloth.

Next came the regular clergy, each order dressed in its traditional costume and each placed according to the antiquity of its foundation in Montpellier: first eight Dominicans, then twelve Cordeliers, three Augustins, three Grands Carmes, twelve Carmes Déchaussés, three Pères de la Merci, thirty Capucins, twenty Récollets, and one Oratorien. The secular clergy followed: three curates and eleven vicars, representing the "cure" (pastoral care) of souls in the three parishes of the city.

At this point a magnificent cross, elaborately wrought in gold and silver, signaled the arrival of the bishop. He marched immediately before the Host, surrounded by the canons of the cathedral; and his profuse pink robes expressed his special eminence, for he was also comte de Mauguio and Montferrand, marquis de la Marquerose, baron de Sauve, and seigneur de la Vérune, with domains worth 60,000 livres in annual revenue. True, other sees in the province were older; Narbonne, Toulouse, and Albi had *arch*bishops. But when the prelates joined in processions of the Provincial Estates in Montpellier, only the bishop of Montpellier marched in pink. The other twenty-three wore black, except for the archbishop of Narbonne, whose preeminence also gave him the right to pink. And in municipal processions, the pink robes of Montpellier's bishop stood out against the deep, black robes and the gray fur hoods of the canons, who marched according to rank: four Dignitaires, four Personnats, and fifteen Simples Chanoines. Then came the most solemn segment of the procession, the Host, displayed in a monstrance mounted on an elaborate processional altar under a canopy carried by the town's six consuls.

The consuls, who occupied the top municipal offices of the town, marked the point in the procession where the religious and civil authorities were joined. Each of them paraded in ceremonial robes of scarlet with purple satin hoods, and each represented a corporate group. The first three were named by the governor of the province from the ranks of "gentlemen," "bourgeois living nobly," and attorneys or notaries, respectively.[11] The second three were selected by the main municipal body, the Conseil de Ville Renforcé, and came from the following groups of corporate bodies: first, merchants, surgeons, apothecaries, or clerks; second, goldsmiths, wig makers, distillers, tapestry makers, or members of another "respectable trade" (*métier honnête*); and third, a master artisan from one of the established trades (*corps de métiers*).[12] The consuls also represented the Third Estate (commoners) of Montpellier at meetings of the Provincial Estates. To be sure, they seemed insignificant in comparison with the bishop on such occasions, for they wore only short robes and could not make speeches. But they collected a ceremonial gift of four watches worth 600 livres, and in municipal processions they cut quite a figure, marching in full regalia beside the Holy Sacrament. In some processions they were accompanied by a dozen robed members of the Archiconfrérie du Saint-Sacrément, who walked alongside the Host carrying candles. A detachment of guards in dress uniform always escorted this section, the heart of the whole parade.

The other leading officials of the town continued the line of march according to their rank and dignity. A company of guards from the Prévôté Générale in ceremonial dress and mounted on horses led the way for the magistrates of the Cour des Aides, the highest court in the area. The Cour actually comprised three chambers, which dealt with different legal and administrative questions, but its members processed according to *places d'honneur*.[13] First came the governor of the province, usually a nobleman of royal blood, who presided over the court on ceremonial occasions as its honorific Premier Président. He was usually flanked by his Commandants and Lieutenants-Généraux, all appropriately robed. Then came the magistrates proper: thirteen Présidents in black silk soutanes under scarlet robes with ermine hoods; sixty-five Conseillers-Maîtres in the same costume but set back a pace; eighteen Conseillers-Correcteurs in robes of black damask; twenty-six Conseillers-Auditeurs in black taffeta; three Gens du Roi (state attorneys) with a Greffier (clerk) in robes like those of the Conseillers-Maîtres, provided they had received a law degree; a Premier Huissier (bailiff) in a silk soutane and a scarlet robe but a hood without fur; and eight Huissiers in pink robes. The Trésoriers de France came next, thirty-one strong, including four Gens du Roi and three Greffiers, all dressed in black satin. They were wealthy and important, for they had the ultimate legal authority over most tax gathering.

The procession closed with a long string of officials from the Présidial or lower court: two Présidents, a Juge-Mage, a Juge-Criminel, a Lieutenant Principal, a Lieutenant Particulier, two Conseillers d'Honneur, twelve Conseillers, a Procureur, an Avocat du Roi, a Greffier en Chef, and an assortment of Procureurs and Huissiers. The Présidents marched in scarlet robes but without hoods or fur trim. The other officers, by virtue of a special privilege, wore black satin.

The procession ended here, at a rather elevated point in the hierarchy of local officials. It could have extended to the other corporate bodies that our author went on to describe in the next sections of his essay: the Prévôté Générale; the Hôtel des Monnaies; the Juges Royaux; the ecclesiastical, feudal, and commercial courts; the Conseil Renforcé and Conseil des Vingt-Quatre; and the swarm of commissaires, inspecteurs, receveurs, trésoriers, and payeurs, who swelled the local branches of the royal bureaucracy. These officials appeared in processions in appropriate costumes on appropriate occasions, but they did not participate in *processions générales,* which were solemn affairs, reserved for the highest *dignités* of the city and the most important holidays of the year, both religious (la Fête-Dieu) and civil (le Voeu du Roi). A *procession générale* provided an impressive display of sound, color, and texture. Trumpets pealed; horses' hoofs clattered over the cobblestones; a throng of dignitaries tramped by, some in boots and some in sandals, some under plumes and some in sackcloth. Different shades of red and blue stood out against the lace and fur trim of the magistrates and contrasted with the dull blacks and browns of the monks. Great sweeps of satin, silk, and damask filled the streets—a vast stream of robes and uniforms winding through the city, with crosses and maces bobbing up here and there and the flames of candles dancing all along its course.

A modern American might be tempted to compare this spectacle with a Rose Bowl or a Macy's Thanksgiving Day parade, but nothing could be more misleading. A *procession générale* in Montpellier did not stir up fans or stimulate trade; it expressed the corporate order of urban society. It was a statement unfurled in the streets, through which the city represented itself to itself—and sometimes to God, for it also took place when Montpellier was threatened by drought or famine. But how can one read it two centuries after the dust has settled and the robes were packed away?

Fortunately, our native informant took great pains to explicate details. He noted, for example, that some members of the Cour des Aides did not wear red, a color reserved for magistrates who had studied law. The court contained a distressing proportion of young men who purchased their office without passing through the university. They stood out to the educated eye, the Présidents marching in black velvet trimmed with ermine and the Conseillers in black satin *erminé*. Our man also knew all about the status and income that corresponded with the color and fabric of the robes. The Présidents possessed full, transmissible nobility; were addressed as *Messire;* had the right of *commitmus* (trial by peers in a sovereign court); enjoyed certain fiscal exemptions (dispensation from *franc-fief* and from *lods et ventes*); and received 6,000 livres plus various fees from their offices, which had cost them 110,000 livres apiece. The Conseillers had the same privileges and the same judicial functions; but their nobility was not fully transmissible until the third generation; they were addressed as *Monsieur;* and their annual income came to only 4,000 livres from offices that had cost 60,000.

The same set of correspondences held for the clergy in the procession. Our author listed all the titles, privileges, incomes, and functions inscribed implicitly in the order of march. The Dominicans, who marched first, had the oldest foundation and received 6,000 livres a year. The Augustins occupied a middle rank and received 4,000, while the *arrivistes* Pères de la Merci, who received only 2,000 and did not have a proper monastery, brought up the end. Our author saw a great deal of fat under the robes. He noted that many monasteries with vast buildings and large endowments sheltered only three or four unproductive priests. Monks had little *dignité* in his eyes.

Professors had a great deal. He observed with approval that the Professeurs Royaux of the University of Montpellier wore crimson satin with ermine hoods. In the law faculty they were known as *Chevaliers ès-Lois,* a title that gave them nontransmissible nobility and the right to be buried in an open coffin wearing their robes and boots with gold spurs. To be sure, they received only 1,800 livres a year (and the lesser Docteurs-Agrégés, who wore only black gowns, got only 200 livres), an income that our author thought incompatible with the "nobility" of their "estate." [14] But "dignity" or "quality" (to use his favorite terms) did not derive from wealth. Professors were knights of the law because of the noble character of their knowledge, and it was more important to go to the grave with golden spurs than to leave a fortune behind.

Thus wealth, status, and power did not join lock-step in a single social code. There were complexities and contradictions in the human comedy as it paraded in the *Description.* The Grands Carmes were more venerable but less rich than the Carmes Déchaussés. The Trésoriers de France owned offices worth far more than those of the Conseillers in the Cour des Aides but enjoyed less esteem and a less prestigious place in the processions. The royal governor, who marched at the head of the Cour and received 200,000 livres a year, had little power in comparison with the intendant, who received only 70,000 livres and did not join in the procession at all.

The nonparaders complicated the picture considerably because although they did not appear in the line of march they inflected the perceptions of the onlookers, or at least of the author of the *Description*. He noted that the Trinitaires, who belonged just below the half-way mark in the hierarchy of religious houses, had fallen on hard times and had ceased to figure in processions. The Jesuits, once rich and powerful, no longer marched behind the Récollets because they had been expelled from the kingdom. The Pénitents Bleus, a new but very popular confraternity, had wanted to march ahead of the Pénitents Blancs; and having lost the dispute, they had to retire from the processions altogether. The three other confraternities in the line of march knew better than to challenge the Blancs; but by accepting a subordinate place, they asserted themselves against eight other confraternities, who also had to stand on the sidelines. Our author carefully listed the eight, noting that they were not "publicly known" owing to their exclusion from the processions.[15] In the same way, he went over the municipal corps who did not participate in the procession—the Prévôté Générale, Hôtel des Monnaies, and so on. Each could walk about the streets, plumed and robed, on other occasions; but in a *procession générale* a line was drawn behind the last Huissier of the Siège Présidial— beyond that no corps possessed enough dignity to march in the supreme civic ceremonies. The excluded stood out in the minds of the observers by their conspicuous absence from the ranks of the paraders. They belonged to negative categories, which were crucial to the meaning of the whole, for one could not read a procession properly without noting the blank spots as well as the units that bulged with pomp and circumstance.

What then was the meaning of the whole? A procession could not be taken literally as a model of society, because it exaggerated some elements and neglected others. The clergy dominated the processions, but they had very little prestige in the eyes of observers like our author, who noted that monks were no longer invited to dinner in polite society, however grand they might appear in the line of march on the Fête-Dieu. He also stressed that Montpellier was a commercial city, where citizens showed a healthy respect for wealth. Yet processions gave a significant place to the poor, while leaving very little room for merchants and none at all for manufacturers. They also omitted nearly all the artisans, day laborers, and servants who formed the bulk of the population; and they excluded all Protestants—one citizen of every six.

But processions did not operate as miniature replicas of the social structure; they expressed the essence of society, its most important *qualités* and *dignités*. In the *Description* a person's "quality" was determined by corporate rank or office rather than by individual characteristics like bravery or intelligence. The text also assumes that society was composed of corporate units, not free-floating individuals, and that the corps belonged to a hierarchy, which was embodied in the processions. The hierarchy did not file by in a straightforward, linear order, however. As the quarrel between the Pénitents Blancs and the Pénitents Bleus demonstrated, precedence was a vital principle, but it took complex forms. The canons followed the curates, who occupied a lower rank within the ecclesiastical hierarchy; yet within the corps of canons the higher ranks marched first. Different segments of the procession followed different lines of division—not merely clerics versus laymen, but regular versus secular clergy; not merely the upper versus the lower tribunals, but the magistrates versus the *Gens du Roi* (state attorneys) within each court.

Nonetheless, a general morphology stood out. The ranks mounted as the procession passed, progressing from the confraternities to the regular clergy, the secular clergy, and the bishop with the canons of the cathedral accompanying the Host—that is, the living presence of Christ. At this point, the most sacred in the procession, the ecclesiastical order shaded off into civil society, for the canopy over the Host was carried by the six Consuls or principal officials of the municipal government. They in turn were divided, the first three coming from the patriciate of noblemen and *rentiers,* the second from the upper ranks of guild masters. In this way the three traditional estates of the realm—clergy, nobility, and commoners—came together in the heart of the procession. And then the procession wound down through a suite of municipal corps, which passed by in descending order of importance. The dignity of the marchers derived from distinctions drawn within the line of march even more than from the contrast between them and the unwashed general public on the sidelines. In Montpellier, as in India, *homo hierarchicus* thrived through the segmentation of society rather than from its polarization.[16] Instead of dividing into classes, the social order rippled past the onlooker in graduated degrees of *dignités*.

The onlooker, as represented by the *Description,* did not merely see the ostensible divisions of rank. He also noticed invisible demarcations, for he knew who had been excluded from the processions as well as who had been included. Exclusion and inclusion belonged to the same process of boundary drawing, a process that took place in men's minds as well as in the streets. But the boundaries acquired their force by being acted out. A *procession générale* ordered reality. It was not merely aimed at some utilitarian objective—the end of a drought or the promotion of the nobility of the robe. It existed the way many statements and works of art exist—as sheer expression, a social order representing itself to itself.

But the language of the processions was archaic. It could not convey the shifting alignments within the social order that resulted from the economic expansion of the mid-century years. Our author knew that his world was changing, though he could not define the changes or find words to express them. He began to grope for an adequate terminology as he neared the second half of his *Description,* which concerned the social and economic life of Montpellier rather than its official institutions. When he reached the half-way point, in a chapter entitled "Nobility, Classes of Inhabitants," he suddenly stopped and changed metaphors. The city no longer appeared as a parade of *dignités.* It became a three-tiered structure of "estates" *(états).*

This manner of speaking came naturally in a province and a kingdom where men were still understood to fit into the three traditional categories of those who prayed (the clergy or First Estate), those who fought (the nobility or Second Estate), and those who worked (the remaining bulk of the population or Third Estate). But our author rearranged the categories so thoroughly as to destroy their traditional meaning. He eliminated the clergy altogether, on the grounds that "it is not much esteemed in this city. It has no influence whatever in daily affairs."[17] Thus in one bold stroke he excluded the group that figured most prominently in the standard version of the three estates and in the first half of his *Description.* Then he elevated the nobility to the rank of "First Estate" (the term must be put within quotation marks to distinguish it from conventional usage). Montpellier had no great feudal families, he explained. Its "First Estate" merely included nobles of the robe—that is, magistrates who had acquired nobility through ownership of important offices as opposed to the older feudal nobles of the sword. Although these recently ennobled bourgeois could be classed juridically as a second division within the "First Estate," they did not differ from other wealthy citizens in the way they lived their everyday lives: "These nobilities [of the robe] give no particular distinction, authority, or privilege in this city, where in general possessions and wealth count for everything."[18]

Next, our author placed the bourgeoisie where the nobility was traditionally located, in the "Second Estate." This was also where he lodged his own loyalties, as his choice of words made clear:

> Bourgeois Estate or Second Estate. The designation *Second Estate* covers magistrates who have not been ennobled, lawyers, doctors, attorneys, notaries, financiers, merchants, tradespeople, and those who live from their revenues without having any particular profession. This class is always the most useful, the most important, and the wealthiest in all kinds of countries. It supports the first [estate] and manipulates the last according to its will.[19]

The author presented the "Third Estate" as an old-fashioned *artisanat* rather than as a working class. He described its members as "the artisans" and "the common people" and divided it into three "branches": artisans who worked with their minds as well as their hands (*artistes*); artisans who worked in mechanical trades (*métiers mécaniques*); and day laborers and agricultural workers, for, like most early modern cities, Montpellier included a great deal of country—gardens and fields that were cultivated by a sizeable labor force.[20] Finally there were domestic servants and the unemployed poor. The author listed them after the laborers, but he excluded them from his classification scheme, because they did not have any corporate existence, except in the case of a few officially licensed beggars and the paupers of the Hôpital Général. They lived outside of urban society and did not constitute an estate, although they could be seen everywhere swarming through the streets.

It was an odd way to describe a social structure—and the second half of the *Description* had a structural aspect to it, something that evoked one of Montpellier's solid town houses in contrast to the procession that had swirled by earlier. The bourgeoisie occupied the main floor of the edifice, having pushed the nobility from the *piano nobile* into the top of the superstructure, while the common people remained below stairs. But the language of estates was no more modern than the language of dignities. Our author used an antiquated set of categories, emptied them of their old meanings, and rearranged them in such a way as to convey the shape of a social order like the one that would emerge openly in the nineteenth century: a society of "notables" dominated by a mixture of the old elite and the *nouveaux riches*; a Balzacian society in which the basic force was wealth, but wealth was derived from traditional sources—land, offices, *rentes,* and trade—rather than from an industrial revolution.

What then was the bourgeoisie? Our author used the word unblushingly. But instead of defining it, he cited examples, most of them professional men—doctors, lawyers, notaries—along with a few merchants and finally the social type who gave the category its name, the "bourgeois" pure and simple: that is, a man who lived from land rents and annuities without exercising any profession. When the term appeared in the *Description,* it had an archaic ring to it: "the bourgeois living nobly," "the bourgeois who lives only from *rentes.*"[21] This species contributed very little to industrialization. True, it included some financiers and merchants, but they operated within a system of commercial capitalism that had existed since the Middle Ages. The entrepreneur, in contrast to the *rentier,* was conspicuous by his absence from the *Description*—all the more so as he already existed, in small numbers, in Montpellier. The *sieurs* Farel and Parlier employed 1,200 workers in their textile *fabriques,* but our author did not mention them or their mills. Instead, he produced an elaborate catalogue of all the trades in the city. Like a botanist enumerating flora and fauna, he distinguished every possible variety of artisan, emphasizing local specialties—glove makers, perfumers, traders in verdigris—and working through the types that proliferated everywhere in early modern cities: cobblers, pewterers, tailors, saddlers, locksmiths, goldsmiths, glaziers, braziers, wig makers, rope makers. The list stretched into hundreds of workshops and lost itself in untranslatable trades—the *mangonniers, romainiers, passementiers, palemardiers, plumassiers,* and *pangustiers*—that have since become extinct. It conveyed a sense of a handicraft economy, cut into tiny units and hedged about by guilds, a little world of artisans and shopkeepers that seemed centuries away from an industrial revolution.

Our author clearly felt at home in this world. He had doubts about the value of industry:

> It is an open question as to whether a great many factories in a city are more of an evil than a good. They certainly provide work for a vast number of people of all ages and both sexes, and keep them and their families alive. But wouldn't the work of such people be more usefully employed in the cultivation of the earth? Although it is scorned by city people and left to peasants, the production of agricultural goods is surely more precious and necessary than the production of textiles and fine liqueurs. After all, one can do without the latter, because they are purely superfluous, often harmful to one's health, and at most susceptible of maintaining a luxurious way of life.[22]

A touch of Physiocratic theory and some fashionable deprecation of luxury colored those remarks, but the author had no sympathy for the taking of risks, the expanding of production, the widening of profit margins, or any other activity that suggested a modern spirit of enterprise. He rejoiced that manufacturing in Montpellier "amounts to very little," and then explained, "Its lack of importance is what keeps it healthy. Our manufacturers only produce as much as they are sure to sell, do not risk the wealth of others, and remain certain of continuing in business. This kind of behavior is very prudent. A small but certain profit, which can be regularly repeated, is doubtless worth more than risky speculations, about which one can never be sure."[23] There spoke a "bourgeois d'Ancien Régime," not a captain of industry or an apologist of capitalism. But if his notions of economics seem downright backward, what was it that tinctured his general view of things in a way that seems irreducibly, unavoidably bourgeois?

Judging from his text, our man felt himself to be bourgeois in his bones; but that feeling, insofar as one can understand it from the *Description,* had little to do with his perceptions and misperceptions of the economic order. It derived from the way he read society. He situated the "Bourgeois Estate" in opposition to the two other main "estates" of Montpellier, the nobility and the common people. Each of them seemed threatening in its own way. So he kept a close watch on their borders and thus defined the position of the bourgeoisie negatively, by reference to its hostile neighbors.

Despite his sensitivity to the importance of the *dignité* attached to social positions, our author rejected the aristocratic notion of honor. Instead, he showed a healthy respect for money. It was wealth not honor that counted in the upper ranks of Montpellier, he emphasized, though things were different in aristocratic cities like Toulouse.

> The small number of persons in this city who belong to chivalric orders confirms me in what I said in the previous chapter, namely that there is a lack of ancient houses and a marked indifference to obtaining honorable distinctions. I could also attribute this to the decided penchant that exists here for lucrative things, things that bring in a solid revenue and that are preferred to honor, which after all produces neither comfort nor distinction in a city where everyone is known solely by the extent of their fortune.[24]

The distinction between noblemen and commoners could ultimately be reduced to a question of wealth, old-fashioned wealth that was calculated in dowries: in the "First Estate" brides brought thirty to sixty thousand livres to their marriages; in the "Second Estate" they brought ten to twenty thousand. Our author saw nothing untoward in using such a crass standard to take the measure of the nobility because he stressed that virtually all the nobles of Montpellier came from the bourgeoisie and had acquired their "quality" by purchasing it in the form of ennobling offices. Once they entered the top rank of society, however, they could not demean themselves by engaging in most kinds of work; for many of them, living "nobly" meant doing nothing at all. But to our author, idleness—*fainéantise,* whether genteel or not—was the height of sin. A citizen should above all be useful. Uselessness compounded by snobbery about losing rank made gentlemen thoroughly despicable, no matter how much they strutted and fretted in processions. The author felt deference for magistrates of the Cour des Aides and for Trésoriers de France, but he deplored the underlying spirit of their estate:

It is especially harmful that persons in the First Estate should consider themselves dishonored if their younger sons took up a useful profession, which would make it possible for them to earn a living honorably, by some real work. It is an erroneous prejudice for a Président, a Conseiller, a Correcteur, an Auditeur, a Trésorier de France, even a magistrate in the Cour Présidial, to consider his younger children dishonored if they adopted the profession of lawyer, doctor, attorney, notary, merchant, or the like. They are full of scorn for such professions, but for the most part they come from them. This fatuousness, which is outrageous in a city where people accept the authority of reason, means that swarms of young men are condemned to idleness and poverty instead of being employed in a useful way, for their good and the good of society.[25]

This tone betrayed a touchiness about aristocratic exclusivity that undercut the author's insistence on the relative unimportance of the "First Estate." He never passed up an opportunity to criticize the nobles' tax exemptions, meager as they were in a province where the main tax (*la taille*) fell on land irrespective of the proprietor's status; or to point out aristocratic privileges, which were equally trivial (the right of *commitmus,* exemptions from duty in the municipal guard and from payment of *franc-fief*); or to deride the lack of professionalism among noble magistrates and the absurdity of practices like dueling over points of honor. His general point of view had many affinities with the demands that the Third Estate in the usual sense of the word—everyone who did not belong to the clergy or nobility—would advance in 1789.

But he did not sound militant. On the contrary, he praised the benign and equitable character of the government, and his political comments could have come from one of the intendant's offices, where politics was seen essentially as a matter of collecting taxes and improving roads. Our man could not imagine a political body composed of autonomous individuals who elected representatives or participated directly in the affairs of state. He thought in terms of corporate groups. Thus it seemed perfectly natural to him that when the province sent delegations to Versailles, it should speak to the king by estate—first through a bishop who remained standing, then through a nobleman who spoke while bowing, and finally through a member of the Third Estate (in the conventional meaning of the term) who addressed the throne while kneeling on one

knee. Similar notions colored his account of the municipal government. He considered Montpellier fortunate because its consuls did
not become ennobled through their offices, unlike their counterparts in Toulouse and Bordeaux. But much as he disapproved of
such ennoblement, he did not question the assumption that the
consuls should represent orders rather than individuals: "It is a
good thing that this privilege [ennoblement through municipal
offices] was not granted, for it would only have produced a swarm
of noblemen, who would have sunk into idleness and poverty.
Furthermore, nomination by ranks is more useful, because in that
way each order and sub-order in the division and subdivision of
citizens has the right to aspire to the municipal government."[26]
Our bourgeois had no use for the nobility as an estate, but he
accepted a hierarchy of estates as the natural organization of
society.

He also seemed willing to accept a certain amount of ennoblement of the bourgeoisie. It was *embourgeoisement* of the common
people that really alarmed him, for the greatest danger to the "Second Estate" lay along its border with the "Third." Rousseau might
have been able to detect virtue among the common people, but our
author knew better: "The common people are naturally bad, licentious, and inclined toward rioting and pillage."[27] He summarized
their wickedness under four headings: (1) they duped and cheated
their employers at the slightest opportunity; (2) they never did a
job right; (3) they knocked off work whenever they spotted an
occasion for debauchery; (4) they ran up debts, which they never
repaid.[28] This indictment read like a negative version of the non-
work ethic propounded to Jerome by the journeymen printers, and
indeed our Montpelliérain seemed to be observing the same sort of
artisanal culture, though from the opposite point of view. He conceded that artisans, unlike noblemen, did something useful: they
worked, however badly. But they were given over to "brutality."[29]
He knew vaguely that the likes of Jerome in his city formed associations with strange initiation rites and endless meals, and he felt
nothing but scorn for their arcane lore, "as pitiful as it is absurd."[30]
It generally issued in violence, for nothing pleased a worker more
after carousing with his mates than to bash an innocent passerby or
to brawl with a rival and equally besotted journeyman's association. The only cure for such behavior was hanging, or deportation

at the very least. But the authorities were far too indulgent. They required proof before meting out punishment and never punished severely enough, whereas the only way to live with the "Third Estate" was to keep it in its place.

These comments betrayed a mixture of fear and incomprehension in the face of an alien way of living. Our author believed that Montpellier was suffering from a crime wave. Bands of youths "from the dregs of the common people" roamed the streets, snatching purses and slitting throats.[31] Cabarets, billiard halls, gambling dens, and houses of ill repute were springing up everywhere. A reputable citizen could not even promenade in the Jardin du Roi of an evening without running into dangerous hordes of lackeys and low-life. In reading the *Description,* one gets the impression that this sense of danger derived from a cultural gap that was opening up between the common people and polite society— that is, a mixed elite of nobles and wealthy bourgeois, whom the author referred to as *les honnêtes gens.*[32] The estates did not inhabit completely separate worlds; in fact our author regretted that the "Third Estate" was not separate enough. But whenever he described it, he noted differences that set it apart from the first two estates—differences in language, dress, eating habits, and amusements. He paid so much attention to this theme in the last part of the *Description* that in the end it turned into a treatise on customs and culture, and the society it depicted no longer seemed to be segmented into three estates but to be divided into two hostile camps: patricians and plebeians.

Everyone in Montpellier spoke the local variation of the *langue d'oc,* but all official activities took place in French; so the first two estates tended to be bilingual, while the "Third Estate" kept to its own dialect. Dress served as a social code in Montpellier as everywhere else in early modern Europe. Gentlemen wore breeches; laborers wore trousers. Ladies dressed in velvet and silk, depending on the season; common women dressed in wool and cotton, and did not coordinate their clothing strictly with the seasons. All kinds of finery, from shoe buckles to wigs, distinguished the first two estates from the "Third" without drawing a line between the "First Estate" and the "Second."

Similar distinctions marked off what, when, and how one ate.

Artisans and laborers ate at all kinds of hours, on the job and off, because they mixed work and diversion in irregular quantities throughout the day. Masons traditionally knocked off eight times for meals during the workday, and journeymen in other crafts usually managed at least four breaks for food. But the bourgeois and nobles of the robe sat down at the same time for the same three meals: breakfast, dinner, and supper. On the rare occasions when they bought a meal, they went to a proper inn, kept by a *hôte majeur,* and paid for the whole dinner at once, whereas an artisan went to a cabaret, kept by a *hôte mineur,* and paid by the plate. The cabaret had become alien territory to the first two estates, although a half century earlier everyone frequented it and got drunk together—or so our author believed. He noted approvingly that the modern bourgeois and the modern nobleman did not drink to inebriation and kept to delicate wines, usually imported from other provinces. Artisans and laborers preferred the local *gros rouge,* which they swilled in huge quantities, gargling to give it a kick.

Montpellier also divided according to the games it played, and our author catalogued them carefully, noting what kind of fun was appropriate for the first two estates. Not *ballon,* nor the *jeu de mail,* which involved violent *mêlées,* suitable only for peasants and laborers; nor billiards, which drew one into bad company; but the ancient game of the *perroquet,* "the most beautiful, the most noble, and the most capable of amusing *honnêtes gens.*"[33] It involved two companies of "knights" from the "Second Estate," who were commanded by officers from the "First Estate" and dressed in costumes of red and blue silk with gold trim and plumed hats. For several days they paraded through town behind a marching band and a large wooden parrot mounted on a pole. Then they attached the parrot to the top of a ship's mast in a grassy moat outside the city walls and held an archery contest. The knight who felled the parrot was proclaimed king. A triumphal arch was raised in front of his house, and the knights danced there with their ladies all night long, then retired for a feast given by the king, while *gros rouge* was distributed to the populace. The bourgeois did not get to play at knights and ladies very often, however. In fact, the "Divertissement du Perroquet" had last taken place two generations ago, at the birth of the Dauphin in 1730. So it did not provide much amusement in comparison with the joyful bashings that the workers administered to themselves every week in the primitive versions of football that they played in the moat.

Judging from the account of games and festivities in the *Description,* the "Third Estate" had all the fun. The "First" and "Second" Estates could parade about solemnly in *processions générales,* but the artisans and laborers got to whoop it up around Le Chevalet, a dummy horse mounted by a popular "king," who set whole neighborhoods dancing in a kind of Beggars' Opera parody of court life that dated back to the sixteenth century. Dancing was a passion for the "little people" (*petites gens*), and it often gave them an opportunity to make fun of the big (*les grands*), especially during carnival time, May Day celebrations, and charivaris. Our author dutifully recorded all these amusements, but he disapproved of them and noted with satisfaction that the bourgeois had left them to the lower orders. "Such amusements have completely gone out of favor in this city and have given way to a concern for making money. Thus no more public *fêtes,* no more Perroquet archery contests or general merry-making. If any take place from time to time, it is only among the common people. *Les honnêtes gens* do not take part."[34]

Hell-raising had even gone out of wedding feasts, except in the "Third Estate." In the upper estates, one invited only the immediate family, not the whole neighborhood. There was no more drunkenness, no more brawling at table, no more smashed furniture and broken pates, no invasions from a rowdy counter-ceremony (*trouble-fête*) or bawdiness exploding from a charivari or a cabaret. "All that used to create such a horrible disorder that if anyone tried to revive it today he would be punished for disturbing the peace. The overall change has had a most salubrious effect. Order and decency now reign during meals. They are required in public festivities; and unless the character of the nation changes, there is every reason to believe that they will last forever."[35]

True, some disturbing strains of Rabelaisianism still existed among the artisans, and our author would have recognized them in the story of Jerome's apprenticeship. But he took heart in the observation that witchcraft, spell casting, and black sabbaths no longer aroused passions in Montpellier. If any superstition remained, it was restricted to the common people, like the violent games and the rowdy festivities. The upper orders had withdrawn from the activities that had engaged the whole population several generations ago, and had shut themselves up within their own cultural forms. "Decent amusements now predominate. The establishment of the Music Academy [a concert society] is one of them, which has pushed the others [popular amusements] into oblivion. The reading of good books, the philosophical spirit that gains ground every day, has made us forget all the inanities of our predecessors."[36] If some inanity survived in the form of popular culture, the *honnêtes gens* seemed to have everything pretty well in hand.

But it would be misleading to imply that urban society had segregated into separate cultural spheres or that our author's consciousness, however bourgeois, remained unperturbed. He had worries, especially about the problem of boundary crossing.

The democratizing effects of wealth extended below as well as above the bourgeoisie. To be sure, most journeymen and laborers could never accumulate enough capital to buy anything more expensive than a watch, but a master artisan—a watchmaker, for instance, or a counterpart of Jerome's "bourgeois"—could live like a member of the "Second Estate." Many wealthy artisans owned silver table settings and ate just as well as the bourgeois. Their wives and daughters took coffee in mid-morning, just like gentlewomen. Women of all classes now wore silk stockings, and one could mistake some shop girls for ladies of quality—unless one paid special attention to fine points of their coiffure, their slightly shorter skirts, and the studied, provocative elegance of their shoes. Worse still, valets sometimes put on clothes every bit as fine as those of their masters and strutted about, swords at their sides, with the finest of company at the public promenades. Distinctions had especially become eroded within the three branches of the "Third Estate." "The most vile artisan behaves as the equal of the most eminent *artiste* or anyone who practices a trade superior to his. They are indistinguishable by their expenditures, their clothes, and their houses. It is only the agricultural laborer who does not leave his estate."[37]

But the crossings from the "Third" to the "Second Estate" were most disturbing. Surgeons, for example, caused notions of quality to blur. They traditionally belonged to the upper ranks of the "Third Estate," for they were *artistes,* members of the barbers' guild. But ten of them taught courses as Professeurs-Démonstrateurs Royaux before large crowds of students in Montpellier's advanced school of surgery, the Saint-Côme des Chirurgiens. They wore only simple black robes and received only 500 livres in salary; but like other professors, they could claim a kind of nobility. So by a special decree, they enjoyed a hybrid status of "notable inhabitant," which fixed "the honor of their estate" as long as they did not open a shop and shave customers.[38] The surgeons who shaved continued to be classified as *artistes,* an estate and a half below.

Education, like money, had a disruptive effect on social categories. Although our author respected it, it made him uneasy; and he positively condemned its existence in the "Third Estate." To his horror, the Frères de la Charité maintained two large schools, where they taught reading and writing free of charge to children of the lower orders. He wanted to close the schools and to abolish instruction in reading among the pauper children in the Hôpital Général as well. Artisans should be forbidden to send their sons to secondary school (*collège*). And at the top of the educational system, the university should enforce its rule against admitting anyone who had exercised a "mechanical trade" into the faculties of law and medicine.[39] Only by keeping learned culture closed to the "Third Estate" could society save itself from having to support a population of unemployed intellectuals, who ought to be walking behind plows or laboring beside their fathers in workshops.

This argument was a commonplace in the eighteenth-century debates on education. Voltaire had often hammered away at it. But what really upset our author was not so much that educated common people would become a burden on the economy as that they would disrupt the divisions between estates. "It is repugnant to the rules of propriety that a sedan-chair bearer, a street porter, a vile and abject man, should have the right to send his son to a secondary school . . . and that children of the common people, who have neither upbringing nor sentiments, should mix with sons of good families, providing bad examples and a contagious source of bad behavior."[40]

The common people were bad enough in themselves, but they were a menace to the whole social order when they stepped out of their estate. The fault lines of society ran along the seams where estates, orders, corporations, classes, and groups of all kinds were joined. Our author therefore recommended reinforcing boundaries at every possible point. Students, a rowdy lot given to rebellion, should be made to wear special uniforms, one for each faculty, so they could not blend in with normal citizens. Parks and promenades should be reserved for certain groups at certain hours. Artisans in certain trades should be required to live in certain neighborhoods. And above all, servants should be forced to wear distinctive badges on their clothing:

> For nothing is more impertinent than to see a cook or a valet don an outfit trimmed with braid or lace, strap on a sword, and insinuate himself amongst the finest company in promenades; or to see a chambermaid as artfully dressed as her mistress; or to find domestic servants of any kind decked out like gentle people. All that is revolting. The estate of servants is one of servitude, of obedience to the orders of their masters. They are not deemed to be free, to form part of the social body with the citizens. Therefore they should be forbidden to mix with the citizenry; and if any such mixing must take place, one should be able to pick them out by a badge indicating their estate and making it impossible to confuse them with everyone else.[41]

But our author took heart from a countervailing tendency toward cultural fusion across the dividing line between the "First" and "Second" estates; for the increase of wealth that looked so dangerous at the bottom of society seemed promising at the top. "Ever since people have begun to get rich rapidly from finance and trade, the Second Estate has won new respect. Its spending and luxury have made it the envy of the First. Inevitably the two have merged, and today there are no more differences in the way they run their households, give dinner parties, and dress."[42] A new urban elite was forming in opposition to the common people. It was not that more bourgeois were buying their way into the nobility but that they were using their wealth to develop a new cultural style, which the nobles also found attractive.

Consider once more the question of dinner, a matter of consequence in France. Our author observed that sumptuosity had gone out of style, that the best houses practiced a "decent restraint" and a "good economy" at table.[43] By that he meant that polite society had abandoned the orgiastic mode of dining that had prevailed under Louis XIV, when banquets were marathon events of twenty or more courses, in favor of what was beginning to emerge as *la cuisine bourgeoise.* Courses had become less numerous but more carefully prepared. Accompanied by appropriate wines and sauces, they appeared according to a standard choreography: *potages, hors d'oeuvre, relevés de potage, entrées, rôti, entremets, dessert, café,* and *pousse-café.* That may sound rather daunting to the modern middle-class eater, but it was simplicity itself in the eighteenth century. And when they had no guests for supper, the patrician family would settle for only one *entrée, rôti, salade,* and *dessert.*[44]

The new taste for simplicity did not imply any disapproval of luxury. On the contrary, the urban elite spent vast sums on dress and furniture. While at her morning toilette, a lady from the "First" or "Second Estate" took her coffee from a special service, *le déjeuné,* which consisted of a platter, a coffee pot, a pot for hot chocolate, a bowl for hot water, a bowl for hot milk, and a set of knives, forks, and spoons—all of it in silver; then a tea pot, a sugar bowl, and cups—all in porcelain; and finally a liqueur cabinet stocked with an assortment of cordials in fine crystal decanters. But all of this was for her private delectation. Instead of being used for public display, luxury became increasingly contained within the domestic sphere of life. It took the form of *boudoirs, fauteuils,* snuff boxes, a whole world of exquisite objects wrought with Pompadourean prettiness. Patrician families cut back on the number of their servants and eliminated livery. They no longer wished to dine in state, surrounded by retainers, but to enjoy a family meal. When they built new houses, they made the rooms smaller and added hallways, so that they could sleep, dress, and converse with a new degree of privacy. The family withdrew from the public sphere and turned increasingly upon itself. When it attended the plays of Sedaine and Diderot, read the novels of Le Sage and Marivaux, contemplated the paintings of Chardin and Greuze, it admired its own image.

Of course, one cannot reduce the art of Louis XV, or even the *drame bourgeois,* to the rise of the bourgeoisie. The point that needs to be stressed—for it has been overlooked in the social history of art—is that the nobility was descending. It did not decline in wealth or abandon its claims to superior birth; quite the contrary. But it led a less exalted life. It relaxed the severe poses it had struck in the seventeenth century and enjoyed the intimacy of a new urban style, one that meant it had a great deal in common with the upper bourgeoisie.

The elaboration of a common cultural style involved a certain commitment to the "high" culture of the age of Enlightenment. Although our author did not find any local painters or poets worthy of note, his civic pride swelled in describing the Académie de Musique, a concert society "composed of almost all the best families in the first and second orders of inhabitants."[45] The members paid sixty livres a year to attend operas, chamber music, and symphonies in a handsome concert hall built by the town. Montpellier also had a well-appointed theater and several Masonic lodges, where persons from both estates mixed. The more serious-minded invested huge sums in cabinets of natural history, where they collected all manner of insects, plants, and fossils. Private libraries also flourished, stimulating a boom in the book trade, though not in local printing. The educated elite, both noble and bourgeois, showed great interest in science and technology. They took pride in their university, with its famous faculty of medicine, and in their Société Royale des Sciences, which claimed to be a peer of the Académie des Sciences in Paris. The academy in Montpellier was a distinguished body, which published its proceedings and met every Thursday to discuss eclipses, fossils, phlogiston, and the latest discoveries in everything from geography to anatomy. It included honorary members—the bishop, intendant, first presidents of the Cour des Aides, and other dignitaries, mainly from the nobility—and regular members, who tended to come from the professional classes. Like other provincial academies, it epitomized the moderate, Enlightenment culture that took root in a mixed elite of urban notables.[46]

Our author himself clearly sympathized with the Enlightenment. He had no use for monks, a parasitic lot who contributed nothing to society and absorbed funds that were needed in commerce. The expulsion of the Jesuits delighted him. He favored the toleration of Protestants and Jews, and felt nothing but scorn for the doctrinal quarrels between Molinists and Jansenists. Theology struck him as so much vain speculation: better to get on with the business of improving life on earth than to worry about questions beyond the reach of reason. His secular orientation did not mean that he had broken with the Catholic Church, for he expressed sympathy for the overburdened and underpaid parish priests and respect for "true piety."[47] But his heart clearly lay with the *philosophes*. "There are no more disputes over Calvinism, Molinism, and Jansenism," he wrote with evident satisfaction. "In place of all that, the reading of philosophical books has taken such a hold on most people, especially young people, that one has never seen so many deists as there are today. It must be said that they are peaceful spirits, who are willing to countenance all sorts of religious practices without adhering to any of them and who believe that the exercise of moral virtue is enough to make one an *honnête homme*."[48]

The ideal of the *honnête homme*, the decent, well-bred citizen ("un honnête homme, qui a un nom et un état"),[49] reappears at several points in the *Description*. It had its roots in the aristocratic, seventeenth-century notion of gentility, but by 1768 it had acquired a bourgeois coloring. It suggested good manners, tolerance, reasonableness, restraint, clear thinking, fair dealing, and a healthy self-respect. Neither an aristocratic honor code nor a bourgeois work ethic, it expressed a new urbanity and marked the emergence of a new ideal type: the gentleman. More often than not, in Montpellier if not everywhere in France, the urban gentleman belonged to the bourgeoisie. The two terms no longer looked like a laughable contradiction, as in the era of Molière. Whatever his uneasiness about being flanked by noblemen on one side and artisans on the other, the bourgeois gentleman had developed his own way of life. Rich, well fed, correctly dressed, surrounded by tasteful objects, certain of his usefulness, and firm in his philosophy, he reveled in the new urbanity. "Happy are those who live in great cities,"[50] concluded our author. The conclusion did not allow for bread lines, *hôpitaux*, madhouses, and gibbets. But it suited those who had taken the lead in the pursuit of happiness, the *honnêtes gens* of the "Second Estate."

That consideration brings us back to our original question: how did someone situated somewhere within the middle classes read a city under the Old Regime? The *Description* actually provided three readings. It presented Montpellier as a procession of dignities, then as a set of estates, and finally as the scene of a style of living. Each of the three versions contained contradictions and contradicted the others—hence the fascination of the document, for through its inconsistencies one can sense a fresh vision of the world struggling to emerge. The author went on for hundreds of pages, piling description upon description, because he was driven by a need to make sense of his world and he could not find a framework adequate to the task. The *processions générales* furnished him with a traditional idiom through which the city represented its hierarchy, but it grossly exaggerated the importance of some groups and completely neglected others. The division into estates made use of another traditional language, which did justice to the corporate character of society, but only by considerable sleight of hand in the juggling of categories. And the account of urban culture revealed a great deal about how people lived, but upon closer inspection it turned out to be a tendentious apology for the bourgeois way of life. When he reached this point, our author had exploded his archaic terminology and had come close to a cultural conception of class, one in which the *cuisine bourgeoise* counted for more than the factory in identifying the new masters of the city. That notion may seem extravagant, but it should be taken seriously. For as a perception of reality, it shaped reality itself, and it was to impose its shape on the next hundred years of French history, the century not only of Marx but also of Balzac.

APPENDIX: SCRAMBLED ESTATES IN PROVINCIAL SOCIETY

The following text comprises chapter XV, "Nobility, Classes of Inhabitants" in the *Etat et description de la ville de Montpeller fait en 1768,* pp. 67–69.

I. *Ancient houses.* One should not expect to find a numerous ancient military nobility in this city. In the days of the Seigneurs de Montpellier there were some great old houses. There are none today, either because they died out or because their survivors have moved away or lost their family names and genealogies.

The gentlemen from old Montpellier houses are the Baschi du

Caila, de Roquefeuil, de Montcalm, de Saint-Véran, de la Croix de Candilhargues (a branch of the house of Castries), Brignac de Montarnaud, Lavergne de Montbasin, Saint-Julien. There are no others whose ancient nobility has been firmly proven.

II. *Nobility of the robe.* This is very extensive. There are many old families in the judiciary, such as the Grasset, Bocaud, Trémolet, Duché, Belleval, Joubert, Bon, Massannes, Daigrefeuille, Deydé, etc. The *Histoire de Montpellier* [by Charles d'Aigrefeuille] gives the chronological sequence of these houses and of the officials they have provided. But the oldest of them does not go back beyond 250 years.

III. *Bourgeois Estate or Second Estate.* The designation *Second Estate* covers magistrates who have not been ennobled, lawyers, doctors, attorneys, notaries, financiers, merchants, tradespeople, and those who live from their revenues without having any particular profession. This class is always the most useful, the most important, and the wealthiest in all kinds of countries. It supports the first [estate] and manipulates the last according to its will. It does the basic business of the city, because trade and finance are in its hands and because the necessities of life are procured through its activity and intelligence.

IV. *Artisans.* The artisans are very numerous. (I will devote a chapter to the craft guilds.) One can divide their class into several branches: first, the *artistes;* second, the mechanical trades; third, the agricultural laborers and workers who hire themselves out by the day. These citizens are extremely useful. The two other estates could not get along without them. It is important to support them and to give them work. But at the same time it is necessary to subject them to standards of probity and lawfulness. For the common people are naturally bad, licentious, and inclined toward rioting and pillage. It is only by keeping them subdued through the rigorous execution of good ordinances that one can succeed in making them do their duty.

V. *Domestic servants.* The ridiculous practice of filling one's house with liveried servants has been abandoned for a long time. Now people settle for having the necessary minimum and do what they can to keep them occupied and useful. But there are still too many of them, which is bad for the state and for the servants themselves. They prefer a soft and lazy life with a master to labor on a farm or in a workshop. They refuse to understand that by taking up a trade they would be able to set up shop for themselves and become their own masters, that they could produce families and thereby serve the fatherland, whereas by remaining in service they can only expect to die in the poorhouse after they grow old. In short, domestic service is a drain on the resources of Montpellier, in the form of wages, gifts, and food—and the worst of it is that there is not a city in the world where one is served so badly.

Observations. What I have just said about the lack of an ancient nobility in Montpellier accounts for the fact that one cannot find in this city a single knight of the Order of Saint-Esprit nor a canon of Lyon, even though they exist in a great many small towns. We have only three families here who have supplied knights of Malta: the Bocaud, Montcalm, and Bon.

As for the armed services, the houses of le Caila, la Chaize, and Montcalm have provided four lieutenants généraux des armées du roi. Others have produced some brigadiers, a great many captains, lieutenant colonels, and knights of Saint Louis, but not colonels. People from here are accused of becoming tired of service in the army, of lacking commitment to it, and of leaving it at an early age. It must be said that in general, once one has been decorated with the cross [of Saint Louis], one begins to pine for retirement. There are far too many examples of this tendency for one to dare deny it.

Ever since people have begun to get rich rapidly from finance and trade, the Second Estate has won new respect. Its spending and luxury has made it the envy of the First. Inevitably the two have merged, and today there are no more differences in the way they run their households, give dinner parties, and dress.

One cannot see any more differences either among the branches of the Third [Estate]. The most vile artisan behaves as the equal of the most eminent *artiste* or anyone who practices a trade superior to his. They are indistinguishable by their expenditures, their clothes, and their houses. It is only the agricultural laborer who does not leave his estate, either because his occupations do not permit it, or because he remains subordinate to the other inhabitants, who own land and hire him to work it, or finally because he earns only just enough to keep himself and his family alive.

However, if there are public works to be done, soldiers to be lodged, or forced labor to be performed in an emergency, those are the ones on whom the full burden falls. To be sure, such is the lot of their estate. But it would be a good thing to compensate them for their hardship, to encourage them, and without letting them become aware of how much we need them to grant them some special marks of favor, even tax exemptions, which in easing their lot would incite them to fulfill their duties better.

The practice of having oneself carried by other men is a great abuse. It contradicts nature, and nothing seems more ridiculous than to see a canon, a bishop, a military officer, a magistrate, or any fop who wants to cut a figure shut himself up in a box and have himself carried on the shoulders of other men, who must stagger through water, mud, ice, and snow, in constant danger of being crushed if they make a false step. This harsh trade occupies a prodigious quantity of mountain peasants, who are sturdy by nature and certainly could employ their strength more usefully by cultivating the earth rather than by carrying around other men who are perfectly capable of walking. They give themselves over to drink, become paralytic after a certain time, and finish by dying in the poorhouse. If preachers spoke out against this abuse instead of declaiming about metaphysical points of doctrine; if the churchmen excommunicated the carriers and the carried instead of excommunicating witches, who don't exist, and caterpillars, who fear nothing less than excommunication, then this ridiculous practice would stop and society would be much the better for it.

Finally, there should be an ordinance requiring every servant, male or female, to wear a clearly visible badge on his clothes. For nothing is more impertinent than to see a cook or a valet don an outfit trimmed with braid or lace, strap on a sword, and insinuate himself amongst the finest company in promenades; or to see a chambermaid as artfully dressed as her mistress; or to find domestic servants of any kind decked out like gentle people. All that is revolting. The estate of servants is one of servitude, of obedience to the orders of their masters. They are not deemed to be free, to form part of the social body with the citizens. Therefore they should be forbidden to mix with the citizenry; and if any such mixing must take place, one should be able to pick them out by a badge indicating their estate and making it impossible to confuse them with everyone else.

Political *propos* in a Parisian café

4

A POLICE INSPECTOR SORTS HIS FILES: THE ANATOMY OF THE REPUBLIC OF LETTERS

WHILE THE BOURGEOIS from Montpellier tried to sort out his fellow citizens, a police officer in Paris was sifting and filing information on another species of urban animal: the intellectual. Although the word for them had not yet been coined, intellectuals were already multiplying in garrets and cafés; and the police were keeping them under surveillance. Our policeman, Joseph d'Hémery, was an inspector of the book trade; so he also inspected the men who wrote books. In fact, he investigated so many of them that his files constitute a virtual census of the literary population of Paris, from the most famous *philosophes* to the most obscure hacks. The files make it possible for one to trace a profile of the intellectual at the height of the Enlightenment, just when he was beginning to emerge as a social type. And they reveal the way a fairly enlightened official of the Old Regime attempted to make sense of this new phenomenon—a matter of imposing a framework on the world as it appeared on a peculiar police beat.[1]

To be sure, d'Hémery did not present his survey as a sociology of culture and did not question its epistemological basis. He merely went about his work, inspecting. In five years, from 1748 to 1753, he wrote five hundred reports on authors, which now lie unpublished in the Bibliothèque Nationale. Just why he undertook such a task is difficult to say. The reports appear in three huge registers under the title "Historique des auteurs," without any introduction, explanation, or textual evidence about the way they were used. D'Hémery, who took up his office in June, 1748, may simply have wanted to build up his files so that he could do an effective job of policing his new administrative territory. But he had some extraordinary books to police during those first five years: *L'Esprit des lois,* the *Encyclopédie,* Rousseau's *Discours sur les sciences et les arts,* Diderot's *Lettre sur les aveugles,* Buffon's *Histoire naturelle,* Toussaint's *Les Moeurs,* and the scandalous thesis by the abbé de Prades. The whole Enlightenment seemed to burst out all at once in print. And at the same time, the tax reforms of Machault d'Arnouville, the Jansenist-Jesuit controversy, the agitation over the *billets de confession,* the struggle between the crown and the *parlements,* and the *frondeur* spirit following France's humiliation in the Peace of Aix-la-Chapelle produced a general heating up of the ideological atmosphere. However absolute the monarchy claimed to be, it had to take account of public opinion and of the men who directed it with their pens.

The new inspector of the book trade clearly had his work cut out for him, and he went about it systematically. He built up dossiers from all kinds of sources: journals, spies, concièrges, café gossips, and interrogations in the Bastille. Then he selected information from the dossiers and transcribed it on standard forms with printed headings, which he filed in alphabetical order and brought up to date as the occasion arose. The procedure was more thorough than anything done before, but it looks primitive in the light of the subsequent history of ideological police work. Instead of adapting data to a computerized program, d'Hémery recounted anecdotes.

In the report on Crébillon fils, for example, he noted: "His father said, 'There are only two things that I regret having done, *Semiramis* and my son.' 'Oh, don't worry,' the son replied. 'No one attributes either of them to you.'" Not only did d'Hémery go about information retrieval with an unscientific sense of humor, he also exercised literary judgment. La Barre wrote passable prose but could not manage verse, he observed. And Robbé de Beauveset sinned in the opposite way: "There is some genius in his poetry, but he writes harshly and has very little taste." D'Hémery would not have gone down well with the Deuxième Bureau or the F.B.I.

It would be a mistake, therefore, to treat d'Hémery's reports as hard data of the kind one can find in a modern census; but it would be a greater mistake to dismiss them for excessive subjectivity. D'Hémery had a more intimate knowledge of the eighteenth-century world of letters than any historian can hope to acquire. His reports provide the earliest known survey of writers as a social group, and they do so at a critical moment of literary history. Moreover, they can be checked against a vast array of biographical and bibliographical sources. Once one has worked through all this material and compiled the statistics, one can enjoy the first clear view of the republic of letters in early modern Europe.

D'Hémery actually reported on 501 persons, but 67 of them never published anything, or anything beyond a few lines in the *Mercure*. So the reports cover 434 active writers. Of them, the date of birth can be established in 359 cases, the place of birth in 312, and the socio-occupational position in 333. The statistical basis of the survey therefore seems wide enough to support some firm conclusions.

But how widely had d'Hémery cast his net in the first place? The only source against which to compare his survey is *La France littéraire,* a literary almanac that purported to list every living French author in 1756. As the list ran to 1,187 names, it seems likely that d'Hémery covered about a third of the total population of French writers. But which third? That question raises the problem of defining a writer. D'Hémery used the term "auteur" without explaining it, and *La France littéraire* claimed to include everyone who had ever published a book. But the "books" it listed were

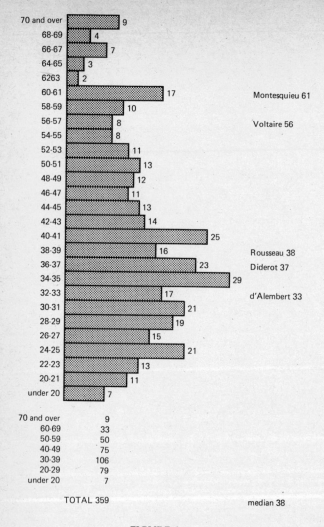

FIGURE 1
Authors' Ages in 1750

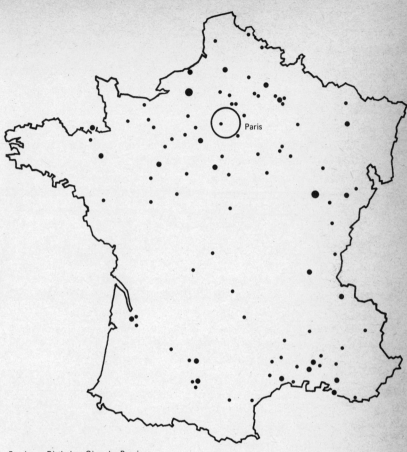

Paris

Provinces: Birthplace Given by Province
Without Specific Location
Anjou (1)
Bourgogne (1)
Bretagne (6)
Champagne (1)
Dauphine (1)
Gascogne (1)
Languedoc (3)
Lorraine (1)
Normandie (2)
Saintonge (1)

Key: Number of Natives
•   1
●   2-5
●   6-11
○   100+

FIGURE 2
Authors' Birthplaces

mainly ephemeral works—sermons by village curés, orations by provincial dignitaries, medical pamphlets by small-town doctors, in fact anything that anyone wanted mentioned—for the authors of the almanac had offered to include in their own lists the names of any books and authors that the general public could supply. As a result, *La France littéraire* favored the minor provincial literati. D'Hémery dealt with a broad range of writers, but he restricted himself almost entirely to Paris. It seems reasonable to conclude that his files covered a major proportion of the active literary population and that the statistics drawn from them give a fairly accurate picture of literary life in the capital of the Enlightenment.[2]

The demographic structure of the group shows up in figure 1. In 1750, the writers ranged in age from ninety-three (Fontenelle) to sixteen (Rulhière), but most of them were relatively young. Rousseau, at thirty-eight, represented the median age exactly. The inner circle of Encyclopedists was composed mainly of men in their thirties, beginning with Diderot, thirty-seven, and d'Alembert, thirty-three. Thus the bulge in the bar graph suggests something akin to a literary generation. With exceptions like Montesquieu and Voltaire, who had one foot in the France of Louis XIV, the *philosophes* belonged to cohorts that reached their prime at mid-century.[3]

The geographical origins of the writers, which are mapped on figure 2, fall into a familiar pattern. The south looks backward, except in urban areas scattered around the Rhône delta and the Garonne. Three-quarters of the writers were born above the celebrated Saint Malo-Geneva line, in northern and northeastern France, where literacy and schools were densest. Paris supplied a third (113) of the writers. So the map does not bear out another cliché of cultural history—namely, that Paris has always dominated the country by soaking up talent from the provinces. There were more home-grown authors than one might expect in the Paris of 1750.[4]

Any attempt to analyze the social composition of a group of Frenchmen who lived two centuries ago is liable to flounder in faulty data and ambiguous classification schemes. But three-quarters of d'Hémery's writers can be identified and classified unambiguously according to the categories in figure 3. The remaining quarter of "unidentified" writers contains a large number of *gens sans*

FIGURE 3
Authors' Socio-Occupational Positions

	Authors in 1750	Authors at unspecified date	Authors total	Percent	Fathers of authors	Percent of total
Upper clergy, secular	3		3	1		
Upper clergy, regular	1		1			
Lower clergy, secular	31		31	9		
Lower clergy, regular	4	1	5	2		
Titled nobility, no office	11		11	3	16	10
Officer, high administration	4		4	1	1	1
Officer, military	20	7	27	8	12	8
Officer, sovereign courts	10	2	12	4	12	8
Officer, high finance	2		2	1	6	4
Officer, lower courts	4	2	6	2	8	5
Lower administration	20	10	30	9	22	14
Lawyer, attorney	26	2	28	8	19	12
Law personnel	3		3	1	1	1
Doctor	6		6	2	1	1
Apothecary		1	1		4	3
Professor	10		10	3		
Lower finance	2	1	3	1	2	1
Merchant	1		1		11	7
Manufacturer						
Rentier	10		10	3		
Journalist	9	11	20	6		
Private teacher	27	8	35	11	4	3
Librarian	6		6	2		
Secretary	15	10	25	8	1	1
Sinecure	10	1	11	3		
Actor	8	1	9	3	1	1
Musician	1		1		1	1
Student	3		3	1		
Employee	5	1	6	2	8	5
Shopkeeper	2		2	1	6	4
Artisan	6	1	7	2	14	9
Servant	1	1	2	1	1	1
Wives, Widows	9		9	3		
Other	1	2	3	1	5	3
TOTAL	271	62	333		156	

Total Number of Writers

Identified Authors, 1750	271
Identified Authors, unspecified date	62
Excluded (nonauthors)	67
Unidentified	101
	501 (434 "writers")

Alternate Breakdown

Probable nobility	60
Tonsured clerics	69
Women	16
Imprisoned	45

état—hacks who drifted from job to job, as Diderot and Rousseau did for many years. Although a good deal of information exists about many of them, they defy classification and statistical analysis. But if one makes allowances for their existence in the unfathomable floating population of the Old Regime, one can take figure 3 as a reliable indication of the social dimensions to the republic of letters in Paris.

The privileged orders occupied a far more important place in d'Hémery's files than they did within the population at large. Seventeen percent of the identified authors were noblemen. Although they included some serious writers, like Montesquieu, they tended to be gentleman amateurs and to write incidental verse or light comedies. As in the case of the marquis de Paulmy, who published novelettes under the name of his secretary, Nicolas Fromaget, they did not often want to be identified with such frothy stuff. Nor did they write for the marketplace. D'Hémery noted that the comte de Saint-Foix "works as a gentleman author and never takes any money for his plays." The aristocratic writers generally appear in the reports as power brokers, channeling patronage toward more lowly *littérateurs*.

Writing also tended to be a secondary activity for the clergymen in the reports, and there were a great many of them: 12 percent of the authors who can be identified. Only four belonged to the upper clergy in contrast to dozens of abbés, among them Condillac, Mably, Raynal, and the threesome of the *Encyclopédie*, Yvon, Pestré, and de Prades. A few priests, like J.-B.-C.-M. de Beauvais and Michel Desjardins, continued to produce court sermons and funeral eulogies in the style of Bossuet. But in general the courtier-cleric had given way to the omnipresent abbé of the Enlightenment.

Although 70 percent of the writers came from the third estate, few of them can be considered "bourgeois" in the narrow sense of the term—that is, capitalists living from trade and industry. They included only one merchant, J. H. Oursel, the son of a printer, and no manufacturers. There was a certain business element—eleven merchants—among their fathers, 156 of whom can be identified. But literature flourished less in the marketplace than in the professions and the royal administration. Ten percent of the writers were doctors or lawyers; 9 percent held minor administrative offices; and 16 percent belonged to the apparatus of the state, if magistrates from the parlements and lower courts are included in the count. The largest group of fathers, twenty-two, came from the lower administration; the next largest, nineteen, were lawyers. After sifting through the statistics and reading hundreds of biographical sketches, one gets the impression that behind many literary careers stood an ambitious, sharp-witted, royal bureaucrat. French literature owes an incalculable debt to the *commis* and the law clerk as well as to the abbé. Prévost epitomized this species. The son of a lawyer turned court official in the bailliage of Hesdin, he was an abbé many times over. "He has been a member of every religious order," d'Hémery observed.

When it came to earning a living, however, the largest group of writers depended upon what may be called the intellectual trades. Thirty-six percent of them worked as journalists, tutors, librarians, secretaries, and actors, or else relied on the income from a sinecure procured for them by a protector. This was the bread-and-butter element in the republic of letters; and as it was dispensed by patronage, the writers knew which side their bread was buttered on. According to d'Hémery, François-Augustin Paradis de Moncrif certainly did:

> He was a tax inspector in the provinces when M. d'Argenson was intendant. The pretty songs he composed made him noticed by d'Argenson, who brought him to Paris and gave him a position. From that time on, he [Moncrif] has always been attached to him. . . . He is also secretary general of the French postal service, a position that brings him in 6,000 livres a year and that M. d'Argenson gave to him as a present.

At a lower level, the literary population contained a surprising proportion, 6 percent, of shopkeepers, artisans, and minor employees. They included both master craftsmen—a printer, an engraver, a painter-enameler—and relatively humble workers—a harness maker, a binder, a gatekeeper, and two lackeys. D'Hémery noted that one of the lackeys, Viollet de Wagnon, published his *L'Auteur laquais* with the help of a valet and a grocer. Charles-Simon Favart reputedly acquired his facility with verse by listening to his father improvise songs while kneading dough in the family's pastry shop.[5] Thus the lower classes played some part in the literary life of the Old Regime—a substantial part, if one considers the writers' fathers. Nineteen percent of them belonged to the *petites gens*; they were ordinary artisans for the most part—cobblers, bakers, and tailors. So the careers of their sons, who became lawyers, teachers, and journalists, showed that exceptional possibilities of social advancement sometimes opened up for young men who could wield a pen. The literary world remained closed, however, to one social group: the peasantry. Of course, d'Hémery did not look for writers in the countryside, but he did not find the slightest peasant element in the background of writers who came to Paris from the provinces. Restif de la Bretonne notwithstanding, literary France seems to have been primarily urban.

It was also mainly male. Women presided over the famous salons and therefore won a few places in the police files. But only sixteen of them ever published anything. Like Mme de Graffigny, the most famous of their number, the female authors often turned to writing after being widowed or separated from their husbands. Most of them were independently wealthy. Two were teachers. One, Charlotte Bourette, *la muse limonadière,* ran a soft-drink shop; and one was a courtesan. The report on the courtesan, Mlle de Saint Phalier, reads like the précis of a novel. After leaving her father, a horse dealer in Paris, she became a chambermaid in the house of a wealthy financier. The son of the house seduced and abducted her, only to be arrested by the father, who then forced him to marry a more suitable woman, leaving Mlle de Saint Phalier in the streets. By the time the police ran across her, she had become a kept woman, consorted with actresses, and was about to publish her first book, *Le Portefeuille rendu,* dedicated to Mme de Pompadour.

D'Hémery had sadder stories to tell when he filled in the entries under the rubric *histoire,* for many careers followed trajectories that led from the garret to the gutter, with stopovers in the Bastille. L.-J.-C. Soulas d'Allainval illustrates the pattern. Unable to support himself by the farces he wrote for the Comédie Italienne, he took up political *libelles* and clandestine journalism, which brought him straight to the Bastille. After his release, he sank deeper into debt.

Ultimately, he was unable even to get paper from his stationer, who cut off the pittance he received from the box office of the Comédie Italienne in order to collect an unpaid bill of sixty livres. D'Allainval began to sleep *à la belle étoile* (in the streets). His health gave out. D'Hémery recounted the rest:

> He was struck down by an attack of apoplexy in September, 1752, while a dinner guest of M. Bertin of the parties casuelles, who put two louis in his pocket and sent him off. As there was no means of nursing him at his place, he was brought to the Hôtel-Dieu [paupers' hospital], where he vegetated for a long while. He finally remained paralyzed and now is reduced to looking for a place at Bicêtre or at the Incurables. What a sad end for a talented man.

D'Hémery expressed less sympathy for François-Antoine Chevrier, "a bad subject, an audacious liar, trenchant, critical, and unbearably pretentious." After failing as a lawyer, soldier, playwright, and poet, Chevrier turned to pamphleteering, underground journalism, and espionage. The police chased him with a *lettre de cachet* through Germany and the Low Countries; but just as they were closing in on him, he died down and out in Rotterdam. The police got their man in the case of Emmanuel-Jean de La Coste, a fifty-nine-year-old defrocked monk, who was condemned to a whipping and the galleys for the rest of his life. He had run off to Liège with a young girl and had supported himself by peddling anti-French pamphlets, counterfeit lottery tickets, and, it seems, the girl herself. These characters belonged to Grub Street, an important ingredient in the republic of letters. To be sure, most writers did not sink so low as d'Allainval, Chevrier, and La Coste; but many shared an experience that marked the men of Grub Street: *embastillement*. Forty-five writers, 10 percent of those in the survey, were locked up at least once in a state prison, usually the Bastille. If the Bastille was almost empty on July 14, 1789, it was full of meaning for the men who made it into the central symbol of radical propaganda before the French Revolution.[6]

Of course, no one could foresee 1789 in 1750. At mid-century the literary population may have been restive, but it was not revolutionary. Most of its members were struggling to get a review in the *Mercure,* an *entrée* in the Comédie française, or a seat in the

Le veritable Portrait tiré d'après nature sur la Place du Palais Royal, d'Emmanuel Jean de la Coste, comdamné par Jugement souverain de M.^r le Lieutenant G.^l de Police, du 28 Aoust 1760. au Carcan pendant 3. jours a la marqû, et aux Galeres a perpétuité.

A *libelliste*, Jean de La Coste, being pilloried

Academy. They supported themselves in dozens of ways, some from *rentes,* some from offices, some from professions, and a great many from the jobs that were open to men of the pen: journalism, teaching, secretaryships, and, for the fortunate, sinecures. They came from all sectors of society except the peasantry and from all corners of the kingdom except the backward areas of the south. They included a small number of women and a large number of bright young men, sons of minor officials and artisans, who won scholarships, published poems, and ended up as lawyers and civil servants—or, in a few cases, full-time writers, living like Diderot, *aux gages des libraires* (in the pay of the booksellers).

It would be satisfying to end on that note, with a pattern firmly established and the *philosophes* located within it. Unfortunately, however, literary theorists have taught historians to beware of texts, which can be dissolved into "discourse" by critical reading, no matter how solid they may seem. So the historian should hesitate before treating police reports as hard nuggets of irreducible reality, which he has only to mine out of the archives, sift, and piece together in order to create a solid reconstruction of the past. The reports are constructions of their own, built on implicit assumptions about the nature of writers and writing at a time when literature had not yet been recognized as a vocation.

In drafting his reports, d'Hémery acted as a kind of writer himself. He, too, played a role in the republic of letters while at the same time remaining subordinate to the Lieutenant-Général de Police and other officials in the French state. The reports show a combination of literary sensitivity and bureaucratic orderliness that would be unthinkable in most police headquarters today. They contain as many remarks about the quality of the authors' style as about the character of their religious and political opinions. In the report on the marquise de Créquy, for example, d'Hémery included a three-page excerpt of a dialogue she had written, not because it had any relevance to the ideological issues of the day but because it demonstrated her perfect mastery of prose. He praised "taste," "wit," and "talent" wherever he found it, even among "bad subjects" like Voltaire. *Esprit* (cleverness) was his favorite term. It seems to have been the first thing that he looked for in a writer, and it compensated for a good deal of straying from the straight and narrow. The abbé Paul-François Velly was "a very clever man" and a skirt chaser, but so were "almost all monks when they leave the monastery." The same went for Jean-Pierre Bernard, a "clever" priest with a special talent for funeral sermons: "He is a jolly old boy who enjoys pleasure and spends an evening with the girls whenever he gets a chance."

D'Hémery understood the ways of the world. He did not take offense at a little bawdiness or anticlericalism, especially when it was offset by "genius," as in the work of Alexis Piron: "His biting wit and reputation for impiety mean that he is not a member of the Académie Française. M. de Crébillon advised him never to think of being elected. But *Les fils ingrats, Gustave,* and *La métromanie* bear sufficient testimony to his genius. He can succeed in anything he undertakes." D'Hémery admired the *philosophes,* at least the moderate ones, like Fontenelle, Duclos, and d'Alembert. But he was horrified at atheism, and he seems to have sincerely believed in the official orthodoxies. His values show through clearly in all the reports, but especially in off-hand remarks on ordinary writers, like Jean-Baptiste Le Mascrier:

> He was a Jesuit for a long time. He edited *Télliamed* and various other publications for the booksellers. He contributed to the *Cérémonies religieuses* and worked over the *Mémoires de M. de Maillet sur la description de l'Egypte,* which does great honor to him by its style. He turns poems very nicely, as is clear from a prologue to a play that was performed some years ago.
>
> The Benedictines, where he has worked, agree that he is a man of talent. Too bad that he isn't more creative. He has published an excellent work of piety, a book that is useful for every true Christian, but the people who know him most intimately think that the need to produce copy is making him gradually shift to different sentiments.

In short, d'Hémery took stock of the literary world with sympathy, humor, and an appreciation of literature itself. He shared some of the values held by the people under his surveillance, but he did not waver in his loyalty to church and state. Nothing could be more anachronistic than to picture him as a modern cop or to interpret his police work as witch-hunting. It really represents something less familiar and more interesting: information gathering in the age of absolutism. No one expected to uncover revolutionary conspiracies in the mid-eighteenth century, when the Revolution was unthinkable; but many bureaucrats in the Bourbon monarchy wanted to learn as much as possible about the kingdom—about the number of its inhabitants, the volume of its trade, and the output of its presses. D'Hémery belonged to a line of rationalizing officials that extended from Colbert and Vauban to Turgot and Necker. But he operated at a modest level—an inspector of the book trade belonged a notch or two below an inspector of manufactures—and he built up his files on a smaller scale than some of the surveys undertaken by ministers and intendants.[7]

The texts of the reports contain some evidence about the way they were written. They often include remarks such as "See the attached sheets" or "See his dossier," which indicate that d'Hémery kept a file on each writer. Although the dossiers have disappeared, the references to them in the reports reveal the kind of information they contained. They included clippings from journals, prospectuses from booksellers, notes that d'Hémery made when he went on his rounds, records of interrogations in the Bastille, letters from authors who wanted to ingratiate themselves or to undermine their enemies, and reports from spies in the hire of the Lieutenant-Général de Police. Some of the spies had dossiers of their own. The report on Charles de Fieux, chevalier de Mouhy, shows how they worked: "He is a spy for M. Berryer [the Lieutenant-Général de Police], to whom he furnishes a daily report on everything he sees in the cafés, theaters, and public gardens." One can also find traces of Mouhy's activities in other reports, such as the one on Mathieu-François Pidansat de Mairobert: "He has just been arrested and taken to the Bastille for having distributed some [verse] attacking the king and Mme la marquise [de Pompadour] in cafés. Some was even found in his pockets upon his arrest. It was the chevalier de Mouhy who denounced him." Denunciations also arrived from jilted lovers, angry sons, and estranged wives. Booksellers and printers produced a steady flow of information about the sources of their copy—and especially the copy of their competitors. Landladies and curés supplied further details, and at the bottom of many dossiers d'Hémery could find scraps collected from neighborhood gossips, not all of it malicious. Thus Etienne-André

Philippe de Prétot: "As to his conduct, it is fairly good. He is married and has children, which forces him to be orderly. He is well spoken of in his neighborhood."

D'Hémery culled through all this material before composing a report. The sifting and selecting must have been difficult because the dossiers contained such a disparate mixture of hard data and loose gossip. So d'Hémery used standard forms—large folio sheets with six headings printed in bold type: name, age, birthplace, description, address, and *histoire* (story). The headings provided a grid for classifying the information, and the dates and handwriting of the entries under them provide some clues about d'Hémery's mode of composition. Most of the entries are written in a clear, scribal hand, but at later dates d'Hémery added new information in his own scrawl, which can be recognized easily from the letters and memorandums by him in the Bibliothèque Nationale. About half the reports are dated on the first day of the month, many of them on the first of the year. It seems likely, therefore, that d'Hémery set aside special days to work over his files, called in one of the secretaries in the police administration, and dictated the reports, selecting the information that seemed most important to him, dossier by dossier. The whole process suggests an attempt to be systematic, a will to impose order on an unruly world of garret scribblers and salon lions. It corresponds to the same ordering impulse behind the *Description* of Montpellier, but it took a different form: the standardizing, pigeon-holing, filing-and-classifying drive of the modern bureaucracy.

D'Hémery represents an early phase in the evolution of the bureaucrat; so his own voice can be heard quite clearly through the standard format of the reports. He composed in the first person singular and in a casual style, which contrasts markedly with the formal and impersonal tone of his official correspondence. Whereas his memos and letters were often directed to "Monseigneur"— Nicolas-René Berryer, the Lieutenant-Général de Police—his reports seem to have been addressed to himself. While filling in the birthplace of Le Blanc de Villeneuve, for example, he corrected himself off-handedly: "From Lyon. No, I'm wrong; it's Montélimar, the son of a captain." In the report on the chevalier de Cogolin, he noted:

July 1, 1752. I have been informed that he died insane at the house of his brother, the almoner of the King of Poland and Duke of Lorraine.

December 1. That isn't true.

The report on a poet named Le Dieux contained an equally casual remark: "Julie told me that he wrote a great deal of verse. That's true." Occasionally d'Hémery used foul language and spoke of important personages in a tone that would not have been appreciated by his superiors.[8] The closer one studies the reports to see whether they seem to be aimed at an implicit reader located somewhere in the hierarchy of the French administration, the more one comes around to the view that d'Hémery wrote them for himself and used them in his everyday activities, especially during his first years on the job, when he needed points of reference in order to steer a course through the complex subculture of literary factions and publishing intrigues.

Like everyone else, d'Hémery had to see some order in the world, but he also faced the task of finding his way around his beat. How did an inspector "inspect" the republic of letters? As a start, he had to be able to recognize writers; so he took some care in filling out the entries under the rubric *signalement* (description). They suggest the way he looked at the authors under his surveillance. Thus, for example, the *signalement* of Voltaire: "Tall, dry, and the bearing of a satyr." Descriptions involved something more than the impact of an image on an eyeball. They were charged with meaning: "Nasty, toadlike, and dying of hunger" (Binville); "fat, ungainly, and the bearing of a peasant" (Caylus); "nasty, swarthy, small, filthy, and disgusting" (Jourdan). D'Hémery went beyond simple categories like handsome or ugly and short or tall, because he perceived messages in faces. Thus the chevalier de La Morlière: "Fat, full-faced, and a certain something in his eyes." This practice of reading faces for character probably derived from physiognomy, a pseudoscience that had emerged during the Renaissance and had spread everywhere during the subsequent centuries through popular chapbooks.[9] D'Hémery's descriptions contained a great many remarks such as "a harsh physiognomy and character, too" (Le Ratz), "a very honest physiognomy" (Foncemagne), "detestable physiognomy" (Coq), "perfidious physiognomy" (Vieuxmaison), "hideous physiognomy" (Biliena), and "the saddest physiognomy in the world" (Boissy).

Similarly, addresses gave off meanings. Pidansat de Mairobert lived alone "in the rooms of a washerwoman on the third floor, rue des Cordeliers." He was obviously a marginal type, like a student-poet named Le Brun, who lived in the "rue de la Harpe, facing the Collège d'Harcourt, in a furnished room kept by a wig maker, on the second floor at the back" and an equally obscure versifier named Vauger, who lived "in the rue Mazarine in a furnished room kept by the first wig maker on the left, entering from the Carrefour de Buci, on the second floor on the street side, the door facing the stairs." Such men bore watching. They had no fixed *état,* no grounding in property, family, and neighborhood connections. Their addresses alone sufficed to place them.

The rubric *histoire* provided the most room for situating the writers, and d'Hémery accorded it the largest space on his printed forms. It was in composing *histoires* that he had to do the most selecting and organizing of material from the dossiers, for his compositions were narratives, as complex in their way as the folktales of the peasants. Some of them even read like digests of novels. Thus the *histoire* of the playwright Charles-Simon Favart:

He is the son of a pastry-cook, a very clever boy who has composed the prettiest comic operas in the world. When the Opéra Comique was closed, the maréchal de Saxe made him the head of his troupe. Favart made a lot of money there; but then he fell in love with the maréchal's mistress, la petite Chantilly, and married her, although he agreed to let her continue to live with the maréchal. This happy union lasted until the end of the war. But in November, 1749, Favart and his wife quarreled with the maréchal. After having used his influence to get a place in the Comédie Italienne and squeezed a lot of money from him [the maréchal], Mme Favart wanted to leave him. The maréchal obtained an order from the king to have her arrested and to have her husband exiled from the kingdom. They fled, he in one direction, she in another. The wife was captured at Nancy and imprisoned, first at Les Andelys, then with the Pénitentes of Angers. This affair stirred up a terrific storm among the actors, who even sent a deputation to the duc de Richelieu to demand the return of their comrade. He let them cool their heels in his antechamber. Finally, after they had their arrival announced a second time, he agreed to see them; but he gave them a very cold reception and especially mistreated Lélio [Antoine-François Riccoboni], who quit the troupe as a result. So la Favart was not given her liberty until she agreed to go back to the maréchal, who kept her until his death. After that, she returned to her husband, who had been wandering outside France all that time. Soon afterward, she took up a place once more in the Comédie Italienne. Then, when the Opéra Comique was restored, both of them wanted to join it. But the Italians gave her a full share in their troupe and gave him a pension in exchange for a regular supply of parodies; so they are now attached to that theater.[10]

D'Hémery chose simple phrases and organized his narrative around a straightforward chronological line, but he recounted a complicated story. Although he did not embellish it with editorial comments, he got across the notion of two young people from humble origins living by their wits in a world of courtiers and *lettres de cachet*. D'Hémery did not sentimentalize over the plight of the underprivileged. On the contrary, he noted Favart's readiness to share his wife with the maréchal and her ability to turn the situation to her own advantage. But the narrative develops a powerful undertow, which sweeps the reader's sympathies away from the rich and powerful. Favart sets out to make his fortune like a hero from the fairy tales. He is small, poor, and clever ("*Signalement:* short, blond, and with a very pretty face.") After all kinds of adventures in the land of giants—and the maréchal de Saxe was probably the most powerful man in France, aside from the king, in the 1740s—he wins the girl and they live happily ever after in the Comédie Italienne. The structure of the story corresponded to that of many popular tales. Its moral might have come from "Kiot-Jean," "Le Chat botté," or "Le Petit Forgeron." But d'Hémery did not draw a moral. He went on to the next dossier, and one can only wonder whether the world of letters, as he inspected it, fit into a framework that had originally been devised in the world of peasants.

In any case, the construction of a police report involved an element of storytelling, and the "inspection" of writers took place within a frame of meaning. One can therefore read the *histoires* as meaningful stories, which reveal some basic assumptions about literary life under the Old Regime. Few of them are as elaborate as

Favart's. Some contain only two or three sentences, unconnected by a narrative line. But they all proceed from presuppositions about the way the literary world operated, the rules of the game in the republic of letters. D'Hémery did not invent those rules. Like the writers themselves, he took them for granted and then watched them at work in the careers under his surveillance. Despite their subjective character, his observations have some general significance; for they belong to a common subjectivity, a social construction of reality, which he shared with the men he observed. In order to decipher their common code, one must reread the reports for what remains between the lines, assumed and so unsaid.

Consider a typical report about an eminent citizen of the republic of letters, François-Joachim de Pierres, abbé de Bernis. He had sat in the Académie Française from the age of twenty-nine, although he had published only some light verse and an insubstantial treatise, *Réflexions sur les passions et les goûts.* A member of a distinguished family and a favorite of Mme de Pompadour, he was rising rapidly through the offices of church and state, which eventually would lead to a cardinal's hat and the ambassadorship in Rome. What information did d'Hémery select for a report on such a man? After noting Bernis's age (in his prime—thirty-eight), address (good—rue du Dauphin), and looks (also good—"handsome physiognomy"), he stressed six points:

1. Bernis was a member of the Académie Française and count of Brioude and of Lyon.
2. "He is a lecher who has had Madame la princesse de Rohan."
3. He was an accomplished courtier and a protégé of la Pompadour, who had persuaded the pope to grant him a benefice, using the duc de Nivernais as an intermediary.
4. He had written some "pretty pieces in verse" and the *Réflexions sur les passions.*
5. He was related to the maréchal de La Fare, who always advocated his cause at court.
6. He extended his own protection to Duclos, whom he had had named to the position of historiographe de France.

D'Hémery did not pay much attention to the literary works of the abbé. Instead, he situated him in a network of family relations, clientages, and "protections," a key term, which runs through all the reports. Everyone in the police files was seeking, receiving, or dispensing protection, from princes and royal mistresses down to two-bit pamphleteers. Just as Mme de Pompadour got Bernis an abbey, Bernis got Duclos a sinecure. That was how the system worked. The police did not question the principle of influence peddling. They assumed it: it went without saying, in the republic of letters as in society at large.

That it prevailed at the middle and lower ranges of literary life can be appreciated from the reports on writers located well below the abbé de Bernis. Pierre Laujon, for example, followed a well-traveled route through the upper-middle ranks of the republic of letters. Like many writers, he began as a law student and wrote verse for pleasure. The versifying resulted in a hit at the Opéra Comique; the hit attracted protectors; and the protectors procured sinecures. It was a classic success story, whose stages stand out clearly in d'Hémery's narrative:

> This young man is very clever. He wrote some operas, which were performed at the [Opéra Comique] and the Petits Apartements of Versailles, which won him the protection of Mme de Pompadour, of M. le duc d'Ayen, and of M. le comte de Clermont, who gave him the post of Secrétaire des Commandements. That prince also made him Secrétaire du Gouvernement de Champagne, a position worth 3,000 livres a year.

To be sure, Laujon had natural assets: wit, good looks ("*Signalement:* blond and with a very pretty face"), an attorney for a father, and a relative who was the mistress of the comte de Clermont. But he played his cards right.

So did Gabriel-François Coyer, though he had a weaker hand and never rose above a middle rung in the literary hierarchy. Without wealth, family connections, or a pleasing face ("disagreeable and elongated physiognomy"), he nonetheless persevered in turning out books and belles-lettres. Finally a source of steady income opened up, and he snatched it.

> He is a priest who is clever, although a little inclined toward pedantry. For a long time he haunted the streets of Paris, broke and without employment. But at last he found a place as tutor for the prince de

Turenne. Having served in it to the satisfaction of the prince, the latter rewarded him with the post of Aumonier du Colonel Général de la Cavalerie. As the revenue of that post now goes to the comte d'Evreux, M. de Turenne has provided him with a pension of 1,200 livres, which he will collect until the death of d'Evreux.

One of Bernis's protégés, Antoine de Laurès, occupied a precarious position on a lower-middle rung of the ladder. When he drafted the original report on Laurès, d'Hémery could not predict which way the young man's career would turn. On the one hand, he came from a good family: his father was Doyen de la Chambre des Comptes in Montpellier. On the other, he had run out of money. In fact, he would starve in his garret if his odes to the king and to Mme de Pompadour did not bring in some patronage soon. But according to a note added later to the report, the verse seemed to be working.

> He managed to get himself introduced to the marquise [de Pompadour], thanks to the credit of the abbé de Bernis, and he has boasted that she gave him permission to look out for an affair that will bring in some money and that she will make him succeed. Some time later he managed to get an introduction to the comte de Clermont, to whom he now pays court, thanks to the intervention of M. de Montlezun, his relative.[11]

On a still lower rung, Pierre-Jean Boudot, the son of a bookseller, compiled, abridged, and translated prodigiously. But he depended on protectors for his living. "He is very clever and is very protected by the président Hénault, who got a job in the Bibliothèque du Roi for him," d'Hémery noted, adding that Boudot was believed to have written most of the *Abrégé de l'histoire de France* that appeared under Hénault's name. Meanwhile, Pierre Dufour, the twenty-four-year-old son of a café owner, was trying to make his way at the bottom of the literary world. He worked as an errand boy in a printing shop. He peddled prohibited books. He insinuated himself among the actors and playwrights of the Comédie Italienne and the Opéra Comique, thanks to the favor of Favart, his godfather. And somehow he attached himself to the comte de Rubanprez, who gave him lodging and some ineffectual protection. D'Hémery put Dufour down as a suspicious character, a scrambler and hustler, who would write and peddle underground literature, while pretending to keep an eye on it for the police: "He is a devious little guy, and very slippery." Dufour actually wrote a great deal—a half-dozen plays and skits, a book of poems, and a novel. But he failed to parlay any of it into a position; so he finally gave up writing and settled for a job in a bookstore.

The constant, unremitting quest for protection stands out everywhere in d'Hémery's accounts of literary careers. François Augier de Marigny hears a position has opened up in the Invalides and dashes off some poems in praise of the comte d'Argenson, who will name someone to it. Charles Batteux cultivates the doctor of Mme de Pompadour and therefore wins a vacant professorship in the Collège de Navarre. Jean Dromgold notes that the valor of the comte de Clermont is not adequately celebrated in a poem about the battle of Fontenoy. He attacks the poem in a pamphlet and is promptly named Secrétaire des Commandements de Mgr. le comte de Clermont.

Such were the facts of literary life. D'Hémery recorded them unblinkingly, without any moralizing about toadyism among the writers or the vanity of protectors. On the contrary, he sounded shocked when a protégé deviated from the unswerving loyalty he owed to his patron. Antoine Duranlon had won the favor of the house of Rohan, which had him named principal of the Collège de Maître Gervais after he had served the family satisfactorily as a tutor. But once he was installed, Duranlon sided with a faction in the Sorbonne that opposed the Rohans in a quarrel over some honorific rights claimed by the abbé de Rohan-Guéménée. The Rohans had Duranlon stripped of his post and exiled to Bresse—and it served him right, d'Hémery observed, for the protégé had responded to the protector with "the blackest ingratitude." How laudatory, by contrast, was the behavior of F.-A. P. de Moncrif. Moncrif owed everything to the comte d'Argenson, who as already mentioned had seen him through all the stops of an ideal literary career: three secretaryships, a cut in the revenue of the *Journal des savants,* a seat in the Académie Française, an apartment in the Tuileries, and a position in the postal service worth 6,000 livres a year. When Moncrif uncovered some satires against the king and Mme de Pompadour emanating from the anti-d'Argenson, pro-Maurepas faction of the court, he promptly denounced their authors—and rightly so: not only should a writer never bite the hand that fed him, he should also smite all hands in the enemy camp.

Thus protection functioned as the basic principle of literary life. Its presence everywhere in the reports makes another phenomenon, the literary marketplace, look conspicuous by its absence. Occasionally d'Hémery mentioned a writer who attempted to live by his pen. Gabriel-Henri Gaillard, for example, ventured into the market for a while in 1750, after living from jobs dispensed by Voltaire (for established writers also functioned as protectors themselves): "He was sub-librarian in the Collège des Quatres Nations, an unimportant position, which he quit in order to take up a job as a children's tutor, which M. de Voltaire arranged for him. He only stayed in it for six months, and now he lives from his writing. . . . His last works are full of praise for Voltaire, to whom he is completely dedicated." But soon afterward he took up a job on the *Journal des savants,* which kept him solvent for the rest of his career. D'Hémery also mentioned a pamphleteer named La Barre, who tried to write himself out of a state of "frightful indigence" when the Peace of Aix-la-Chapelle put an end to his employment as a propagandist in the ministry of foreign affairs. "Having no resources whatsoever after the end of the war, he gave himself over to La Foliot [a bookseller], who keeps him alive and for whom he writes a few things from time to time." But such cases were rare, not because there was any lack of writers who needed support but because the booksellers were unwilling or unable to provide it. And in a later entry in La Barre's report, d'Hémery noted that he had finally snared "a small job on the *Gazette de France,*" thanks to the intervention of the Lieutenant-Général de Police.

When desperate for money, writers generally fell back on marginal activities, such as smuggling prohibited books or spying on the smugglers for the police. They could not hope to strike it rich with a best-seller because the publishers' monopoly of book privileges and the pirating industry made it impossible to expect much from sales. They never received royalties, but sold manuscripts for lump sums or a certain number of copies of the printed book, which they peddled or gave to potential protectors. Manuscripts rarely fetched much, despite the famous case of the 6,000 livres paid to Rousseau for *Emile* and the 120,000 livres that went to Diderot for twenty years of labor on the *Encyclopédie*. D'Hémery noted that François-Vincent Toussaint received only 500 livres for the manuscript of his best-seller, *Les Moeurs,* although his publisher, Delespine, made at least 10,000 livres from it. Toussaint's case illustrated a general proposition: "He works a great deal for booksellers, which means that he has a hard time making ends meet." D'Hémery remarked that Joseph de La Porte supported himself by his pen, "and has only that to live on," as if that were unusual. The common pattern was to aim at enough *succès de prestige* to attract a protector and land a place in the royal administration or a wealthy household.

One could also marry. Jean-Louis Lesueur did not leave much of a mark in the history of literature, but his career represented an ideal type from the viewpoint of the police: beginning with little more than talent and amiability, he acquired a respectable reputation, a protector, a sinecure, and a wealthy wife.

> He is a clever young man, who wrote some comic operas that were performed with a fair amount of success. M. Bertin de Blagny got to know him at the theater, befriended him, and gave him a job in the parties casuelles worth 3,000 a year. That is where he is now employed.
>
> He just married a woman who has brought him something of a fortune. He certainly merits it, because he is a nice boy with a most amiable character.

D'Hémery did not take a sentimental view of matrimony. He treated it as a strategic move in the making of a career—or else as a mistake. Writers' wives never appeared as intelligent, cultivated, or virtuous in the reports; they were either rich or poor. Thus d'Hémery did not waste any sympathy on C.-G. Coqueley de Chaussepierre: "He married an unimportant girl from his village, who has neither birth nor wealth. Her sole merit is that she is related to the wife of the former Procureur Général, who only married her [the relation] as a matter of conscience, after having kept her for a long time as his mistress." Similarly, Poiteven Dulimon seemed unlikely to scribble his way out of obscurity because "he made a bad marriage in Besançon." "Bad" marriages produced children rather than money, and so the reports show a succession of unhappy *pères de famille* battling against unfavorable demographic odds—Toussaint, reduced to hack writing because he had eleven children; Mouhy, spying for the police because he had five; Dreux de Radier and René de Bonneval, weighed down with offspring and therefore condemned to Grub Street for the rest of their lives.

It followed that writers who needed "good" marriages but could not make them should avoid matrimony altogether. Apparently most of them did. D'Hémery kept an eye on family connections, but he mentioned wives and children in only two dozen reports. Although the information is too scattered for one to draw firm conclusions, it seems that the majority of writers, especially those in the "intellectual trades," never married. And if they did, they often waited until they had acquired a reputation and a sinecure—or even a seat in the Académie Française. Thus the career of J.-B.-L. Gresset, another success story in the eyes of the police: first several hits in the Comédie française, then election to the Académie, and finally, at age forty-four, the daughter of a wealthy merchant in Amiens.

But how was a writer to steer clear of passion while working his way up to immortality? D'Alembert urged all *philosophes* to embrace a life of chastity and poverty.[12] But d'Hémery knew that that was more than flesh would bear. He recognized the existence of love just as he acknowledged the economics of marriage. Marmontel and Favart both appear as *amourachés* (in love) in their reports—each with an actress kept by the maréchal de Saxe. Marmontel's *histoire* is as rich in intrigues as Favart's; in fact, it reads like a plot from one of their plays: The young playwright falls in love with the actress, Mlle Verrière, behind the back of the old maréchal. They dismiss a lackey so that they can give full rein to their passion without being observed. The lackey, who operates as a spy for the maréchal and perhaps for the police as well, learns of their liaison nonetheless; and soon they face disaster—the loss of 12,000 livres a year for the actress and the severing of protections for the author. But all ends well because Mlle Verrière apparently succeeds in repairing the damage with the maréchal while Marmontel moves on to one of her colleagues, Mlle Cléron. After looking through a great many keyholes, either directly or through intermediaries, d'Hémery saw quite clearly that most writers would take mistresses.

Easier said than done. Actresses from the Comédie française did not often throw themselves into the arms of impecunious authors, even those with physiognomies like Marmontel and Favart. The men of Grub Street lived with women from their own milieu—servants, shop girls, laundresses, and prostitutes. The setting did not tend to produce happy households, and few of d'Hémery's *histoires* had happy endings, especially if seen from the woman's point of view. Consider the love life of A.-J. Chaumeix, an unknown author who arrived in Paris with little money and great expectations. At first he survived by part-time teaching in a boarding school. But the school collapsed, and he retreated to a rooming house, where he seduced the servant girl, after promising marriage. He soon fell out of love with her, however. And as he had begun to make some money by writing anti-Enlightenment tracts for the bookseller Herissant, the jilted fiancée, who was probably pregnant, demanded reparations from Herissant and managed to collect 300 livres from Chaumeix's account. Chaumeix then took up with the sister of another free-lance teacher. This time he did not escape from marriage, even though the woman was "a she-devil, who is worth nothing and from whom he got nothing," according to d'Hémery. But some years later, he ran off to a tutoring job in Russia, leaving his wife and a baby daughter behind.

Liaisons were dangerous for a man of letters because he might marry his mistress, no matter how "bad" the match. D'Hémery reported that A.-G. Meusnier de Querlon fell in love with a procuress and married her in order to get her out of prison. Before long he had his back to the wall and a family to support. An appointment to the *Gazette de France* followed by the editorship of the *Petites affiches* saved him from destitution; but he never accumulated enough to provide for himself in his old age, when he had to be saved once again by a pension granted by a financier. Several other authors lost their hearts in brothels, according to the accounts of their private lives that appeared in d'Hémery's files. A poet named Milon found himself unable to escape from a passion for the procuress of an establishment at the Carrefour des Quatre Cheminées, where he was a regular customer. The playwright and future journalist Pierre Rousseau lived with the daughter of a prostitute, whom he passed off as his wife. And two other hacks, the compiler F.-H. Turpin and a pamphleteer named Guenet, not only frequented prostitutes but married them. Grub Street marriages occasionally worked out. D'Hémery noted that Louis Anseaume had been living down and out as a part-time teacher until he married the sister of an actress in the Opéra Comique—"a marriage that he made from need rather than from inclination." Two years later he was doing quite well, writing and producing comic operas. But marriage usually dragged an author down. The normal pattern shows up clearly in two, brutal sentences in the report on the indigent playwright Louis de Boissy: "He is a gentleman. He married his laundress." Seen from the perspective of the other reports, the marriages of Rousseau and Diderot—to a semiliterate laundry maid and to the daughter of a washerwoman, respectively—do not look unusual.

If writers could not expect to live by their pens and to lead respectable family lives, how did writing itself appear as a career? The dignity of men of letters and the sanctity of their calling had already emerged as a leitmotiv in the works of the *philosophes*,[13] but no such theme can be found in d'Hémery's reports. Although the police recognized a writer when they saw one and sorted him out from other Frenchmen by giving him a place in d'Hémery's files, they did not speak of him as if he had a profession or a distinct position in society. He might be a gentleman, a priest, a lawyer, or a lackey. But he did not possess a *qualité* or *condition* that set him apart from nonwriters.

As the French phrases suggest, d'Hémery used an ancient social vocabulary, which left little room for modern, free-floating intellectuals. He may have been out of date in comparison with Diderot and d'Alembert, but his language probably corresponded pretty well with the conditions of authorship in the mid-eighteenth century. The police could not situate the writer within any conventional category because he had not yet assumed his modern form, freed from protectors, integrated in the literary marketplace, and committed to a career. Given the conceptual cloudiness surrounding this uncertain position, what sort of status did he have?

Although the police reports do not provide a clear answer to that question, they contain some revealing remarks. For example, d'Hémery often referred to writers as "boys" (*garçons*). The expression had nothing to do with age. Diderot appeared as a "boy" in his report, although he was then thirty-seven, married, and a father. The abbé Raynal, the abbé de l'Ecluse-des-Loges, and Pierre Sigorgne were all "boys" in their mid-thirties; and Louis Mannory was a "boy" of fifty-seven. What set them apart from writers classified implicitly as men, and often explicitly as gentlemen, was their lack of social distinction. Whether journalists, teachers, or abbés, they occupied vague and shifting positions in the lower ranks of the republic of letters. They moved in and out of Grub Street and clustered in the sector of the socio-occupational spectrum referred to above as the "intellectual trades." One must fall back on that anachronism because the Old Regime did not have a category for people like Diderot. "Boy" was the best d'Hémery could do. He would never think of applying such a term to the marquis de Saint-Lambert, a military officer, who was only thirty-three at the writing of d'Hémery's report on him, or to Antoine Petit, a doctor, who was thirty-one. "Boy" implied marginality and served to place the unplaceable, the shadowy forerunners of the modern intellectual, who showed up in the police files as *gens sans état* (people without an estate).

D'Hémery's use of language should not be attributed to the peculiarities of a status-conscious bureaucrat; he shared the prejudices of his time. Thus in the report on Pierre-Charles Jamet, he remarked as a matter of course, "He is said to be from a good family"; and he noted that Charles-Etienne Pesselier, a tax farmer, was "a man of honor [galant homme], which is saying a lot for a poet and a financier." But d'Hémery was no snob. In his report on Toussaint, he wrote, "He is hardly well born, since he is the son of a shoemaker in the parish of Saint Paul. He is no less an estimable person for all that." When the reports disparage writers, they do not seem to express d'Hémery's personal views so much as attitudes embedded in his surroundings. Of course, one cannot distinguish clearly between the personal and the social ingredients in such statements. But in some places, especially in off-guard moments or casual asides, d'Hémery seemed to articulate general assumptions. For example, in the *histoire* of Jacques Morabin, he observed in a matter-of-fact manner, "He is clever and is the author of a book in two volumes in-quarto entitled *La Vie de Cicéron,* which he dedicated to M. le comte de Saint Florentin, who protects him and for whom he was a secretary. It is this lord who gave him to M. Hénault." A writer could be passed from one protector to another, like a thing.

The tone of such remarks corresponded to the treatment that ordinary writers received. The drubbing given Voltaire by the servants of the chevalier de Rohan is often cited as an example of disrespect for authors at the beginning of the century. But writers who offended important personages were still beaten up in the era of the *Encyclopédie.* Pierre-Charles Roy, a fairly distinguished elderly playwright was nearly killed by a pummeling from a servant of the comte de Clermont, who wanted to exact revenge for a satirical poem written during a disputed election to the Académie Française. G.-F. Poullain de Saint-Foix terrorized audiences throughout the 1740s by bashing anyone who jeered his plays. He was rumored to have dispatched several critics in duels and to have threatened to cut off the ears of any reviewer who panned him. Even Marmontel and Fréron got involved in a brawl. While the *beau monde* strolled between acts in the foyer of the Comédie française, Marmontel demanded satisfaction for some satirical remarks that Fréron had leveled at him in the *Année littéraire.* Fréron suggested that they step outside. After crossing swords a few times, they were separated and turned over to the maréchaux de France, who handled affairs of honor. But the maréchal d'Isenquien dismissed them as "small game, good only for the police," and the affair appeared in d'Hémery's reports as "comic." To d'Hémery as to everyone else, there was something laughable about the notion of a writer's honor and the spectacle of writers defending it as if they had been gentlemen.

Of course, many writers did not need to worry about being protected, beaten up, or made into the butt of jokes. It was unthinkable for them to marry prostitutes or to be called "boy"; for they had an independent *dignité,* an established position as magistrates, lawyers, or government officials. But the common writer remained exposed to the brutalities of a rough-and-tumble world, and his contemporaries did not put him up on a pedestal. While the *philo-*

sophes laid the foundation of the modern cult of the intellectual, the police expressed a more ordinary, down-to-earth view of their "game." Writing might embellish the career of a gentleman and lead to a sinecure for a commoner. But it was more likely to produce good-for-nothings. D'Hémery sympathized with the family of Michel Portelance, a bright young man who might make something of himself, if only he could give up his penchant for poetry: "He is the son of a domestic servant, and he has an uncle who is a canon, who made him study and intended to make something of him. But he has given himself over completely to poetry, which has driven the uncle to despair."

At the same time, d'Hémery admired talent. To him, Fontenelle was "one of the most beautiful geniuses of our century"; and Voltaire was "an eagle in his spirit but a very bad subject in his opinions." Although the voice of the police inspector could be heard in that remark, it contained a note of respect. D'Hémery gave quite a sympathetic account of Montesquieu's difficulties with *L'Esprit des lois* and of Montesquieu himself: "He is an extremely clever man, terribly troubled with poor eyesight. He has written several charming works, such as the *Lettres persanes, Le Temple de Gnide,* and the celebrated *L'Esprit des lois.*"

Such remarks would have been unthinkable under Louis XIV, when Vauban and Fénelon were exiled from court for less-daring publications and when Racine gave up writing in order to take up gentility. Nor would they have been in place in the nineteenth century, when Balzac and Hugo established the heroic style of authorship and Zola consummated the conquest of the marketplace. D'Hémery expressed an in-between stage in the evolution of the writer's status. He did not think of writing as an independent career or a distinct estate. But he respected it as an art—and he knew it bore watching as an ideological force.

Although ideology did not exist as a concept for d'Hémery, he ran into it every day—not as a downward streaming of Enlightenment or an upward surging of revolutionary consciousness, but as a form of danger that he encountered at street level. The notion of "danger" appears in several reports, usually in connection with remarks on suspicious characters. D'Hémery used a graduated scale of epithets: "good subject" (Fosse), "fairly bad subject" (Olivier,

Febre, Néel), "bad subject" (Courtois, Palmeus), and "very bad subject" (Gournay, Voltaire)—or "not suspicious" (Boissy), "suspicious" (Cahusac), and "extremely suspicious" (Lurquet). He seemed to measure his language carefully, as if he were gauging the degree of danger in each dossier. And the context of his remarks suggests that he associated "danger" with "bad subjects" in a way that was peculiar to police work under the Old Regime. Palmeus was "a dangerous, bad subject" because he wrote anonymous letters against his enemies to people in authority. Mlle Fauque de la Cépède looked just as bad because she had embroiled two lovers by counterfeiting their handwriting in fake letters—an intrigue that might seem trivial today but that d'Hémery took seriously: "That talent is very dangerous in society." The ability to compromise someone seemed especially threatening in a system where individuals rose and fell according to their *crédit* or reputation. Those most *en crédit*, the placemen or *gens en place*, had most to lose by falling from favor. So d'Hémery was especially wary of persons who collected information in order to damage reputations in high places. Thus P.-C. Nivelle de La Chaussée: "He has never done anything suspicious, yet he is not liked because he is considered dangerous and capable of hurting people secretly."

Secret hurting—an idea transmitted by verbs such as *nuire* and *perdre* (to harm, to ruin)—usually took the form of denunciation, the contrary principle to protection, which operated throughout the system as a countervailing force. D'Hémery encountered denunciations everywhere he went. An impecunious poet named Courtois hired himself out to an army captain, who wanted to put an enemy behind bars by providing information in an anonymous letter to the police. A Mme Dubois quarreled violently with her husband, a sales clerk in a tailor's shop, and then tried to get him shut up in the Bastille by means of a letter under a false name, saying she had seen him reading a violent poem against the king to a crowd during the Mardi Gras celebrations. A banker, Nicolas Jouin, had his son's mistress thrown in prison; and the son retaliated with an anonymous letter, which brought the father to the Bastille by revealing that he had written a series of Jansenist tracts, including a pamphlet against the archbishop of Paris.

The surveillance of this slander was a full-time job for the police. D'Hémery did not bother with cases where reputations of humble people were at stake. He turned a deaf ear to a café waitress who complained about being pilloried in a pamphlet by her jilted lover, a poet named Roger de Sery. But he paid close attention to Fabio Gherardini, who maligned the genealogy of the comte de Saint-Séverin in a pamphlet; to Pierre-Charles Jamet, who defamed the controller general and his ancestors; and to Nicolas Lenglet du Fresnoy, who wanted to publish a history of the Regency, which was "full of very strong things against families in power." When clans and clientages were slandered, it was an affair of state; for in a system of court politics, personalities counted as much as principles, and personal credit could be sapped by a well-placed pamphlet.

Thus ideological police work was often a matter of hunting down pamphleteers and suppressing *libelles,* the form that slander took when it appeared in print. D'Hémery took special care to protect the reputation of his own protectors—notably the Lieutenant-Général de Police Nicolas-René Berryer and the d'Argenson faction of the court—and the reports sometimes show that in trailing a writer he was acting on orders from his superiors. In the report on Louis de Cahusac, for example, d'Hémery noted that Berryer had "told me that he was considered suspicious in court and that he should be investigated closely." Cahusac did not write revolutionary tracts. But he looked like a "bad subject" because he went through a succession of clientages—from the comte de Clermont, to the comte de Saint Florentin, to the financier la Poplinière—and came out with a pseudo-Japanese novel, *Grigri,* which contained enough information to ruin a great many reputations in court. Similarly, Berryer warned d'Hémery to keep an eye on J.-A. Guer, a "bad subject" in the Machault faction of the court, because he had recently traveled to Holland in order to arrange for the printing of some "suspicious manuscripts."

Adjectives like "suspicious," "bad," and "dangerous" proliferated in the reports on such characters. D'Hémery described L.-C. Fougeret de Montbron as particularly "bad" because he specialized in *libelles:*

> He recently had printed in The Hague a work of eight to nine sheets entitled *Le Cosmopolite, citoyen du monde.* It is a satire against the government of France and especially against M. Berryer and M. d'Argens, who is a particular target of his resentment, because he thinks that he

[the marquis d'Argens] had him run out of Prussia, where he used to live.

The most dangerous *libellistes* aimed at the most elevated figures in the kingdom, firing from beyond its borders. In April, 1751, d'Hémery noted that L.-M. Bertin de Frateaux "is presently in London and was formerly in Spain. He is still saying bad things about his country and has banded with a group of bad subjects to produce satires against it." A year later d'Hémery reported that Bertin was in the Bastille. After seizing some manuscripts that he had hidden in Paris, the police had sent an agent to lure him out of London and had captured him in Calais. He remained in prison for two and a half years for having written "*libelles* of the greatest violence against the king and the entire royal family."

D'Hémery's job, as he understood it, involved the protection of the kingdom by the suppression of anything that could damage the authority of the king. The scurrilous pamphlets about Louis XV and Mme de Pompadour, which may strike a modern reader as little more than rumor mongering, looked like sedition to him. So he reserved his strongest language for *libellistes* like Nicolas Lenglet du Fresnoy, "a dangerous man, who would overthrow a kingdom," and for the pamphleteers and parliamentary *frondeurs* who gathered in the salons of Mme Doublet and Mme Vieuxmaison, "the most dangerous [society] in Paris." These groups did not merely gossip about court intrigues and politics; they wrote up the most damaging news in *libelles* and manuscript gazettes, which circulated "under the cloak" everywhere in France. A half dozen of these primitive journalists (*nouvellistes*) figure in d'Hémery's reports. He took them seriously because they had a serious effect on public opinion. His spies heard echoes of their "nouvelles" in cafés and public gardens, and even among the common people, where news traveled by word of mouth. Thus a spy's account of a harangue by Pidansat de Mairobert, a key *nouvelliste* from the Doublet salon and "the worst tongue in Paris," according to d'Hémery: "Mairobert said in the café Procope, while talking about the recent reforms [the vingtième tax], that someone from the army ought to wipe out the whole court, whose sole pleasure is to devastate the common people and perpetrate injustice."

Police agents were always picking up seditious talk (*propos*), and writers were often jailed for it. D'Hémery kept track of it all in his files, where one often runs into suspicious characters like F.-Z. de Lauberivières, chevalier de Quinsonas, a soldier turned *nouvelliste* who was "extremely free in his *propos*"; J.-F. Dreux du Radier, exiled "for *propos*"; F.-P. Mellin de Saint-Hilaire, sent to the Bastille "for having made *propos* . . . against Mme de Pompadour"; and Antoine Bret, also in the Bastille for "seditious *propos* against the king and Mme de Pompadour." Sometimes one can almost hear the talk. D'Hémery's report on Pierre-Mathias de Gournay, a priest, geographer, and "very bad subject," reads like a stenographic account of what was in the air in public places:

> On March 14, 1751, while walking through the gardens of the Palais Royal and talking about the police, he said that there had never been a more unjust and barbarous inquisition than the one that rules over Paris. It is a tyrannical despotism, which everyone holds in contempt. The source of it all, he said, is a feeble and sensual king, who doesn't care about any affairs except those that give him a chance to besot himself with pleasure. It is a woman who holds the reins. . . . It wasn't possible to hear the rest.

The same theme appeared in the poem that the sales clerk's wife, Mme Dubois, sent to the police in order to inculpate her husband and in several other poems that were set to the tunes of popular songs and sung throughout the streets. Police agents heard people from every milieux singing verse such as:[14]

> *Lâche dissipateur des biens de tes sujets,*
> *Toi qui comptes les jours par les maux que tu fais,*
> *Esclave d'un ministre et d'une femme avare,*
> *Louis, apprends le sort que le ciel te prépare.*
>
> *Indolent dissipator of your subject's wealth,*
> *You, who reckon the days by the evil that you do,*
> *Slave of a minister and of an avaricious woman,*
> *Louis, hear what heaven has in store for you.*

The king was getting a bad press in all the media of the time—in books, pamphlets, gazettes, rumors, poems, and songs. So the kingdom looked rather fragile to d'Hémery. If the supreme protec-

Nouvellistes clustered in a café

tor lost command of his subjects' loyalty, the whole protection system might collapse. D'Hémery did not foresee a revolution; but in inspecting the republic of letters, he saw a monarchy that was becoming increasingly vulnerable to hostile waves of public opinion. While courtiers rose and fell through shifting clientages, pamphleteers eroded the respect for the regime among the general public; and danger lurked everywhere—even in the shabby room off the Place de l'Estrapade, where a "boy" named Diderot was scribbling on a *dictionnaire encyclopédique.*

On the face of it, however, it seems odd that d'Hémery should have associated Diderot with danger. Diderot did not write *libelles* but Enlightenment tracts, and the Enlightenment does not appear as a threatening force in the reports. In fact, it does not appear at all. D'Hémery never used terms like *Lumières* and *philosophe.* Although he compiled dossiers on virtually all the *philosophes* who had published anything by 1753, he did not treat them as a group; and he often gave them a clean bill of health as individuals. Not only did he write respectfully about older, distinguished figures like Fontenelle, Duclos, and Montesquieu; but he also described d'Alembert as "a charming man, both in his character and in his wit." Rousseau figures in the reports as a prickly character but a person of "eminent merit" and "great intelligence," who had a special talent for music and literary polemics. Even Voltaire, "a very bad subject," appears primarily as a notoriety and intriguer in the world of letters and the court. D'Hémery mentioned only two of the famous philosophic salons—those of Mme Geoffrin and the marquise de Créquy—and he referred to them only in passing, while completely neglecting the important groups of intellectuals who clustered around Mlle de Lespinasse, Mme du Deffand, Mme de Tencin, and the baron d'Holbach. Apparently he did not identify a philosophic milieu and did not conceive of the Enlightenment as a coherent movement of opinion, or did not conceive of it at all. The intellectual tide that appears as a mainstream of cultural history in most textbooks does not surface in the police reports.

It is there, however—below the surface. Unlike the *libellistes* and *nouvellistes,* Diderot represented an insidious variety of danger: atheism. "He is a young man who plays the wit and prides himself on his impiety; very dangerous; speaks of the holy mysteries with scorn," d'Hémery noted. The report explained that after having written such horrors as *Les Pensées philosophiques* and *Les Bijoux indiscrets,* Diderot had gone to prison for the *Lettre sur les aveugles* and now was working on the *dictionnaire encyclopédique* with François-Vincent Toussaint and Marc-Antoine Eidous. Those writers had dossiers of their own in d'Hémery's files, and so did their predecessor in the original *Encyclopédie* enterprise, Godefroy Sellius, as well as the booksellers who financed it. They all appeared as dubious characters, who lived in Grub Street fashion, turning out a compilation here and a translation there, with bits of pornography and irreligion in between. Thus d'Hémery noted that Eidous had furnished some of the salacious material for Diderot's *Bijoux indiscrets,* which one of the *Encyclopédie* publishers, Laurent Durand, had put out clandestinely in 1748, while another Encyclopedist, Jean-Baptiste de la Chapelle, had supplied impieties for the *Lettre sur les aveugles*: "He pretends that Diderot took the conversation of Saunderson from him, which is the strongest thing against religion in the *Lettre sur les aveugles.*"

The cross references in the reports certainly made it look as though Diderot kept bad company, and the company reflected badly on the *Encyclopédie,* especially after one of Diderot's collaborators, the abbé Jean-Martin de Prades, was run out of France for heresy. In early 1752, just as the second volume of the *Encyclopédie* was being published, the professors of the Sorbonne discovered impieties scattered throughout the thesis that de Prades had recently defended successfully for a *licenciate* in their own faculty of theology. It was distressing enough to find philosophical rot—not to mention lax examination procedures—in the temple of orthodoxy, but de Prades seemed to take his text from the *Discours préliminaire* to the *Encyclopédie.* He actually supplied Diderot with copy on theological questions and shared rooms with two other collaborators, the abbés Yvon and Pestré. Moreover, the trio of abbé-Encyclopedists had ties with abbé-*philosophes*: the abbé Edme Mallet, another contributor to the *Encyclopédie*; the abbé Guillaume-Thomas-François Raynal, later notorious as the author of the outspoken *Histoire philosophique et politique des établissements et du commerce des Européens dans les deux Indes*; and the abbé Guillaume-Alexandre Méhégan, who later became an editor of the *Journal encyclopédique* and went to the Bastille in 1752 for his *Zoroastre,* which d'Hémery described as "an atrocious *libelle* against religion, which he dedicated to M. Toussaint." De Prades and Yvon escaped the same fate only by fleeing from France, but they did not lose contact with their former associates. D'Hémery noted that Yvon continued to write for the *Encyclopédie* from his place of refuge in Holland and that Pestré was correcting proofs for a pamphlet vindicating de Prades, who had settled safely with Frederick II in Prussia.

The combination of heretical abbés and garret atheists made the *Encyclopédie* look suspicious; but unlike subsequent commentators, such as the abbé Barruel, d'Hémery did not detect any conspiracy behind it. He apparently made no special effort to track down its contributors. Only twenty-two of them appear in his reports—less than 10 percent of all those who had written at least one article by 1765, when the final volumes of the text were published. Between 1748 and 1753, the book had not yet become anathema to the authorities and a symbol of the Enlightenment to the reading public. It was still a legal enterprise, protected by d'Hémery's superior, Lamoignon de Malesherbes, the Director of the Book Trade, and dedicated to the comte d'Argenson, Minister of War. So d'Hémery did not treat it as a serious ideological threat, although he kept an eye on the original nucleus of its authors.

But he did see danger in Diderot—not because of *Encyclopédisme,* a concept that does not appear in the reports, but because Diderot contributed to a current of free thinking that seemed to be flowing everywhere in Paris. D'Hémery took special note of the fact that Diderot was reported to mock the sacraments: "He said that when he gets to the end of his life, he will confess and receive [in communion] what they call God, but not from any obligation; merely out of regard for his family, so that they will not be reproached with the fact that he died without religion." The distressing thing, as d'Hémery saw it, was that plenty of other writers shared that attitude. Several of them appear in the reports with the epithet *libertin* (freethinker) attached to their names: thus L.-J.-C. Soulas d'Allainval, Louis-Mathieu Bertin de Frateaux, and Louis-Nicolas Guéroult. D'Hémery turned up popularizers of science, like Pierre Estève, who wrote a materialist tract on the origins of the universe; historians like François Turben, who transformed a history of England into a general indictment of religion; and a whole flock of impious poets—not merely well-known *libertins* like Voltaire and Piron, but obscure versifiers like L.-F. Delisle de la Drevetière, J.-B. La Coste, an abbé Ozanne, an abbé Lorgerie, and a clerk named Olivier. D'Hémery knew what manuscripts these men kept in their portfolios and what they were currently writing: Lorgerie had just completed "an epistle against religion," and Delisle was working on "a poem in which religion is mistreated." As he received reports on what was being said in salons and cafés, d'Hémery also knew that the comte de Maillebois had recited an obscene poem about Jesus Christ and John the Baptist at a dinner party, that the abbé Méhégan openly preached deism, and that César Chesneau Du Marsais was an outright atheist. Surveillance of religion was an important part of police work, and for d'Hémery it seemed to be a matter of measuring a rising tide of irreligion.

How this policing took place and why it was important can be illustrated by a final example, the report on Jacques le Blanc, an obscure abbé who wrote antireligious tracts from a room in Versailles. After completing a treatise entitled *Le Tombeau des préjugés sur lesquels se fondent les principales maximes de la religion,* le Blanc began to look for a publisher. He ran into a man called Valentin, who claimed to know his way around the Parisian book industry and offered to act as his agent. But a reading of a synopsis of the manuscript convinced Valentin that he could make more money by denouncing le Blanc to the archbishop of Paris in return for a reward. The archbishop sent him to the police with instructions to set a trap to catch the abbé *en flagrant délit.* Valentin and d'Hémery concocted a fake rendez-vous in an eating house at the rue Poissonière in Paris. Then Valentin instructed le Blanc to come in disguise, so he would not be recognized, and to bring the manuscript, because two booksellers were eager to buy it. The abbé changed his clerical gown for an old black suit and an ancient wig. Looking like a down-at-the-heels highwayman, according to d'Hémery's rather sympathetic account, he arrived at the appointed time. Valentin introduced him to the booksellers, who were actually policemen in disguise. Then, just as they were about to close the deal, d'Hémery swooped in, gathered up the manuscript, and hauled le Blanc off to the Bastille. The masquerade could have made an amusing *histoire*, but it appears sad and serious in D'Hémery's narrative. Valentin is a nasty adventurer, le Blanc a misguided victim, and the manuscript a work of iniquity. D'Hémery summarized its propositions as follows: the Bible is a collection of fairy tales; the miracles of Christ are fables, used to dupe the credulous; Christianity, Judaism, and Islam are equally false; and all proofs of the existence of God are absurdities "invented for political reasons." The political implications of the episode seemed especially important to d'Hémery: "At the bottom of his manuscript is written, 'Done in the city of the sun,' which is Versailles, where he lived when he wrote it, 'in the harem of hypocrites,' which is his monastery."

D'Hémery did not separate impiety from politics. Although he had no interest in theological arguments, he believed that atheism undercut the authority of the crown. Ultimately, then, *libertins* constituted the same threat as *libelles*, and the police needed to recognize danger in both forms, whether it struck below the belt as personal defamation or spread through the atmosphere from the garrets of *philosophes*.

Diderot therefore appears as the incarnation of danger in the files of the police: "He is a very clever boy but extremely dangerous." Seen in the light of five hundred other reports, he also seems to fit into a pattern. Like many other writers, he was a male, in early middle age, born to a family of educated artisans in a small city outside Paris. He had married a woman of equally humble origins, and he had spent three months in the prison of Vincennes as well as a great deal of time in Grub Street. Of course, many other patterns can be seen in the reports. No sociological formula will do justice to them all, for the republic of letters was a vague, spiritual territory; and authors remained scattered through society, without a clear professional identity. Nonetheless, in identifying Diderot, d'Hémery distinguished a critical element in the Old Regime and one that especially needed watching from the perspective of the police. By watching the police watch the likes of Diderot, one can see the dim figure of the intellectual take on a perceptible shape and emerge as a force to be reckoned with in early modern France.[15]

APPENDIX: THREE HISTOIRES

The following three reports show how lives were lived in the lower reaches of the republic of letters and how the police observed them. They illustrate the world that Diderot dramatized in *Le Neveu de Rameau* and that he inhabited while working on the *Encyclopédie*. And they indicate the way d'Hémery organized material from his dossiers under the six printed headings of his standard forms, adding new entries as he acquired new information.

I. DENIS DIDEROT

NAME: Diderot, author. 1 January 1748.

AGE: 36.

BIRTHPLACE: Langres.

DESCRIPTION: Medium size, a fairly decent physiognomy.

ADDRESS: Place de l'Estrapade, in the house of an upholsterer.

STORY:

He is the son of a cutler from Langres.

He is a very clever boy but extremely dangerous.

He wrote *Les Pensées philosophiques, Les Bijoux,* and other books of that sort.

He also did *L'Allée des idées,* which he has in manuscript at his house and which he has promised not to publish.

He is working on a *Dictionnaire encyclopédique* with Toussaint and Eidous.

9 June 1749. He did a book entitled *Lettre sur les aveugles à l'usage de ceux qui voient.*

24 July. He was arrested and taken to Vincennes on that account.

He is married, yet had Mme de Puysieux as a mistress for some time.

[A supplementary sheet reads as follows:]

The year 1749.

Author of books against religion and good morals.

Denis Diderot, native of Langres, author living in Paris.

Entered the dungeon of Vincennes on 24 July, 1749; released from the dungeon and given the castle as prison by an order of 21 August.

Left on 3 November of the same year.

For having written a work entitled:

Lettre sur les aveugles à l'usage de ceux qui voient clair [and also] *Les Bijoux indiscrets, Pensées philosophiques, Les Moeurs, Le Sceptique ou l' allée des idées, L' Oiseau blanc, conte bleu,* etc.

He is a young man who plays the wit and prides himself on his impiety; very dangerous; speaks of the holy mysteries with scorn. He said that when he gets to the end of his life, he will confess and receive [in communion] what they call God, but not from any obligation; merely out of regard for his family, so that they will not be reproached with the fact that he died without religion.

> Commissioner De Rochebrune
> D'Hémery, exempte de robe courte

II. ABBÉ CLAUDE-FRANÇOIS LAMBERT

NAME: Lambert (abbé), priest, author. 1 December 1751.

AGE: 50.

BIRTHPLACE: Dôle.

DESCRIPTION: Small, ill shaped, the bearing of a satyr, and a face full of pimples.

ADDRESS: Rue de la verrerie, in the shop of the mistress-dyers, on the fourth floor.

STORY:

He was a Jesuit for sixteen to seventeen years. He is a very bad subject, a drunkard and a whorer.

In 1746 he lived with the daughter of a certain Antoine, an employee in the commissariat department. He passed her off as his wife; and taking the name of Carré, lodged with her in a furnished room in the boarding house of the widow Bailly, where she gave birth to a boy. Then they took off, without paying a bill of 850 livres. After seven years, the widow Bailly discovered his new residence and brought a complaint against him with the Lieutenant-Général de Police. So he was forced to make arrangements to repay that sum over two years.

The woman and her little boy are now living with him. She calls herself his housekeeper.

In 1744 he published *Lettres d'un seigneur hollandais,* in three volumes, in which he discussed the interests of the princes in the last war. He wrote this work at the behest of the comte d'Argenson, who arranged to have him rewarded for it. Since then he has published a *Recueil d'observations,* in fifteen volumes duodecimo, with Prault fils. It is a very bad compilation taken from various authors, full of errors and very badly written. After that, he spent some time in Switzerland in the entourage of the marquis de Paulmy. Upon his return, he published a bad novel entitled *Histoire de la princesse Taïven, reine de Mexique,* put out as a translation from the Spanish by Guillyn. And finally, he just published a *Histoire littéraire du règne de Louis XIV,* three volumes in-quarto, which he had printed at his own cost, as no bookseller wanted to take it on. Mansart, the architect of the king, advanced him the necessary funds for this enterprise. It seems very unlikely that he'll get his money (12,000 livres) back, because they have sold only 100 copies from a printing of 1,200. It's a poorly done work. Only the discourses are good, and they aren't by the abbé Lambert but by various artists who supplied him with discourses on their art.

In return for this work, he received a pension of 600 livres, which d'Argenson procured for him. It appears that this minister values him more as a spy than as an author.

III. LOUIS-CHARLES FOUGERET DE MONTBRON

NAME: Montbron (Fougeret de), author. 1 January 1748.

AGE: 40.

BIRTHPLACE: Péronne.

DESCRIPTION: Tall, well built, brown complexion and a hard physiognomy.

ADDRESS: Rue du chantre, at the hôtel . . .

STORY:

He is an impudent character, the son of a postmaster in Péronne. He has a brother who is an employee in the tax farms.

He was a guard and later a valet de chambre of His Majesty, but had to give up that position because of his bad character. Then he went to various foreign courts in the entourage of ambassadors, and has recently returned. He is a clever boy, the author of *La Henriade travestie,* of an essay on sensual pleasure—a little brochure entitled *Le Canapé*—and he has done a translation, *Le Voyage de l'amiral Binck.*

7 November 1748. He was arrested for having done a bad novel entitled *Fanchon, ou Margot la ravaudeuse, ou la Tribade, actrice de l'Opéra.* The manuscript of this work was confiscated at his lodging at the time of his arrest.

5 December. He was exiled to a distance of fifty leagues from Paris by virtue of an order of the king dated December first.

1 June 1751. He recently had printed in The Hague a work of eight to nine sheets entitled *Le Cosmopolite, citoyen du monde.* It is a satire against the French government, and especially against M. Berryer and M. d'Argens, who is a particular target of his resentment, because he thinks that he [the marquis d'Argens] had him run out of Prussia, where he used to live.

This Montbron travels to Péronne, his hometown, four times a year in order to collect 3,000 livres that he has in *rente.* He is much feared there. He has an uncle who is a canon and whom he throws into a rage by his impious talk. He normally stays there eight days during each journey.

The Sanctuary of Truth, an allegory of the arts and
sciences from the frontispiece of the *Encyclopédie*

PHILOSOPHERS TRIM THE TREE OF KNOWLEDGE: THE EPISTEMOLOGICAL STRATEGY OF THE *ENCYCLOPÉDIE*

THE NEED TO SORT and classify phenomena extended far beyond the files of the police who tried to keep track of men like Diderot; it lay at the heart of Diderot's greatest enterprise, the *Encyclopédie*. But when it expressed itself in print, it assumed a form that may escape the attention of the modern reader. In fact, the supreme text of the Enlightenment can look surprisingly disappointing to anyone who consults it with the expectation of finding the ideological roots of modernity. For every remark undercutting traditional orthodoxies, it contains thousands of words about grinding grain, manufacturing pins, and declining verbs. Its seventeen folio volumes of text include such a jumble of information on everything from *A* to *Z* that one cannot help wondering why it raised such a storm in the eighteenth century. What set it apart from all the learned compendia that preceded it—from the imposing *Dictionnaire de Trévoux*, for example, or the much vaster *Grosses vollständiges Universal-Lexicon aller Wissenschaften und Künste* published in sixty-four folio volumes by Johann Heinrich Zedler? Was it, in the words of one authority, a "reference work or *machine de guerre*"?[1]

One could answer that it was both and dismiss the problem as a *question mal posée*. But the relation between information and ideology in the *Encyclopédie* raises some general issues about the connection between knowledge and power. Consider, for example, a totally different kind of learned book, the Chinese encyclopedia imagined by Jorge Luis Borges and discussed by Michel Foucault in *The Order of Things*. It divided animals into: "(a) belonging to the Emperor, (b) embalmed, (c) tame, (d) sucking pigs, (e) sirens, (f) fabulous, (g) stray dogs, (h) included in the present classification, (i) frenzied, (j) innumerable, (k) drawn with a very fine camelhair brush, (l) *et cetera*, (m) having just broken the water pitcher, (n) that from a long way off look like flies."[2] This classification system is significant, Foucault argues, because of the sheer impossibility of thinking it. By bringing us up short against an inconceivable set of categories, it exposes the arbitrariness of the way we sort things out. We order the world according to categories that we take for granted simply because they are given. They occupy an epistemological space that is prior to thought, and so they have extraordinary staying power. When confronted with an alien way of organizing experience, however, we sense the frailty of our own categories, and everything threatens to come undone. Things hold together only because they can be slotted into a classificatory scheme that remains unquestioned. We classify a Pekinese and a Great Dane together as dogs without hesitating, even though the Pekinese might seem to have more in common with a cat and the Great Dane with a pony. If we stopped to reflect on definitions of "dogness" or on the other categories for sorting out life, we could never get on with the business of living.

Pigeon-holing is therefore an exercise in power. A subject relegated to the *trivium* rather than the *quadrivium*, or to the "soft" rather than the "hard" sciences, may wither on the vine. A mis-shelved book may disappear forever. An enemy defined as less than human may be annihilated. All social action flows through boundaries determined by classification schemes, whether or not they are elaborated as explicitly as library catalogues, organization charts, and university departments. All animal life fits into the grid of an unconscious ontology. Monsters like the "elephant man" and the "wolf boy" horrify and fascinate us because they violate our conceptual boundaries,[3] and certain creatures make our skin crawl because they slip in between categories: "slimy" reptiles that swim in the sea and creep on the land, "nasty" rodents that live in houses yet remain outside the bounds of domestication. We insult someone by calling him a rat rather than a squirrel. "Squirrel" can be a term of endearment, as in Helmer's epithet for Nora in *A Doll's House*. Yet squirrels are rodents, as dangerous and disease-ridden as rats. They seem less threatening because they belong unambiguously to the out-of-doors. It is the in-between animals, the neither-fish-nor-fowl, that have special powers and therefore ritual value: thus the cassowaries in the mystery cults of New Guinea and the tomcats in the witches' brews of the West. Hair, fingernail parings, and feces also go into magic potions because they represent the ambiguous border areas of the body, where the organism spills over into the surrounding material world. All borders are dangerous. If left unguarded, they could break down, our categories could collapse, and our world dissolve in chaos.[4]

Setting up categories and policing them is therefore a serious business. A philosopher who attempted to redraw the boundaries of the world of knowledge would be tampering with the taboo. Even if he steered clear of sacred subjects, he could not avoid danger; for knowledge is inherently ambiguous. Like reptiles and rats, it can slip from one category to another. It has bite. Thus Diderot and d'Alembert took enormous risks when they undid the old order of knowledge and drew new lines between the known and the unknown.

Of course, philosophers had rearranged mental furniture since the time of Aristotle. Reordering the *trivium* and *quadrivium,* the liberal and mechanical arts, the *studia humanitatis* and all the branches of the ancient curriculum was a favorite game for schematizers and synthesizers during the Middle Ages and the Renaissance. The debate about "method" and correct "disposition" in the ordering of knowledge shook the entire republic of letters in the sixteenth century. Out of it emerged a tendency to compress knowledge into schemata, usually typographical diagrams, which illustrated the branches and bifurcations of disciplines according to the principles of Ramist logic. Thus a diagrammatic impulse—a tendency to map, outline, and spatialize segments of knowledge— underlay the strain of encyclopedism that stretched from Ramus to Bacon, Alsted, Comenius, Leibniz, Chambers, Diderot, and d'Alembert.[5] But the diagram at the head of Diderot's *Encyclopédie,* the famous tree of knowledge derived from Bacon and Chambers, represented something new and audacious. Instead of showing how disciplines could be shifted within an established pattern, it expressed an attempt to raise a boundary between the known and the unknowable in such a way as to eliminate most of what men held to be sacred from the world of learning. By following the *philosophes* in their elaborate attempts to trim the tree of knowledge that they had inherited from their predecessors, one can form a clearer idea of how much was at stake in the Enlightenment version of encyclopedism.

Diderot and d'Alembert alerted the reader to the fact that they were engaged in something more momentous than Ramist doodling by describing their work as an encyclopedia, or systematic account of "the order and concatenation of human knowledge,"[6] and not merely as just another dictionary, or compendium of information arranged according to the innocent order of the alphabet. The word encyclopedia, Diderot explained in the *Prospectus,* derived from the Greek term for circle, signifying "concatenation [enchaînement] of the sciences."[7] Figuratively, it expressed the notion of a world of knowledge, which the Encyclopedists could circumnavigate and map. "Mappemonde" was a crucial metaphor in their description of their work. Still more important was the metaphor of the tree of knowledge, which communicated the idea that knowledge grew into an organic whole, despite the diversity of its branches. Diderot and d'Alembert mixed the metaphors at key points. Thus in explaining the difference between an encyclopedia and a dictionary, d'Alembert described the *Encyclopédie* as:

a kind of world map which is to show the principal countries, their position and their mutual dependence, the road that leads directly from one to the other. This road is often cut by a thousand obstacles, which are known in each country only to the inhabitants or to travelers, and which cannot be represented except in individual, highly detailed maps. These individual maps will be the different articles of the *Encyclopédie* and the Tree or Systematic Chart will be its world map.[8]

The mixing of metaphors suggested the unsettling effect of conflating categories. The very attempt to impose a new order on the world made the Encyclopedists conscious of the arbitrariness in all ordering. What one philosopher had joined another could undo. So the *Encyclopédie* might not fix knowledge more permanently than the *Summa* of Thomas Aquinas had done. Something like epistemological *Angst* showed through the language of the *Prospectus,* even when it advanced its most aggressive claims to make the older syntheses obsolete:

This tree of human knowledge could be formed in several ways, either by relating different knowledge to the diverse faculties of our mind or by relating it to the things that it has as its object. The difficulty was greatest where it involved the most arbitrariness. But how could there not be arbitrariness? Nature presents us only with particular things, infinite in number and without firmly established divisions. Everything shades off into everything else by imperceptible nuances. And if, on this ocean of objects surrounding us, there should appear a few that seem to break through the surface and to dominate the rest like the crest of a reef, they merely owe this advantage to particular systems, to vague conventions, and to certain events that have nothing to do with the physical arrangement of beings and with the true institutions of philosophy.[9]

If the encyclopedic tree was but one of an infinite number of possible trees, if no map could fix the indeterminate typography of knowledge, how could Diderot and d'Alembert hope to establish the "true institutions of philosophy"? Essentially because they thought they could limit the domain of the knowable and pin down a modest variety of truth. True philosophy taught modesty. It demonstrated that we can know nothing beyond what comes to us from sensation and reflection. Locke made feasible what Bacon had begun, and Bacon had begun by sketching a tree of knowledge. Thus a Lockean version of Bacon's tree could serve as a model for the modern *Summa* of everything known to man.

Diderot and d'Alembert could have picked out other trees in the forest of symbols of systematic knowledge. Porphyry and Raymond Lull had anticipated Bacon, and Hobbes had succeeded him. More to the point, a fully developed tree stood at the beginning of Ephraim Chambers's *Cyclopaedia,* which Diderot and d'Alembert took as their main source. Not only did they begin their work as a translation of his, they derived their conception of an encyclopedia from him. Diderot acknowledged their debt freely in the *Prospectus:*

> We realized, with our English author, that the first step we had to take toward the rational and fully understood execution of an encyclopedia was to form a genealogical tree of all the sciences and of all the arts, one which would show the origin of each branch of knowledge and the connections each has with the others and with their common stalk, and which would help us relate the different articles to their main rubrics.[10]

Chambers himself had insisted on the importance of presenting knowledge systematically rather than as an unordered mass of information:

> The difficulty lay in the form and economy of it, so to dispose such a multitude of materials as not to make a confused heap of incoherent parts but one consistent whole. . . . Former lexicographers have scarce attempted anything like structure in their works, nor seem to have been aware that a dictionary was, in some measure, capable of the advantages of a continued discourse.[11]

In short, Chambers distinguished himself from his predecessors by propounding a view of knowledge as an integrated whole. He would produce not merely a "dictionary" arranged from *A* to *Z,* but a "cyclopaedia," which would encompass the entire circle of learning.

Like Bacon, Chambers represented the divisions of knowledge as branches of a tree, which he derived from the three principal faculties of the mind: memory, the source of historical knowledge; imagination, the source of poetry; and reason, the source of philosophy. The faculties disappeared, however, when he depicted the tree in a diagram. The diagram merely showed how knowledge branched and twigged into a luxuriant foliage of forty-seven arts and sciences. Theology, for example, grew out of the main trunk, "knowledge," in the following manner:[12]

$$
\text{knowledge} \leftarrow
\begin{cases}
\text{natural and scientifical} \leftarrow
\begin{cases}
\text{sensible} \\
\text{rational} \leftarrow
\begin{cases}
\text{physics} \\
\text{metaphysics} \\
\text{pure mathematics} \\
\text{religion} \leftarrow
\begin{cases}
\text{ethics} \\
\text{theology}
\end{cases}
\end{cases}
\end{cases} \\
\text{artificial and technical}
\end{cases}
$$

Was such a picture of theology likely to find favor among the Encyclopedists? If it did not quite make her the queen of the sciences, it placed theology at the crowning point of a series of bifurcations drawn out diagrammatically in the old-fashioned Ramist manner. It also allocated more articles to theology than to any other subject, as the reader could tell by consulting notes attached to every branch of the sciences. To be sure, a freethinker like Diderot might have been expected to welcome a system that seemed to derive theology from the rational and the "scientifical" branches of thought. But the bough labeled "rational" issued in four subbranches, which accorded equal dignity to those sciences that he wanted to belittle, metaphysics and religion, and to those sciences that he wanted to elevate, mathematics and physics. Worse, the tree had no branch for philosophy as such. The sacred and the secular ran together through all its ramifications. And in the general confusion, a vital, Baconian point was lost: the arts and sciences seemed to grow out of each other, not to derive from the operations of the mind. Diderot and d'Alembert wanted to root knowledge in epistemology; so they abandoned their immediate source, Chambers, and went back to Bacon.

To return to Bacon was to leap over Locke. As d'Alembert noted in the *Discours préliminaire,* Bacon still used scholastic language, still groped for light in the depths of medieval darkness.[13] Yet much of Bacon's thought—the emphasis on induction, the distinction between perception and reflection, the turning away from metaphysical systems and toward the investigation of the immediate world of sense experience—had an affinity with the empiricism that was later to emerge with Locke. Bacon's tree of knowledge, unlike that of Chambers, really did suggest that the arts and sciences grew from the faculties of the mind. So Bacon provided Diderot and d'Alembert with the model they needed, and they followed it so closely that they were accused of plagiarism.[14] But they also deviated from it at several significant points, as they emphasized repeatedly in the *Prospectus* and the *Discours préliminaire.* They devised a "mappemonde" to suit their own purposes, just as Bacon created "a small globe of the intellectual world" to suit his.[15] By superimposing their map on his, one can see shifts in the topography of knowledge, which may serve as clues to the underlying strategy of the *Encyclopédie.*

Like Bacon, Diderot and d'Alembert began with history, the branch of knowledge derived from memory; and like him, they divided it into four subbranches: ecclesiastical, civil, literary, and natural (see appendix to this chapter). But the proportions of their schema differed completely from his. To them, ecclesiastical history was a minor branch, which they hurried over in one sentence in the body of the *Discours préliminaire* and failed to mention at all in the commentary on Bacon's tree printed at its end. For Bacon, ecclesiastical history had a rich set of subdivisions, including the history of Providence, which demonstrated the hand of God at work in human affairs, to "the confuting of those which are as without God in the world."[16] The place of natural history on the two trees is exactly the reverse. Bacon considered it a "deficient" branch, one that needed developing, especially in the area of the mechanical arts.[17] Those arts occupied a vast area of the encyclopedic tree and constituted the most extensive and original part of the *Encyclopédie* itself. Diderot and d'Alembert did not seek out the hand of God in the world but rather studied men at work, forging their own happiness.

Of course, Bacon also advocated the study of the workaday world, but he did not cut it off from Providence, while the Encyclopedists attributed its improvement entirely to the influence of intellectuals like themselves; hence their version of the distinction between civil and literary history: "The history of man has for its object either his actions or his knowledge, and consequently is civil or literary. In other words, it is divided between the great nations and the great geniuses, between the kings and the men of letters, between the conquerors and the philosophers."[18] This formulation cast the *philosophes* in a grand role. History followed a glorious trajectory from the philosophers of the Renaissance to the philosophers of the Enlightenment, according to the sketch that d'Alembert included in the *Discours préliminaire*. To Bacon, however, literary history (the "just story of learning" as opposed to "poesy" or the arts of the imagination)[19] did not reveal the progressive march of reason. It was so deficient as hardly to exist at all: "The history of the world seemeth to me to be as the statue of Polyphemus with his eye out; that part being wanting which doth most show the spirit and life of the person."[20] Diderot and d'Alembert drew a different conclusion from the same metaphor, strategically misconstrued: "The sciences are the work of the reflection and of the natural light of men. Chancellor Bacon was therefore justified in saying in his admirable work *De dignitate et augmento scientiarum* that the history of the world without the history of scholars is the statue of Polyphemus with his eye torn out."[21] Where Bacon saw darkness, they saw light and gloried in their role as purveyors of Enlightenment.

The arts derived from the imagination, rather misleadingly labeled poetry, look pretty much the same on the two trees, except that the *Encyclopédie* pursued their ramifications through plastic arts that Bacon did not mention. The greatest differences appeared among the sciences derived from reason, that is, philosophy, the third of the three main divisions of knowledge. In defending the encyclopedic tree against the attacks of the Jesuit journalist, Guillaume-François Berthier, Diderot insisted on the originality of "the philosophical branch, which is the most extensive, the most important of our system, and of which almost nothing can be found in Chancellor Bacon."[22] The observations on Bacon's tree at the end of the *Discours préliminaire* made the same point, adding cryptically, "It is for philosophers, that is to say, for a very small number of persons, to judge us on this point."[23] To a philosopher of Diderot's stripe the point would be obvious, for in the tree of the *Encyclopédie* philosophy was not so much a branch as the principal trunk. Out of it, on a rather remote twig, grew "revealed theology" amidst a cluster of dubious subjects: "superstitions," "divination," "black magic," "the science of good and evil spirits." The Encyclopedists conveyed a message merely by positioning things, as in the notorious cross references of their articles (for example, ANTHROPOPHAGY: "See EUCHARIST, COMMUNION, ALTAR, etc."[24]) A new dimension had developed around the mapping of knowledge. Shape yielded significance, and morphology turned into irony.

Diderot and d'Alembert could also hide their meaning by claiming that they shaped their tree after Bacon's. Like him, they divided philosophy into three parts, divine, natural, and human; and by putting the science of God at the top, they seemed to preserve its place as the queen of the sciences. In fact, however, they completely undermined Bacon's system. He included only pagan "natural theology" within philosophy and emphasized its imperfection. It sufficed to confound atheism, because the contemplation of God's works compelled one to acknowledge His existence. But inductive reasoning from observed phenomena—arguments for theism from design—never could lead to knowledge of the true, Christian God. "We ought not to attempt to draw down or to submit the mysteries of God to our reason," Bacon warned. So he separated religion from philosophy, underscoring "the extreme prejudice which both religion and philosophy hath received by being commixed together; as that which undoubtedly will make an heretical religion and an imaginary and fabulous philosophy."[25]

Nothing could be further from the reasoning of Diderot and d'Alembert. By subjecting religion to philosophy, they effectively dechristianized it. Of course, they professed orthodoxy. They noted that God had revealed Himself in "sacred history." Revelation therefore was an impeccable fact, which could be culled from memory and submitted to reason like anything else: "Thus, to separate theology from philosophy [as Bacon had done] would be to cut the offshoot from the trunk to which it is united by its very nature."[26] The premises sounded pious, but the conclusion smacked of heresy because it seemed to subordinate theology to reason, which they described in a Lockean manner, as if one could arrive at knowledge of God by building sensations into ever more complex and abstract ideas. Indeed, when they came to the "science of God" in their account of the tree of knowledge, Diderot and d'Alembert advanced an argument that could have come straight out of *An Essay Concerning Human Understanding*:

> The natural progress of the human mind is to rise from individuals to species, from species to genera, from closely related genera to distantly related ones, and to create a science at each step; or at least to add a new branch to some science already in existence. Thus the concept, which we meet in history and which sacred history announces to us, of an uncreated and infinite intelligence, etc.[27]

To pursue induction so far was impiety, according to Bacon. He guarded against it by placing "divine learning" on a separate tree, which had no connection with "human learning" and the faculties of the mind. Thus Bacon actually envisaged two trees of knowledge, one for revealed and one for natural theology, while the Encyclopedists grouped revealed and natural theology together on a single tree and subordinated both to reason.

The implications of all this pruning, grafting, and uprooting of Bacon became clear in d'Alembert's *Discours préliminaire*. D'Alembert expounded the tree of knowledge in the central section of his essay, which dealt with the systemic connections of the arts and sciences. He situated this section between a discussion of the genesis of knowledge within individual minds, on the one hand, and an account of its development within society, on the other. Thus the *Discours préliminaire* can be seen as a triptych, in which the central panel provides a morphological picture of knowledge, while the side panels present epistemological and historical views.

The three-sided structure of the *Discours préliminaire* is not easy to discern, however. Although the essay certainly deserves to be considered as a major manifesto of the Enlightenment, it is not a model of clarity. Like Bacon, d'Alembert set out to produce a "mappemonde" by circumnavigating the world of knowledge; but he wandered off course, ran into contradictions, and floundered in inconsistencies as he tried to find a way through everything that had accumulated since Bacon's time. It was the difficulties that made the journey so momentous. So its zigs and zags are worth following in some detail.

D'Alembert embarked on a bold, Lockean tack. All knowledge derived from sensation and reflection, he explained. Ideation began with the buzzing of the senses rather than from some introspective unpacking of innate ideas: I feel, therefore I am. From knowledge of the self, I advance to knowledge of external objects, the experience of pleasure and pain, and thence to notions of morality. At this point, d'Alembert seemed to root ethics in a kind of utilitarianism, and he shifted from the consideration of how ideas developed in the individual to the question of how individuals formed societies. This tack took him back to the beginning, to man in the state of nature. Presocial men lived like Hobbesian brutes, by "the barbarian right of inequality called the law of the strongest,"[28] rather than by Lockean natural law. But their experience of oppression awakened their moral sense and drove them to protect their legitimate rights by organizing in societies. Once engaged in social life, they began to question the source of their newly acquired morality. It could not come from the physical world, so it must come from some spiritual principle dwelling within us, which had forced us to reflect on justice and injustice. We recognize two principles at work, mind and body; and in the act of recognition, we sense our imperfection, which implies a prior notion of perfection itself. In the end, therefore, we arrive at a conception of God.

It was an odd argument. After a brush with Hobbes, which anticipated Rousseau, d'Alembert became entangled with Descartes. His mode of exposition shifted from hypothetical history to epistemological introspection. He argued that the dawning of ethical thought forced man to examine his own thinking substance or soul, which he immediately recognized as having nothing in common with his body. That is, he induced Descartes's dualism; and in the next, swift leap, he derived Descartes's God: "This mutual slavery [of body and soul], which is so independent of us, together with the reflections that we are compelled to make on the nature of the two principles and on their imperfection, lifts us to the contemplation of an all-powerful Intelligence to whom we owe our being and who consequently requires our worship."[29]

D'Alembert had taken a Lockean route to a Cartesian God. After following Locke's argument about the combination of increasingly complex and abstract ideas, he had reversed himself and arrived at the supreme abstraction in the manner of Descartes, by a direct jump from the consciousness of imperfection to the logically prior notion of perfection. From this high ontological ground, Descartes had gone on to derive the world of extension, ending where Locke began. D'Alembert proceeded in the opposite direction, beginning where Locke did; so his epistemology ran forward and his metaphysics backward. Indeed, the recapitulation of his argument reads like a series of non sequiturs:

> It is therefore evident that the purely intellectual concepts of vice and virtue, the principle and the necessity of laws, the spiritual nature of the soul, the existence of God and of our obligations toward him—in a word, the truths for which we have the most immediate and indispensable need—are the fruits of the first reflective ideas that our sensations occasion.[30]

D'Alembert may have been less than orthodox in religion, but he was no fool. Why did he compress such incompatible propositions into a single argument? The rather casual style of his exposition suggests that he did not mean the *Discours préliminaire* to be read as a formal treatise in philosophy. He intended it to serve as an introduction to an encyclopedia, and so he moved fast. Thus he noted that a perceptive knowledge of the soul came "naturally" from considerations of morality, as if one could shift from an ethical to an epistemological argument with no difficulty at all. "It is not necessary to probe deeply," he added, in order to recognize the dualism between body and soul.[31] He dashed through Descartes's proof of the existence of God in a sentence, almost in a parenthetical remark. The hasty turns of phrase suggested that the modern philosopher could dispatch with metaphysical questions quickly, or at least that he need not tarry over them. Malebranche and others had erected Cartesianism into a new orthodoxy. By echoing their arguments, d'Alembert established his own credentials as a good Catholic; and by splicing the arguments with inconsistencies, he undercut them, perhaps intentionally. As noted above, the *Discours préliminaire* ended with a revised version of the *Prospectus,* which argued about God as if it were a gloss on *An Essay Concerning Human Understanding.* Having appeared confusedly Cartesian in one place, the *Encyclopédie* sounded audaciously Lockean in another. The reader could draw his own conclusions.

But it would be wrong to conclude that d'Alembert meant to

becloud his argument by fogging it over with incompatible propositions. Arguments often burst at the seams with incompatibilities, not because their author intended them to but because he unconsciously utilized different idioms. D'Alembert wrote at a time when scholastic, Cartesian, and Lockean language jostled one another in philosophic discourse. He easily slipped from one idiom to another whenever he dropped his guard or needed to negotiate around a difficult point. In fact, a certain amount of slippage suited the meandering character of the *Discours préliminaire.* In the section following his epistemological account of knowledge, d'Alembert spoke out against excessive coherence in scientific method. Instead of laying out a rigorously consistent set of premises and proceeding deductively, he maintained, philosophers ought to take nature as they found it, reduce its phenomena down to their underlying principles, and then reconstruct those principles systematically. This *esprit systématique* rested on the postulate that underlying principles really existed, but it did not, like the *esprit de système,* take their existence as its starting point. Still, it could be objected that d'Alembert's postulate—expressed at its most dramatic in his contention that "the universe, to someone who could embrace it from a single point of view, would be so to speak only a single fact and one great truth"[32]—was a matter of faith, not knowledge. How did he know that knowledge ultimately would cohere?

Instead of confronting that question directly, d'Alembert tried to demonstrate the cohesion of the arts and sciences by surveying all their branches. He shifted from an epistemological to a morphological mode of argument, which culminated in his discussion of the tree of knowledge. Even so, the argument continued to sway between incompatible types of exposition. At times it developed a "philosophical history"[33] of the arts and sciences, continuing the earlier discussion of their genesis from the state of nature. At times it took them up according to their "philosophical order"[34] or logical relations.

D'Alembert began with logic itself because he considered it first in importance, even though it did not rank first in the order of discovery. At the same time, he proclaimed his intention of discussing the sciences according to a hypothetical chronology of their development. Continuing in this inconsistent manner, he picked his way through grammar, eloquence, history, chronology, geography, politics, and the fine arts until he arrived at the encyclopedic tree. It provided him with an overview of everything, because it emblematized the totality of knowledge both in "the encyclopedic order" and in "the genealogical order"[35]—that is, it brought together the two modes of argument that had threatened to fly apart from the very beginning of the *Discours préliminaire*. Bacon had shown how to turn this trick. His tree demonstrated that knowledge grew into an organic whole while emanating from the faculties of the mind. But it did not illustrate a full-blown epistemological argument. Insofar as it suggested any epistemology at all, it conjured up notions from Aristotle and Aquinas. D'Alembert and Diderot wanted to bring the old faculty psychology up to date. So they trimmed Bacon's tree in the Lockean manner and thereby brought morphology into line with epistemology.

This second trick more than doubled the power of the argument because it ruled out of bounds any knowledge that could not be derived from sensation and reflection. D'Alembert prudently left room for "revealed facts"[36] under the rubric of history, but he subjected revelation to reason under philosophy, the most important division of knowledge. Of course, it might be argued that Aquinas had done as much. But the *Summa* of Aquinas embraced everything that could fit within the predicate of a syllogism, while the *Summa* of Diderot and d'Alembert excluded everything that could not reach reason through the senses. On their tree, unlike Bacon's, "natural theology" (balanced by "religion") received equal billing with "revealed theology" (balanced by "superstition"). It was difficult to find any place at all for the traditional doctrines of the church. Although memory might summon them out of history, they would look no more reasonable than Stoicism or Confucianism in the realm of philosophy. In fact, they had ceased to be knowledge altogether. The morphological and epistemological arguments combined to cut orthodox religion off the map, to consign it to the unknowable, and thus to exclude it from the modern world of learning.

The historical argument completed the job. D'Alembert presented history as the triumph of civilization and civilization as the work of men of letters. The last section of the *Discours préliminaire* propounded a kind of great-man view of history in which all the great men were philosophers.[37] After deploring the Dark Ages and celebrating the Renaissance, it concentrated on the greatest of the great: Bacon, Descartes, Newton, and Locke.

Bacon appeared in this grand tableau as the progenitor of philosophy, the first man to dissipate darkness and to restrict reason to its proper sphere, the study of natural phenomena. To be sure, he failed to break completely with scholasticism. That task fell to Descartes, who destroyed the fetters that had held back philosophy since the time of Aquinas, if not Aristotle. D'Alembert hailed Descartes the doubter, not Descartes the metaphysician. The doctrine of innate ideas actually represented a step backward, he explained, for it led reason astray into a world beyond sense experience, whereas the scholastics at least "retained from the peripatetic sect the sole truth that it had taught, namely that of the origin of ideas in the senses."[38] Although this formulation made Aquinas sound like Locke, it had the advantage of undercutting neo-orthodoxy in metaphysics; and it cleared the way for Newton, who "gave to philosophy a form that it seems certain to conserve."[39] D'Alembert's Newton served as the perfect modern philosopher not merely because he discovered the fundamental law of the solar system but because he restricted philosophy to the study of observed phenomena. Unlike Descartes, who tried to know everything, he limited knowledge to the knowable; he was Newton the modest. From this Newton, the Newton of Voltaire's *Lettres philosophiques* rather than of the Book of Revelation, it was but one step to Locke and "the experimental physics of the soul."[40] Locke represented the ultimate in modesty, the definitive reining-in of philosophy, because he fixed the final limits to the knowable. By reducing all knowledge to sensation and reflection, he at last eliminated extra-terrestrial truth from the world of learning.

Once these great men had established the frontiers of knowledge, it remained for their successors to fill in the gaps. D'Alembert surveyed the leading ranks of scientists and philosophers, passing rapidly from Galileo, Harvey, Huyghens, and Pascal to Fontenelle, Buffon, Condillac, Voltaire, Montesquieu, and Rousseau. It was an impressive array, but d'Alembert had difficulty keeping the men in line. He suggested that each thinker consolidated part of the territory conquered by Bacon, Descartes, Newton, and Locke; so that history since the Renaissance demonstrated the progressive march of reason. But some of the philosophers had come before the four *chefs de file,* and others, though they followed, marched to different tunes. Pascal could hardly be passed off as a partisan of natural religion or Leibniz as an adversary of the *esprit de système.* So Pascal appeared as an experimental physicist with a weakness for theology and Leibniz as a mathematician who lapsed into metaphysics. Rousseau presented a particularly embarrassing problem, because his *Discours sur les sciences et les arts* undercut the whole encyclopedic enterprise. D'Alembert skirted that difficulty by remarking that Rousseau's collaboration on the *Encyclopédie* effectively repudiated his paradoxical deprecation of the value of the arts and sciences. Despite their differences, therefore, the entire population of philosophers seemed to advance in the same direction, sweeping superstition before them and carrying enlightenment in triumph, right up to the present—that is, to the *Encyclopédie* itself.

To d'Alembert it was a stirring story, though to the modern reader it may look a little unilinear. The *Discours préliminaire* abounds in violent and heroic metaphors: the breaking of chains, the rending of veils, the clashing of doctrines, the storming of citadels. Thus Descartes:

> Descartes dared at least to show intelligent minds how to throw off the yoke of scholasticism, of opinion, of authority—in a word, of prejudices and barbarism. . . . He can be thought of as a leader of conspirators who, before anyone else, had the courage to rise against a despotic and arbitrary power and who, in preparing a resounding revolution, laid the foundations of a more just and happier government, which he himself was not able to see established.[41]

This version of the past cast the *philosophes* in a heroic role. Persecuted or disdained, they battled alone, fighting for future generations who would grant them the recognition that their contemporaries had refused. D'Alembert acknowledged the existence of real generals waging real wars, but he wrote as if there were no history but intellectual history and the *philosophes* were its prophets.

This theme emerged in tandem with the cult of the *philosophe* throughout Enlightenment literature in the mid-eighteenth century. D'Alembert carried it further in his *Essai sur la société des gens de lettres et les grands,* published a year after the *Discours préliminaire.* Here again he celebrated the man of letters as the lone warrior in the struggle for civilization, and went on to issue a declaration of independence for *gens de lettres* as a social group. Although they had been humiliated and ignored, they deserved well of mankind because they had carried the cause of Enlightenment forward since the Renaissance and especially since the reign of Louis XIV, when the "philosophic spirit" began to set the tone in polite society.[42] This view of history owed a great deal to Voltaire, who had proclaimed the importance of men of letters in the *Lettres philosophiques* (1734) and then identified them with the progressive drive in history in *Le siècle de Louis XIV* (1751). Voltaire's own contributions to the *Encyclopédie,* notably in the article GENS DE LETTRES, developed the same theme and made its implications clear. History advanced through the perfection of the arts and sciences; the arts and sciences improved through the efforts of men of letters; and men of letters provided the motive force for the whole process by functioning as *philosophes.* "It is this philosophic spirit that seems to constitute the character of the men of letters."[43] The article PHILOSOPHE made much the same point. It was adapted from the celebrated tract of 1743, *Le Philosophe,* which established an ideal type—the man of letters committed to the cause of Enlightenment.[44] Throughout the 1750s, in pamphlets, plays, journals, and treatises, the *philosophes* came to be recognized or reviled as a kind of party, the secular apostles of civilization, in opposition to the champions of tradition and religious orthodoxy.[45] Many of them contributed to the *Encyclopédie*—so many, in fact, that *Encyclopédiste* and *philosophe* became virtual synonyms, and both terms crowded out their competitors—*savant, érudit, gens d'esprit*—in the semantic field covered by the general expression *gens de lettres.*[46] D'Alembert contributed to this shift in meaning by glorifying his fellow *philosophes* as the ultimate in *gens de lettres,* the heirs to Newton and Locke, at the end of the *Discours préliminaire.* The entire *Encyclopédie* proclaimed itself to be the work of "a society of men of letters" on its title page, while its friends and enemies alike identified it with *philosophie.*[47] It seemed to embody the equation civilization =*gens de lettres*=*philosophes* and to funnel all the progressive currents of history into the party of Enlightenment.

Thus the historical argument of the *Discours préliminaire* completed the work undertaken in the epistemological and morphological arguments. It legitimized the *philosophes* by identifying them with *gens de lettres* and by presenting *gens de lettres* as the moving force in history. Just as the first parts of the essay demonstrated that there was no legitimate knowledge beyond the branches of the Baconian tree, the last part showed that there were no legitimate *gens de lettres* outside the circle of *philosophes.* Part two had trimmed the tree to fit the requirements of sensationalist epistemology, and part one had excluded all knowledge without an empirical base. So nonempirical knowledge, the doctrine taught by the Church, was ruled out of bounds, and the boundary keepers turned out in part three to be the *philosophes.*

Despite their tensions and inconsistencies, the segments of the *Discours préliminaire* interlocked in the execution of a single strategy. It succeeded in dethroning the ancient queen of the sciences and in elevating philosophy to her place. Far from being a neutral compendium of information, therefore, the modern *Summa* shaped knowledge in such a way as to remove it from the clergy and to put it in the hands of intellectuals committed to the Enlightenment. The ultimate triumph of this strategy came with the secularization of education and the emergence of the modern scholarly disciplines during the nineteenth century. But the key engagement took place in the 1750s, when the Encyclopedists recognized that knowledge was power and, by mapping the world of knowledge, set out to conquer it.

APPENDIX: THREE TREES OF KNOWLEDGE

The following schematic pictures of all human knowledge come from the *Encyclopédie* of Diderot and d'Alembert reprinted from Denis Diderot's *The Encyclopedia: Selections* edited and translated by Stephen J. Grendzier (New York: Harper Torchbook, 1967), the *Cyclopaedia* of Ephraim Chambers, and *The Advancement of Learning* by Francis Bacon. The first two represent the tree of knowledge typographically as a diagram. Bacon developed his in the form of an outline from which a diagram has been drawn.

The Tree of Diderot and d'Alembert
Detailed System of Human Knowledge

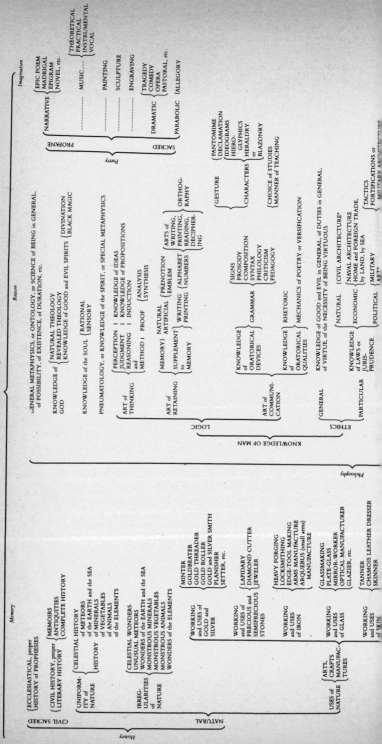

METAPHYSICS of BODIES, or GENERAL PHYSICS of EXTENSION, IMPENETRABILITY, MOVEMENT, the VOID, etc.

KNOWLEDGE OF NATURE

MATHEMATICS

PURE

- ARITHMETIC
  - NUMERICAL
  - ALGEBRA
    - ELEMENTARY
    - TRANSCENDENTAL
      - ELEMENTARY INFINITESIMAL
        - DIFFERENTIAL
        - INTEGRAL
- GEOMETRY
  - ELEMENTARY
  - TRANSCENDENTAL
    - MILITARY ARCHITECTURE, TACTICS
    - THEORY of CURVES

APPLIED

- MECHANICS
  - STATICS
    - STATICS, proper
    - HYDROSTATICS
  - DYNAMICS
    - DYNAMICS, proper
    - BALLISTICS
    - HYDRODYNAMICS
      - HYDRAULICS
      - NAVIGATION, NAVAL ARCHITECTURE
- GEOMETRIC ASTRONOMY
  - COSMOGRAPHY
  - CHRONOLOGY
  - GNOMONICS
    - URANOGRAPHY
    - GEOGRAPHY
    - HYDROGRAPHY
- OPTICS
  - OPTICS, proper
  - DIOPTRICS, PERSPECTIVE
  - CATOPTRICS
- ACOUSTICS
- PNEUMATICS
- ART OF CONJECTURING, ANALYSIS of CHANCE

PHYSICO-MATHEMATICS

PHYSICS (NATURAL PHILOSOPHY)

GENERAL

- PHYSICAL ASTRONOMY, ASTROLOGY
  - JURIDICAL ASTROLOGY
  - PHYSICAL ASTROLOGY
- METEOROLOGY

PARTICULAR

- COSMOLOGY
  - URANOLOGY
  - AEROLOGY
  - GEOLOGY
  - HYDROLOGY
  - AGRICULTURE
  - GARDENING
- BOTANY
- MINERALOGY
- ZOOLOGY
  - ANATOMY
    - SIMPLE
    - COMPARATIVE
  - PHYSIOLOGY
  - MEDICINE
    - HYGIENE
      - HYGIENE, proper
      - COSMETICS (ORTHOPEDICS)
      - ATHLETICS (GYMNASTICS)
    - PATHOLOGY
    - SEMIOTICS
    - THERAPEUTICS
      - DIET
      - SURGERY
      - PHARMACY
  - VETERINARY
  - HORSEMANSHIP
  - HUNTING
  - FISHING
  - FALCONRY

CHEMISTRY
- CHEMISTRY, proper
- METALLURGY
- ALCHEMY
- NATURAL MAGIC
  - PYROTECHNICS, DYEING, etc.

*These divisions can also be referred to the branch of mathematics which deals with their principles.

WORKING and USES of STONE, PLASTER, SLATE, etc.
- PRACTICAL ARCHITECTURE
- PRACTICAL SCULPTURE
- MASON
- ROOFER, etc.

WORKING and USES of SILK
- EXTRACTION
- THROWING
- PRODUCTS, such as VELVET
- BROCADED FABRICS, etc.

WORKING and USES of WOOL
- DRAPERY
- HOSIERY, etc.

WORKING and USES, etc.

The Two Trees of Bacon

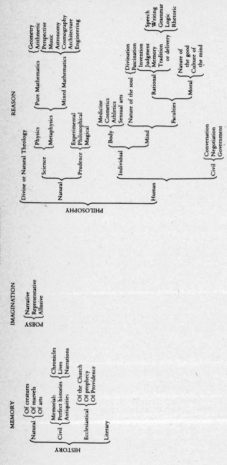

HUMAN LEARNING

MEMORY

HISTORY

Natural { Of creatures / Of marvels / Of arts

Civil { Memorials / Perfect histories { Chronicles / Lives / Narrations / Antiquities

Ecclesiastical { Of the Church / Of prophecy / Of Providence

Literary

IMAGINATION

POESY { Narrative / Representative / Allusive

REASON

PHILOSOPHY

Divine or Natural Theology

Natural { Science { Physics / Metaphysics } Pure Mathematics { Geometry / Arithmetic / Perspective / Music / Astronomy / Cosmography / Architecture / Engineering } Mixed Mathematics

Prudence { Experimental / Philosophical / Magical

Human

Individual { Body { Medicine / Cosmetics / Athletics / Sensual arts } Mind { Nature of the soul / Faculties { Rational { Divination / Fascination / Invention / Judgment / Memory / Tradition or delivery { Speech / Writing / Grammar / Logic / Rhetoric } } Moral { Nature of the good / Culture of the mind } } }

Civil { Conversation / Negotiation / Government

DIVINE LEARNING

THE NATURE OF REVELATION

Limits { Inspiration of persons / Inspiration of the Church / Use of reason

Sufficiency { Fundamental points / Perfective points

Acquisition { Methodical interpretation of Scripture / Interpretation of Scriptures solute

THE MATTER REVEALED

Belief { Faith { Nature of God / Attributes of God / Works of God } Manners { Law of nature / Moral law / Positive law }

Service { Liturgy / Government of the Church

The Tree of Chambers

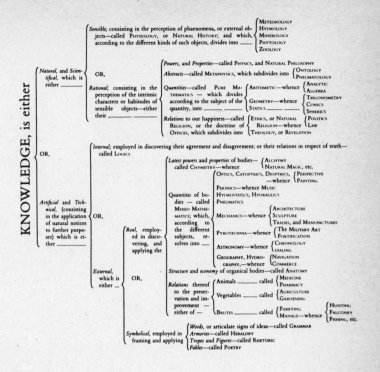

KNOWLEDGE, is either

Natural, and Scientifical, which is either ——

  Sensible; consisting in the perception of phaenomena, or external objects—called Physiology, or Natural History; and which, according to the different kinds of such objects, divides into ——
- Meteorology
- Hydrology
- Minerology
- Phytology
- Zoology

  OR,

  Rational; consisting in the perception of the intrinsic characters or habitudes of sensible objects—either their —— ——
- Powers, and Properties—called Physics, and Natural Philosophy
- Abstracts—called Metaphysics, which subdivides into
  - Ontology
  - Pneumatology
- Quantities—called Pure Mathematics — which divides according to the subject of the quantity, into ——
  - Arithmetic—whence
    - Analytic
    - Algebra
  - Geometry—whence
    - Trigonometry
    - Conics
    - Spherics
  - Statics ——
- Relations to our happiness—called Religion, or the doctrine of Offices, which subdivides into
  - Ethics, or Natural Religion—whence
    - Politics
    - Law
  - Theology, or Revelation

OR,

Artificial and Technical, (consisting in the application of natural notices to further purposes) which is either ——

  Internal; employed in discovering their agreement and disagreement; or their relations in respect of truth—called Logics

  OR,

  External, which is either ——

    Real, employed in discovering, and applying the ——
- Latest powers and properties of bodies—called Chymistry—whence
  - Alchymy
  - Natural Magic, etc.
- Quantities of bodies — called Mixed Mathematics; which, according to the different subjects, resolves into ——
  - Optics, Catoptrics, Dioptrics,—whence
    - Perspective
    - Painting
  - Phonics—whence Music
  - Hydrostatics, Hydraulics
  - Pneumatics
  - Mechanics—whence
    - Architecture
    - Sculpture
    - Trades, and Manufactures
  - Pyrotechnia—whence
    - The Military Art
    - Fortification
  - Astronomy—whence
    - Chronology
    - Dialing
  - Geography, Hydrography,—whence
    - Navigation
    - Commerce
- Structure and economy of organical bodies—called Anatomy
- Relations thereof to the preservation and improvement — either of —
  - Animals —— called
    - Medicine
    - Pharmacy
  - Vegetables —— called
    - Agriculture
    - Gardening
  - Brutes —— called
    - Farrying
    - Manage—whence
      - Hunting
      - Falconry
      - Fishing, etc.

  OR,

  Symbolical, employed in framing and applying
- Words, or articulate signs of ideas—called Grammar
- Armories—called Heraldry
- Tropes and Figures—called Rhetoric
- Fables—called Poetry

The joys of motherhood by Moreau Le Jeune

READERS RESPOND TO ROUSSEAU: THE FABRICATION OF ROMANTIC SENSITIVITY

W<small>HEN THE</small> *philosophes* set out to conquer the world by mapping it, they knew that their success would depend on their ability to imprint their world view on the minds of their readers. But how was this operation to take place? What in fact was reading in eighteenth-century France? Reading still remains a mystery, although we do it every day. The experience is so familiar that it seems perfectly comprehensible. But if we could really comprehend it, if we could understand how we construe meaning from little figures printed on a page, we could begin to penetrate the deeper mystery of how people orient themselves in the world of symbols spun around them by their culture. Even then, we could not presume to know how other people have read in other times and places. For a history or anthropology of reading would force us to confront the otherness in alien *mentalités*.[1] As an example, consider the place of reading in the death rites of Bali.

When the Balinese prepare a corpse for burial, they read stories to one another, ordinary stories from collections of their most familiar tales. They read them without stopping, twenty-four hours a day, for two or three days at a time, not because they need distraction but because of the danger of demons. Demons possess souls during the vulnerable period immediately after a death, but stories keep them out. Like Chinese boxes or English hedges, the stories contain tales within tales, so that as you enter one you run into another, passing from plot to plot every time you turn a corner, until at last you reach the core of the narrative space, which corresponds to the place occupied by the corpse within the inner courtyard of the household. Demons cannot penetrate this space because they cannot turn corners. They beat their heads helplessly against the narrative maze that the readers have built, and so reading provides a kind of defense fortification surrounding Balinese ritual. It creates a wall of words, which operates like the jamming of radio broadcasts. It does not amuse, instruct, improve, or help to while away the time: by the imbrication of narrative and the cacophony of sound, it protects souls.[2]

Now, reading may never have been so exotic in the West, although our use of the Bible—in the taking of oaths, confirmations, and other ceremonies—might look extravagant indeed to the Balinese. But the Balinese example illustrates an important point: nothing could be more misleading in an attempt to recapture the experience of reading in the past than the assumption that people have always read the way we do today. A history of reading, if it can ever be written, would chart the alien element in the way man has made sense of the world. For reading, unlike carpentry or embroidery, is not merely a skill; it is an active construal of meaning within a system of communication. To understand how the French read books in the eighteenth century is to understand how they thought—that is, those of them who could participate in the transmission of thought by means of printed symbols.

The task may seem impossible because we cannot look over the shoulders of eighteenth-century readers and question them as a modern psychologist can question a reader today. We can only ferret out whatever remains of their experience in libraries and archives, and even then we can rarely get beyond the retrospective testimony of a few great men about a few great books: Rousseau's recollections of reading Plutarch and Stendhal's of reading Rousseau. But one dossier—the only one of its kind that exists in the archives of France and Switzerland, or anywhere else as far as I know—makes it possible to follow the readings of an ordinary bourgeois in the course of an ordinary life in provincial France during the last two decades before the French Revolution.

I would like to present the dossier, making due disclaimers about its representativeness or the possibility of locating any typical Frenchman under the Old Regime. It comes from the archives of the Société Typographique de Neuchâtel (STN), an important Swiss publisher of French books in the prerevolutionary period, and it concerns Jean Ranson, a merchant from La Rochelle.[3] In 1774 when he began to correspond with the STN, Ranson was twenty-seven. He had taken over his family's business in the silk trade after the death of his father, and he lived with his mother in the heart of the Rochelais Protestant community. The Ransons were well off, though not as wealthy as some of the families who lived from the Atlantic trade. Jean had inherited 20,000 livres from his father. When he married in 1777, his wife was to bring him a dowry of 10,000 livres. After her death, a second marriage in 1788 would produce an equivalent amount (8,000 livres and an annuity based on a capital of 2,000 livres). And by then Ranson's own fortune, excluding dowries, would come to 66,000 livres—a fairly handsome sum, especially if one takes into account the slump produced in the local economy by the American war.[4] While his business prospered, Ranson occupied an increasingly important place in his town and church. He was an officer (lieutenant du prévôt de la Monnaie) of the local mint. He directed the Protestant hospital founded by his father in 1765. And during the Revolution, he supervised poor relief as president of the Bureau de bienfaisance, in addition to serving on the Conseil municipal and the Conseil des prisons once the Terror had passed.

Ranson's position in the core of La Rochelle's merchant oligarchy shows up clearly in his marriage contract of 1777. Seventy-six witnesses signed the contract; all but three of the men identified themselves as merchants (*négociants*). They included a former mayor, the director of the Chambre de commerce, two previous directors of the Chambre, and the flower of the Rochelais trading families: Raboteaus, Seignettes, Belins, Jarnacs, Roberts, and the Ransons themselves. All of Ranson's male relatives appeared in the contract as *négociants,* and so did those of his bride, Madeleine Raboteau—not surprisingly, for she was his second cousin.

Ranson's letters in Neuchâtel confirm the impression given by the documents in La Rochelle. They suggest that he was serious, responsible, hard-working, civic-minded, and rich—the very picture of the provincial bourgeois. Above all, he was Protestant. Like most members of the r.p.r. (religion prétendue réformée) in France, his parents had made a formal avowal of Catholicism in order to provide their children with a civil status, for the state did not legally recognize the existence of Protestants, though it had allowed them to hold services in La Rochelle since 1755. The Ransons also wanted their son to have a solid Calvinist education. They therefore sent him to the *collège* (secondary school) in Neuchâtel, where he studied with Frédéric-Samuel Ostervald, a learned local notable, who was to found the STN a few years later, in 1769. The French student developed a strong attachment to his Swiss master. So when he returned to La Rochelle, Ranson kept in touch by letter; and when Ostervald took up publishing, Ranson bought books from him. He bought a great many because he was an avid reader and the STN, which did a huge business as a wholesale bookdealer in addition to its printing, could supply him with almost everything he wanted. Unlike the STN's other correspondents, who were mainly booksellers, Ranson chatted about his literary interests and family life when he sent in his orders. Thus his dossier—forty-seven letters amidst the fifty thousand of the STN papers—stands out in the commercial correspondence of the STN precisely because it was so uncommercial. It provides a rare view of a reader discussing his reading while going about the everyday affairs of life in a quiet corner of the provinces.

In confronting the dossier, the first question to ask is: what did

Ranson read? One cannot reconstruct his library, because he owned a great many books that he did not order from the STN. He received some from his family and bought others from Guillaume Pavie, his favorite bookseller in La Rochelle. But his letters to the STN—which include orders for fifty-nine titles over a period of eleven years—provide enough information for one to form a general idea of his taste and reading habits. The orders fall into the following pattern (for bibliographical details, see the appendix):

I. Religion (12 titles)
   Holy Scripture, devotional works
      La Sainte Bible
      Psaumes de David
      Abrégé du catéchisme d'Ostervald
      Recueil de prières, Roques
      Nourriture de l'âme, Ostervald
      Morale évangélique, Bertrand
      Dévotions chrétiennes
   Sermons
      Année évangélique, Durand
      Sermons sur les dogmes, Chaillet
      Sermons, Bertrand
      Sermons, Perdriau
      Sermons, Romilly

II. History, travel, geography (4 titles)
      Histoire philosophique, Raynal
      Voyage en Sicile et à Malte, Brydone
      Voyage dans la Suisse, Sinner
      Description des montagnes de Neuchâtel, Ostervald

III. Belles-lettres (14 titles)
   Works
      Molière
      La Harpe
      Crébillon père
      Piron
      Rousseau (1775)
      Rousseau (1782)
      Oeuvres posthumes de Rousseau
   Novels
      Histoire de François Wills, Pratt
      Le Paysan perverti, Restif de la Bretonne

> *Adèle et Théodore*, Mme de Genlis
> *Don Quichotte*, Cervantes
> Other
> *Théâtre de société*, Mme de Genlis
> *L'An 2440*, Mercier
> *Mon bonnet de nuit*, Mercier

IV. Medicine (2 titles)
> *Soins pour la conservation des dents*, Bourdet
> *Avis contenant une remède contre la rage*

V. Children's books, pedagogy (18 titles)
> Amusement
> *Théâtre d'éducation*, Mme de Genlis
> *Nouveaux Contes moraux*, Mme Leprince de Beaumont
> *Magasin des enfants*, Mme Leprince de Beaumont
> *L'Ami des enfants*, Berquin
> *Fables de La Fontaine*
> *Les Hochets moraux*, Monget
> *Les Jeux d'enfants*, Feutry
> *Lectures pour les enfants*
> *Conversations d'Emilie*, Mme d'Epinay
> *Entretiens, drames et contes moraux*, Mme de Lafite
> Instruction
> *Annales de la vertu*, Mme de Genlis
> *Cours de géographie élémentaire*, Ostervald
> *Les Vrais Principes de la lecture*, Viard
> *Abrégé de l'histoire universelle*, Lacroze
> Pedagogy, moral education
> *Legs d'un père à ses filles*, Gregory
> *Dissertation sur l'éducation physique*, Ballexserd
> *Education morale*, Comparet
> *Instructions d'un père à ses enfants*, Trembley

VI. Other (9 titles)
> *Encyclopédie*, Diderot and d'Alembert
> *Le Socrate rustique*, Hirzel
> *Le Messager boiteux*
> *Mémoires secrets*, Bachaumont
> *Relation des derniers jours de J.-J. Rousseau*, Le Bègue de Presles
> *Discours sur l'économie politique*, Rousseau
> *Lettres de Haller contre Voltaire*
> *Tableau de Paris*, Mercier
> *Portraits des rois de France*, Mercier

The above rubrics correspond to the categories in the catalogues of eighteenth-century libraries, but they exclude a good deal of the standard fare in the literature of the time. Ranson did not order any classics, any legal works, or anything in the natural sciences, except two volumes of popular medicine. True, he may have procured books on those subjects from other sources, although he could have got them from the STN. But his main interests were limited to the following topics:

Children's literature and pedagogy. These books provide the biggest surprise in the dossier. Although they do not seem to have occupied much of a place in the (admittedly few) eighteenth-century libraries that have been studied by historians,[5] they represent almost a third of the works that Ranson ordered from the STN. Their importance can be explained by his interest in his own children, but there is more to it than that, as we shall see.

Religion. Ranson's letters indicate that he was a devout Protestant, and his books suggest that his piety shaded off into pietism. He showed no interest in theology, but he wanted Holy Scripture—a new Protestant edition of the Bible, the Psalms—and especially sermons. He kept calling in his letters for "good new sermons; France has been famished for them for a long time."[6] He favored the moralistic preaching of Swiss and Dutch divines, which occasionally summon up the religion of Rousseau's Savoyard vicar.

History, travel, and general nonfiction. Ranson's religious principles did not prevent him from ordering the *Encyclopédie* or the equally outspoken and encyclopedic *Histoire philosophique et politique des établissements et du commerce des Européens dans les deux Indes* by the abbé Raynal. Travel and history books, a favorite category in eighteenth-century libraries, often provided a screen upon which Enlightenment authors projected criticisms of contemporary society. Ranson even bought two forbidden books that made the criticism explicit: Mercier's *Tableau de Paris* and Bachaumont's *Mémoires secrets pour servir à l'histoire de la république des lettres*. But he avoided the racier and more radical works in the STN's catalogue, concentrating instead on the sentimental and moralistic books that were becoming increasingly popular during the preromantic era.

Belles-lettres. Those books stand out in Ranson's orders for fiction. Although he bought some seventeenth-century classics (Molière, Cervantes), he favored contemporary writers like Mme de Genlis, Mercier, and Restif de la Bretonne. But the one who occupied most of the space on his shelves and most of the discussions in his letters was Rousseau—"*l'Ami* Jean-Jacques" as Ranson called him, although Jean-Jacques was a friend whom he had never met and could know only through the printed word. Ranson devoured everything he could find by Rousseau. He ordered two editions of the complete works and a twelve-volume set of the posthumous writings. The first edition, published by Samuel Fauche of Neuchâtel in 1775, was the best Ranson could obtain during Rousseau's lifetime, but it contained only eleven volumes in octavo. The second, put out by the Société typographique de Genève in 1782, ran to thirty-one volumes and contained a great many previously unpublished works. Ranson ordered it unbound and stitched, "so as to have the full enjoyment of the work as soon as it arrives and not to wait upon the binder, who is very negligent."[7] He was as hungry for information about the writer as for copies of the writings. "I thank you, Monsieur," he wrote to Ostervald in 1775, "for what you were so kind as to tell me about *l'Ami* Jean-Jacques. You give me great pleasure every time you can send me anything about him."[8] Ranson was the perfect Rousseauistic reader. But how did he read?

To pass from the *what* to the *how* of reading is an extremely difficult step. One can approach it indirectly by posing a second preliminary question: how did Ranson look at a book when he took it in his hands? Books as physical objects were very different in the eighteenth century from what they are today, and their readers perceived them differently.

Ranson's perceptions can be surmised from his letters to the STN, for he often discussed the physical aspects of books. For example, before undertaking a new edition of the Bible, Ostervald sounded him out on the format that would be preferred in La Rochelle; and after consulting his friends Ranson replied, "Everyone pronounced in favor of the in-folio. It is more majestic and more imposing in the eyes of the multitude for whom this divine book is intended."[9] Ranson showed a great concern for typographical niceties in discussing a project to reprint a *Cours de géographie élémentaire:* "I hope it will be done with more handsome type and finer paper than that of the third edition, which in those respects is far inferior to the second edition printed in Bern."[10] He especially cared about the raw material of books. "Handsome paper so far as can be had," he reiterated in his orders.[11] And he emphasized the importance of harmonizing paper, print, and binding. When Ostervald asked him to inspect some books that the STN had recovered from a bankrupt dealer in La Rochelle, he reported: "How could you have spent three livres fifteen sous on the binding for books printed so badly on such bad paper, which you sell for fifteen sous in sheets? I might eventually be able to find someone willing to take those in basan [a relatively cheap sheepskin binding], but I have little hope for the others."[12]

Such comments were common in the eighteenth century. The STN often received letters from customers who complained about sloppy printing and from booksellers who worried that the choice of a type face or a kind of paper would make a book unsellable. For example, after offering the *Système de la nature* to Pavie, Ranson's bookseller in La Rochelle, the STN received a reply indicating that the material quality of the book mattered as much as its intellectual content:

> I know of four editions of the *Système de la nature*. The first is from Holland, a magnificent edition. The second and the third are quite comparable. The fourth, from which I include a sample sheet, has been execrably produced, both in the printing, which is full of mistakes, and in the paper, which is detestable. I wouldn't give thirty sous for it. If the one you are offering is like the fourth edition, you needn't bother to send it. You can easily compare them from the sample. But as you say that yours is from a very beautiful edition, I presume it is from one of the first three. In that case, you can send me ten copies, in sheets or stitched.[13]

This typographical consciousness has disappeared now that books are mass-produced for a mass audience. In the eighteenth century they were made by hand. Every sheet of paper was produced individually by an elaborate procedure and differed from every other sheet in the same volume. Every letter, word, and line was composed according to an art that gave the artisan a chance to express his individuality. Books themselves were individuals, each copy possessing its own character. The reader of the Old Regime approached them with care, for he paid attention to the stuff of literature as well as its message. He would finger the paper in order to gauge its weight, translucence, and elasticity (a whole vocabulary existed to describe the esthetic qualities of paper, which usually represented at least half the manufacturing cost of a book before the nineteenth century.) He would study the design of the type, examine the spacing, check the register, evaluate the layout, and scrutinize the evenness of the printing. He would sample a book the way we might taste a glass of wine; for he looked *at* the impressions on the paper, not merely across them to their meaning. And once he had possessed himself fully of a book, in all its physicality, he would settle down to read it.

That brings us back to our initial question: how did Ranson read? The answer may seem as far away as ever, but we can pursue it down another path, one that leads toward an understanding of reading as it was taught in eighteenth-century schools and depicted in eighteenth-century textbooks. Fortunately, Ranson mentioned his own favorite textbook in his letters. He ordered several copies of it, for the use of his family and his friends. Its title (translated into English) suggests that it conveyed a view of the world as well as a means of mastering the printed word: *The true principles of reading, of spelling, and of French pronunciation, followed by a little treatise on punctuation, the first elements of grammar and of French prosody, and by different reading selections suitable for providing simple and easy notions of all the branches of our knowledge,* by Nicolas-Antoine Viard.

Viard's textbook probably left a mark on several generations of French readers. The Bibliothèque Nationale contains five editions of it from the eighteenth century and nineteen editions from the period 1800 to 1830. It seems doubtful that Ranson himself learned to read from the textbook, as the earliest surviving copy comes from 1763, when he had already reached the age of fifteen. But his letters indicate that he used it during his schooling in Neuchâtel—presumably as an aid for reviewing grammar—and that he meant to use it to teach his own children how to read. One aspect of it, however, was insupportable to him—its ultraorthodox Catholicism, which stands out clearly in some of the reading selections.[14] Ostervald must have expurgated those passages for the students in Neuchâtel, because in ordering the book Ranson specified that he wanted "some copies of the *Principes de la lecture* by Viard that I would be glad to have with the changes you have made in it."[15] And in a later letter he stressed that he was ordering the *"Principes de lecture corrigés pour les réformés."*[16] I have not been able to locate this Protestant Viard, but the classical Viard, minus some of the religious texts among its reading exercises, seems adequate as a starting point for studying eighteenth-century reading.

Viard himself starts with the smallest units of sound. He shows how they are linked with letters, syllables, and words, progressing from the simple to the complex and avoiding all irregularities, so that the connections between sounds and typographical symbols become firmly fixed in the student's mind. Reading must be learned orally, he insists; writing can come later. "The entire operation consists in simplifying the sounds and in not doing any spelling; it is the only way to make the combination of sounds meaningful to children."[17] Viard requires some memorizing; but for all his drills and scrambled alphabets, his main concern is to get the child to think: "The memory easily retains things read several times; so after having had a child read a short passage, one can begin to question him about it and to help him understand it."[18] Reading is not passive for Viard. He does not see it as a mechanistic process of deciphering but as an active construction of the intellect.

Nonetheless, Viard will disappoint anyone who consults him in the hope of finding a contemporary strategy for understanding books. He says nothing about *explication de texte* or ways of formulating interpretations. Wholly absorbed with the problem of extracting sense from combinations of letters, he concentrates on exercises like the following:[19]

Les bons livres s'impriment   Les mauvais livres se suppriment
      soigneusement.   promptement.*

---

* This is a drill to help the pupil overcome inconsistencies between sounds and combinations of letters, in this case the suffix *ment*. Although the point gets lost in translation, the phrases may be rendered in English as follows: "Good books are printed carefully. Bad books are suppressed promptly."

For Viard, understanding means mastery of words. If the reader can get the simplest elements straight, he can make sense of entire treatises; for meaning inheres in small semantic units rather than in grammar or in structure. Viard therefore remains at the level of the word, as if the understanding of texts would come of itself.

He does provide some texts, but they hardly illustrate his point; for they are saturated with ideological undercurrents. Thus "La Salutation Angélique" and "La Confession des péchés" in his reading exercises are stripped of ambiguous syllables but loaded down with Counter-Reformation doctrine. And other selections—"Blason," "Généalogie," "Politique," "Le Monde"—read like apologies for the status quo in social and political questions. Viard expected the teacher to bring out the significance of such subjects in discussions with the pupils: "The object is to give the children some simple notions about the arts, sciences, religion, war, trade, and everything else about which one needs to have clear and precise ideas. It is important for the child that the master pause and consider with him each of these subjects, turning them over so to speak beneath his gaze. Each will germinate like a seed, which if cultivated skillfully will make his mind rich and fertile."[20] There is no mistaking the conservative character of the text, but the metaphor could have come from *Emile*. Like Rousseau, Viard insists on the importance of patience and gentleness on the part of the teacher. Instead of being crammed with useless information, children should learn according to the natural development of their faculties. Above all, they should learn to be good. For reading is a kind of spiritual exercise: it trains one not for literature but for life.

Despite its orthodoxy, then, Viard's primer might well have seemed attractive to a Rousseauistic reader. But it does not reveal much about the actual process of reading. In fact, it suggests that children learned to sound out words in eighteenth-century France pretty much as they do today. Rousseau himself had no patience for such pedagogy. He insisted in *Emile* that the child learn to read late, when he was ripe for learning, without artificial exercises: "Any method will do for him."[21] Yet reading is a theme that appears everywhere in Rousseau's works. It obsessed him. If we can understand his understanding of it, we might be able to get beyond the point where Viard left us and to find a third angle from which to attack the problem of eighteenth-century reading.

Rousseau discussed his own induction into reading in the first pages of the *Confessions*:

> I don't know how I learned to read; I only remember my first readings and their effect on me: it is from that time that I date without interruption my consciousness of myself. My mother had left some novels. [She had died a few days after Jean-Jacques's birth.] My father and I began to read them after supper, at first only with the idea of using some amusing books for me to practice reading. But soon we took such a strong interest in them that we read without a break, taking turns throughout the whole night. We could never stop before reaching the end of a volume. And sometimes my father, hearing the swallows at the crack of dawn, would say shamefacedly, "Let's go to bed; I am more of a child than you."[22]

Having exhausted their stock of novels, they took volumes of Bossuet, Molière, La Bruyère, Ovid, and Plutarch from the libraries of the relatives of Jean-Jacques's mother, who came from a more cultivated milieu than his father, a watchmaker. While the father worked in his shop, the son read to him and they discussed the readings. Jean-Jacques's imagination caught fire, especially when he declaimed from Plutarch. He became the heroes that he read about, and he played out the dramas of antiquity in his Genevan apartment as if he had lived them in Athens and Rome. In retrospect it seemed to him that this experience had marked him for life. On the one hand, he never learned to distinguish between literature and reality, having filled his mind with "bizarre and romantic notions, which experience and reflection never cured me of." On the other, he developed a fiercely independent spirit: "From this absorption in reading and the talks to which it gave rise between my father and me, I developed that free and republican spirit, that proud and indomitable character, so incompatible with subjection and servitude, that has been the torment of my life."[23]

The characters in Rousseau's great novel, *La Nouvelle Héloïse*, throw themselves into reading with the same abandon. Because it is an epistolary novel, the plot unfolds through the exchange of letters. Living cannot be distinguished from reading, nor loving from the writing of love letters. Indeed, the lovers teach one another how to read just as they teach one another love. Saint-Preux instructs Julie: "To read little and to meditate a great deal upon our reading, or to talk it over extensively between ourselves, that is the way to thoroughly digest it."[24] At the same time, he learns to read from her. Like the tutor of Emile, he devises a "method" especially suited to the independent spirit of his pupil: ". . . to you who put into your reading more than you take out of it and whose active mind makes another and sometimes better book of the book you read. In this way we will exchange our ideas. I will tell you what others have thought about the subject; you will tell me what you yourself think about it; and I will often leave the lesson better instructed than you."[25] This was how Rousseau learned to read from his father—and how he later read with Mme de Warens: "Sometimes I read beside her. I took the greatest pleasure in it; it exercised me in reading well. . . . We read La Bruyère together: it pleased her more than La Rochefoucauld. . . . When she drew morals from the text, she sometimes lost the thread a little in her reverie; but kissing her from time to time on the mouth or the hands, I was patient, and her interruptions did not bother me."[26] Reading, living, and loving, they were inseparable to the writer who lived more intensely in his imagination than he did in the rounds of daily life.

Thus the great enemy of "method" really had one of his own, the one he had learned from his father. It consisted in "digesting" books so thoroughly that they became absorbed in life. But Rousseau did not merely describe reading as he and the characters of his books experienced it. He directed the reading of his readers. He showed them how to approach his books. He guided them into the texts, oriented them by his rhetoric, and made them play a certain role. Rousseau even attempted to teach his readers how to read and, through reading, tried to touch their inner lives. This strategy required a break with conventional literature. Instead of hiding behind the narrative and pulling strings to manipulate the characters in the manner of Voltaire, Rousseau threw himself into his works and expected the reader to do the same. He transformed the relation between writer and reader, between reader and text. If we can form an adequate idea of this transformation, we should be able to picture the ideal reader envisaged by Rousseau and then to compare that ideal with an actual individual, the reader Jean Ranson.

Consider two key texts, the dual prefaces to *La Nouvelle Héloïse,* where Rousseau discusses reading and the way to read his novel at some length. Both prefaces—one is a brief introduction to the book, the other is a dialogue in which Rousseau represents himself defending his work to a skeptical critic—confront an objection that could be expected from any reader of Rousseau: how could Jean-Jacques do anything as wicked as to publish a novel? The question may seem absurd today, but it fit squarely into the preoccupations of an age in which novels were seen as a moral danger, especially when they dealt with love and their readers were young ladies. Rousseau had won notoriety by denouncing all the arts and sciences for their effect on morals. Yet here he was, shamelessly displaying his name on the title page of the most corrupting kind of literature—not merely a novel, but a story about a tutor who seduces his pupil and later joins her husband in a *ménage à trois!*

Rousseau met the objection head-on in the first sentence of the first preface: "Theaters are necessary for large cities and novels for corrupt peoples."[27] The argument echoed his *Lettre à d'Alembert sur les spectacles,* which condemned theatres, novels, and all modern literature, including the work of the Encyclopedists, for undermining civic virtue in healthy republics like Geneva, yet conceded that they could be of some use in decadent monarchies like France. Rousseau wrote both *La Nouvelle Héloïse* and the *Lettre à d'Alembert* during the great crisis of 1757/58, which resulted in his break with Diderot and the party of the *philosophes.* But both books expressed a theme—the corruptive nature of contemporary culture—that went back to the work that first made Rousseau famous, the *Discours sur les sciences et les arts* (1750). It was a theme that weighed on his whole life and that had to be faced at the point of entry into the story of the modern Héloïse. This great novelist had always preached against novels. How then could he write one?

Rousseau's reply in the prefaces is deceptively simple: "This novel is not a novel."[28] It is a collection of letters, which Rousseau presents in the role of an editor, as the subtitle and "editor's" name on the title page make clear: "*Letters of two lovers living in a small town at the foot of the Alps.* Collected and published by J.-J. Rousseau." But that pretense would satisfy no one, least of all Rousseau, who was proud of his work and could not refrain from talking about it: "Although I have only the title of an editor here, I have worked on this book myself, and I do not hide that fact. Have I done the whole thing, and is the entire correspondence a fiction? Readers from high society [*gens du monde*], what does it matter to you? For you it is certainly fiction."[29] Behind this *coquetterie,* Rousseau strategically shifts the question from the role played by him to the role expected of the reader. The book will seem contrived to members of the socio-cultural elite (*le monde*, an expression charged with meaning for Rousseau and other men of letters); but to those who can read it with innocent eyes, it will appear as truth itself. Where does Rousseau locate this truth? As far away from salon society as possible: "This book is not made to circulate in society [*le monde*] and is suitable for very few readers. . . . It will displease religious bigots, libertines, and *philosophes*."[30] The ideal reader must be able to divest himself of the conventions of literature as well as the prejudices of society. Only then can he enter into the story in the manner prescribed by Rousseau: "Whoever resolves to read these letters must arm himself with patience about the incorrectness of their language, the overblown character of their style, the ordinary quality of the ideas expressed in their inflated phrasing. He must say to himself in advance that those who wrote them are not French, not sophisticates, not academicians nor *philosophes* but rather provincials, foreigners, recluses, young people, almost children, who in their romantic imaginations take the innocent frenzy of their minds to be philosophy."[31]

These distinctions have a social and political edge to them, for Rousseau saw literature as an element in a power system peculiar to the Old Regime. He rejected it, all of it, *belles-lettres* along with the *beau monde;* and in doing so he broke with the *philosophes*. In his eyes, Diderot, d'Alembert, and the other Encyclopedists belonged to the fashionable world of theaters and salons. Philosophy itself had become a fashion, the ultimate in Parisian sophistication; and as it spread beyond Paris, it endangered the healthiest segments of the body politic. D'Alembert's article on Geneva in the *Encyclopédie* epitomized this process. By deriding the old-fashioned puritans who opposed Voltaire's project to establish a theater in their city, it showed that the cultural cancer was attacking the last bastion of virtue, Calvin's republic—and Rousseau's. The article cut "Jean-Jacques Rousseau, citizen of Geneva"[32] to the quick, not merely because he identified with his fatherland but also because the disease that threatened it had also ravaged him. Had he not sunk deeper into depravity with every step that led away from his original innocence? Had he not attempted to break into *le monde?* And had he not used music, theater, literature, and philosophy as a means of entry? He had lived the formula he invented: culture = corruption. So he would invent another cultural form, an antiliterary literature, in which he could defend the cause of virtue by appealing directly to the unsophisticated. Rousseau found his prophetic voice in *La Nouvelle Héloïse*, but he spoke only to those who had ears to hear—which in fact meant those with eyes to read.

La Nouvelle Héloïse therefore required a new kind of reading, one that would succeed in proportion to the reader's spiritual distance from Parisian high society. "In moral matters, I hold that there is no reading that can be of use to society people [*gens du monde*]. . . . The further one moves away from business, big cities, crowded social gatherings, the more the obstacles [to morally effective reading] diminish. At a certain point, books can have some usefulness. When one lives alone, one does not hurry through books in order to parade one's reading; one varies them less and meditates on them more. And as their effect is less mitigated by outside influences, they have a greater influence within."[33] Here was a reply to Diderot's terrible phrase, which had precipitated his break with Rousseau: "Only the evil man lives alone."[34] Rousseau's rhetoric opened up a new channel of communication between two lonely beings, the writer and the reader, and rearranged their roles. Rousseau would be Jean-Jacques, citizen of Geneva and prophet of virtue. The reader would be a provincial youth, a country gentleman, a woman stifled by the refined conventions of society, an artisan excluded from refinement—it did not matter, provided he or she could love virtue and understand the language of the heart.

Thus Rousseau did not demand that the reader try to turn himself into a Swiss peasant but rather that he reject the dominant values of literature and society. Anyone who wanted to read the lovers' letters as they deserved to be read would have to place himself spiritually "at the foot of the Alps," where literary niceties made no sense. The letters were not written to "please" in Paris— *plaire* being a refinement idealized in the seventeenth century—but to give free rein to feeling.

If you read them as the work of an author who wants to please [*plaire*], or who takes pride in his writing, they are detestable. But take them for what they are, and judge them according to their kind. Two or three young people, simple but sensitive, speak to one another about the interests of their hearts. They never think of trying to cut a fine figure in each other's eyes. They know and love each other too well for vanity [*amour-propre,* another key word for Rousseau] to have a place in their exchanges. They are children; should they think as adults? They are foreigners; should they write correctly? They are recluses; should they be familiar with the ways of society [*le monde*]? . . . They know nothing of such things. They know how to love; they refer everything to their passion.[35]

The letters of Julie and Saint-Preux lack refinement because they are genuine. They have nothing to do with literature because they are true. Like music, they communicate pure emotion from one soul to another: "They are no longer letters; they are hymns."[36] Rousseau offered the reader access to this kind of truth, but only if he would put himself in the place of the correspondents and become in spirit a provincial, a recluse, a foreigner, and a child. In order to do so, the reader would have to jettison the cultural baggage of the adult world and learn to read all over again, as Jean-Jacques had read with his father, who knew how to become "more of a child than you." Thus Rousseauistic reading would explode the conventions established at the height of the classical period by Boileau. It would revolutionize the relation between reader and text, and open the way to romanticism. At the same time, it would revive a way of reading that seems to have prevailed in the sixteenth and seventeenth centuries: reading in order to absorb the unmediated Word of God. Rousseau demanded to be read as if he were a prophet of divine truth, and Ranson understood him in that way: thus the emphasis on religious literature in Ranson's orders did not contradict his Rousseauism but rather complemented it. What set Rousseauistic reading apart from its religious antecedents—whether they were Calvinist, Jansenist, or pietistic—was the summons to read the most suspect form of literature, the novel, as if it were the Bible. By exploiting this paradox, Rousseau would regenerate *le monde*.

But the new style of reading ran into another paradox, as it struggled for expression in the preface to *La Nouvelle Héloïse*. Rous-

seau insisted on the authenticity of the lovers' letters, but he wrote
them himself, using all the devices of a rhetoric that he alone could
command. He presented his text as the unmediated communication of two souls—"It is thus that the heart speaks to the
heart"[37]—yet the actual communication took place between the
reader and Rousseau himself. This ambiguity threatened to undercut the new relation between writer and reader that he wanted to
establish. On the one hand, it tended to falsify Rousseau's position
by making him appear as a mere editor. On the other, it left the
reader looking on from the sideline, virtually as a voyeur. To be
sure, such ambiguities, and a heavy dose of voyeurism, exist in all
epistolary novels. The genre had been established long ago in
France and was undergoing a revival, thanks to the popularity of
Richardson. But Rousseau could not hide behind the conventions
of the genre because he meant his text to be nonliterary and "true."
He could not deny his authorship of the letters without offending
truth, and he could not acknowledge the careful craftsmanship that
went into them without spoiling their effect.

The problem may look like a false dilemma to the modern reader,
but it obsessed Rousseau's contemporaries. Many readers of *La
Nouvelle Héloïse* believed and wanted to believe in the authenticity
of the letters. Rousseau understood their need in advance. So he
had his questioner, the sophisticated man of letters "N" in the
second preface or *préface dialoguée,* return again and again to the
query: "Is this correspondence real, or is it a fiction?"[38] "N" cannot let go of it; it "torments" him, he explains.[39] By letting him
give vent to his doubts, Rousseau appeared to square with the reader
and to face up to the paradox inherent in the epistolary genre.
Although he could not resolve the paradox, he seemed to subsume
it in an attempt to reach a higher truth. He asked the reader to
suspend his disbelief and to cast aside the old way of reading in
order to enter into the letters as if they really were the effusion of
innocent hearts at the foot of the Alps. This kind of reading required a leap of faith—of faith in the author, who somehow must
have suffered through the passions of his characters and forged
them into a truth that transcends literature.

Ultimately, then, the power of Rousseau's novel derived from
the force of his personality. He initiated a new conception of the

author as Prometheus, one that would go far in the nineteenth century. So in *La Nouvelle Héloïse* instead of hiding behind the scene, he strode to the front of the stage. He related everything in the prefaces to himself, his "I". And after refusing to deny that he might have written the letters, he told "N" that he is their editor:

> R [Rousseau]: Does a man of integrity hide himself when he speaks to the public? Does he dare to publish something that he will not dare acknowledge? I am the editor of this book, and I will name myself in it as editor.
> N: You will name yourself in it? You?
> R: I, myself.
> N: What! You will put your name to it?
> R: Yes, Monsieur.
> N: Your real name? *Jean-Jacques Rousseau* spelled out in full?
> R: *Jean-Jacques Rousseau* spelled out in full.[40]

Rousseau then explained that he not only intended to assume responsibility for what he wrote, but "I do not want to be considered any better than I am."[41] It was the same position that he would adopt in the *Confessions.* By confessing his moral failures, he underlined his honesty and at the same time created an ideal Jean-Jacques who could speak directly from the heart to the ideal reader envisioned in the text. Author and reader triumphed together over the artifice of literary communication. This metaliterary impulse, which was to find its ultimate expression in the *Confessions,* drove Rousseau to fly his Jean-Jacques openly over *La Nouvelle Héloïse*— an unusual gesture in an age when authors rarely put their names on novels. But Rousseau did not aspire to be novelesque. He wanted to reach through literature into life, his own and that of his readers.

The impact of Rousseauism therefore owed a great deal to Rousseau. He spoke to the most intimate experiences of his readers and encouraged them to see through to the Jean-Jacques behind the texts. It hardly seems surprising that many of them tried to make contact with him in person—so many that he needed a trap door to escape those who sought him out in his retreat on the Ile Saint-Pierre. Rousseau broke down the barriers separating writer from reader. He created the art that he recommended in *Emile:* "the art of speaking to those who are absent and of hearing them, the art of communicating to those far away, without any mediation, our feelings, will, desires."[42] He developed that art, but how did his readers respond to it—real readers, not merely those envisioned in the text? That question brings us back to Jean Ranson.

From the beginning of his correspondence, Ranson made it clear that "l'Ami Jean-Jacques" fascinated him as much as Rousseau's writing. Ostervald was well placed to satisfy that interest, because the Swiss publisher sometimes made business trips to Paris, and after gathering literary gossip he sent reports to his young friend in La Rochelle. Unfortunately, Ostervald's side of the correspondence is missing, but it probably contained some accounts of meetings with Rousseau; for Ranson kept calling for news of his *ami* and complained when it failed to arrive: "What! You have seen *l'Ami* Jean-Jacques and you do not tell me all about it! I hope you have only postponed the report for another letter."[43] Ranson was equally anxious to receive Rousseau's works. Much as he fussed about the quality of the printing, he cared most of all about the authenticity of the texts. "One thing that makes me hesitate to purchase more of them," he explained to Ostervald, "is the disavowal that that great unhappy man made of all the editions that were being sold two or three years ago; he would acknowledge only the first edition, which he helped to produce himself and which has been out of print for years."[44] In the spring of 1777, when Ostervald was about to leave for another trip to Paris, Ranson wrote, "No doubt you will see *l'Ami* Jean-Jacques. Please find out from him whether we will be able to have a good edition of his works. And I beg of you especially to send me some word about his health before you return."[45] The man and the works, they always went together in Ranson's letters.

Ranson also accompanied the references to Rousseau with remarks on his own life. In June, 1777, when he was about to turn thirty, he wrote, "I am sure, Monsieur, that you will be happy to hear that I am about to end my bachelorhood. I have chosen and have been accepted by a Miss Raboteau, my cousin, the sister of the young lady who M. Rother of Nantes married last year. She is also, on her father's side, a relative of Jarnac to the same degree that I am. The happy character of this dear person combined with all considerations of propriety makes me hope in this commitment for the most [here there is a hole in the paper]" Then he moved directly to his favorite subject: "Although I have begged you again and again, Monsieur, to send me news about *l'Ami* Jean-Jacques, in whom I take the deepest interest, you are so cruel as to say nothing about him. Haven't you had a chance to see him and to benefit from a few words with him in Paris? Tell me about it at the first possible moment, I insist, if you don't want me to bear a grudge."[46]

Ranson's association of his marriage and his *ami* did not take place by accident. In his next letter he explained:

I send you my warmest thanks for your good wishes concerning my new estate. My wife is as touched as I am by what you wrote to me on her account. I hope it will not be difficult for me to fulfill my duties toward this dear spouse in the fashion that you prescribe and that I have prescribed for myself. If I have been able to do without women until the age of nearly thirty, though I have certainly never looked upon the fair sex with an indifferent eye, I am sure that one will be enough for me for the rest of my life. Everything that *l'Ami* Jean-Jacques has written about the duties of husbands and wives, of mothers and fathers, has had a profound effect on me; and I confess to you that it will serve me as a rule in any of those estates that I should occupy."[47]

The reference to Rousseau remained implicit in a letter that Ranson wrote a few months later. This time he was the one sending congratulations: "I congratulate you warmly, you and Monsieur and Madame Bertrand [Ostervald's son-in-law and daughter], on the happy birth of your granddaughter, which no doubt the mother will nurse herself as she has done for her other children."[48] At the end of the year, Ranson learned that he, too, was to become a father. He prepared himself for his new responsibilities by reading: "Please procure for me, if possible, an excellent dissertation on the physical education of children published by M. Ballexserd of Geneva. I am about to become a father, and am thinking of how I can best fulfill my duties."[49] We have moved from a traditional world, where children are raised according to family lore, to the world of Doctor Spock, where they grow up under instructions from the printed word. Ranson sought guidance above all from Rousseau, the prophet of breast-feeding and maternal love. In May,

1778, he wrote joyfully, "My wife has made me the father of a girl, who is doing beautifully and who is being nursed by her mother with the greatest success."[50]

But soon afterward he learned that his spiritual guide had died.

So, Monsieur, we have lost the sublime Jean-Jacques. How it pains me never to have seen nor heard him. I acquired the most extraordinary admiration for him by reading his books. If some day I should travel near Ermenonville, I shall not fail to visit his grave and perhaps to shed some tears on it. Tell me, I pray, what you think of this famous man, whose fate has always aroused the most tender feelings in me, while Voltaire often provoked my indignation. . . . He said some years ago that none of the new editions of his works were correct, but rather that all were full of falsifications, cuts, and changes, even the edition of Rey, which he complained about bitterly. I hope he has left behind some manuscripts that will make it possible for one to have an edition free of all those faults. If you learn anything about that, or anything else concerning Rousseau, please share it with me. You would give me the greatest pleasure.

Then, without breaking stride, comes the news of the family: "We are very touched, my wife and I, by the kind things you say about the birth of our daughter, whom the mother continues to nurse with the greatest success and without feeling the slightest discomfort."[51]

Ranson went on to talk about Rousseau in a long string of letters. He wanted to know everything about the life and death of his *ami*. He devoured every anecdote he could get his hands on, comparing versions in the *Courier de l'Europe, L'Année littéraire,* the *Mercure de France,* the *Annales* of Linguet, and many other periodicals. He hung an engraving of the tomb at Ermenonville on the wall of his study. He bought up eulogies, pamphlets, and even scraps of unpublished manuscripts that were attributed to Rousseau and began to circulate after his death. Ranson also collected rumors, especially those that passed through the shop of his bookseller, Pavie. Some said that Jean-Jacques had died from poisoning. But was it not more probably from stomach trouble, as the *Courier de l'Europe* had claimed? Or did it come as a result of the agony produced by the disappearance of the manuscript of the *Confessions*? The Keeper of the Seals was said to have procured a copy and to have sum-

The tomb of Rousseau at Ermenonville

moned Jean-Jacques to explain how it could be circulating, since he had promised never to release it. Thérèse Levasseur must have sold it behind his back. They needed money desperately at the end, when Jean-Jacques had given up copying music. But why in the world had no one come forth to save them from their misery? Had not Jean-Jacques offered in an open letter of February, 1777, to leave his manuscripts to any patron who would rescue them? The pension that Thérèse received from Marc Michel Rey—and Ranson knew all about the details of Rousseau's domestic life—did not provide enough for them to live on. Perhaps Thérèse would turn to Rey for the publication of the manuscripts now that her husband was dead. According to Pavie, some Parisian booksellers were already offering manuscript copies of the *Confessions* for fifteen louis.

What a treasure those *Confessions* must be! Ranson burned with the desire to read them and everything else that Rousseau had left behind. He wanted to know every secret of his mentor's soul, every detail of his past, every product of his pen, down to the annotations of his music, which Ranson especially requested from the STN. The letters between La Rochelle and Neuchâtel are full of references to plans for the publication of Rousseau's works because the STN was competing with the Société typographique de Genève and a pack of other publishers who wanted to get their hands on the manuscripts left with the marquis de Girardin and Alexandre Du Peyrou. The scramble to put out a full edition of Rousseau's works produced the last great free-for-all in the publishing history of the Old Regime. But to Ranson it did not matter terribly whether the Genevans or his friends in Neuchâtel should win the prize, provided that a complete and accurate edition should appear as soon as possible. He wanted above all to possess the complete Rousseau, to absorb it into his inner world, and to express it in his daily life.

Thus the references to Rousseau continued to appear in his letters as a kind of gloss on the reports about his family. In September, 1778, he linked a long discussion of Rousseau's death and posthumous works to some reflections on the new baby:

> I can see from the tenderness that my daughter inspires in me how much the happiness of children must influence that of fathers. How I wish that I knew more, so that I could give my own children lessons;

for no master can teach with the dedication of a father. But if I can teach them the lesson of good morals, if they repay my efforts in that respect alone, I can do without the rest. I speak of my children, and I have only a five-month-old daughter.[52]

A son was to come in February, 1780, another one in December, 1782. The Ransons named the first Jean Isaac after his maternal grandfather. They named the second Emile. That gesture represented a significant break with family tradition, for the Ransons and Raboteaus had almost always kept to a limited stock of family names—a few Jeans, Pierres, and Pauls among a profusion of the Old Testament variety favored by Protestants: Abraham, Isaac, Elie, Benjamin, Samuel, and Joachim.[53] Little Emile was to be a living testimony to his parents' faith in Rousseau's doctrine of education, and human nature in general.

As the children arrived, Ranson sent off announcements of their births accompanied with remarks on their nursing and discussions of Rousseau. He was aware of this double obsession: "I ask your pardon for going on so often and at such length about Jean-Jacques, but I like to tell myself that the enthusiasm he inspires in me, and which is produced entirely by his own enthusiasm for virtue, will excuse me in your eyes and that it will compel you to write to me from time to time about this friend of virtue."[54] And later, in connection with his daughter: "How much pleasure I take in watching this young creature grow! And how much happiness I will have if she continues to live and if, by a good education, I can make the most of the goodness of her nature. You are a father, Monsieur, and so you will excuse my dwelling on such details, which would have no interest for a man who isn't one."[55]

Ranson's approach to fatherhood explains the importance of the pedagogical and children's literature in his orders with the STN. Those books represented a new attitude toward children and a new desire to oversee their education on the part of parents.[56] A century earlier, Charles Perrault had produced his tales of Mother Goose to amuse an audience of salon sophisticates. Ranson's favorite authors, notably Mme de Genlis and Mme Leprince de Beaumont, wrote for the children themselves and did so not merely to amuse them but to develop their virtue. The moralistic emphasis of the new children's books stands out in their titles: *Moral playthings, or tales for infants* and *Reading for children, or a selection of short tales equally suited to amuse them and to make them love virtue.* It also dominated the new primers for parents, like *Moral education, or a reply to the question: how should one govern the mind and heart of a child in order to make him develop into a happy and useful adult?* These books began from the Rousseauistic premise that children were naturally good and went on to develop a pedagogy saturated with Rousseauism. In addition to them, Ranson owned at least two copies of *Emile.* The remarkable thing, however, is not that he read this or that treatise on children but that he read any treatises at all. He entered into parenthood through reading and relied on books in order to make his offspring into so many Emiles and Emilies.

This behavior expressed a new attitude toward the printed word. Ranson did not read in order to enjoy literature but to cope with life and especially family life, exactly as Rousseau intended. Seen through his letters, Ranson and his wife appear as the perfect image of the readers to whom Jean-Jacques addressed *La Nouvelle Héloïse*: "I like to imagine two spouses reading this collection together, finding in it fresh encouragement to continue with their daily work and perhaps new ways to make it useful," Rousseau wrote in the second preface. "How could they contemplate the picture of a happy household without wanting to imitate such a sweet model?"[57] Ranson modeled his household in just that way, by reading Rousseau as Rousseau wanted to be read. "My wife sends you her respects," he wrote to Ostervald in September, 1780. "She continues, thank God, to enjoy good health, as does her dear baby, who is doing very well on his mommy's milk. His older sister, a big girl of thirty months, now shows its influence by the best of temperaments. Virtuous Jean-Jacques! It is to thee that I owe this tender obligation."[58]

The rest of the letters in the dossier have the same tone—earnest, intimate, sentimental, and moralistic—the tone set by Rousseau for readers everywhere, however much they differed in their circumstances. Nothing could be more ordinary, perhaps, but the significance of Ranson's letters consists in their ordinariness. They show how Rousseauism penetrated into the everyday world of an unexceptional bourgeois and how it helped him make sense of the things that mattered most in his existence: love, marriage, parenthood—the big events of a little life and the stuff that life was made of everywhere in France.[59]

Ranson's way of reading is unthinkable today. And *La Nouvelle Héloïse* is unreadable—if not for everyone, at least for a great many "ordinary" readers of the modern variety, who cannot wade through six volumes of sentiment unrelieved by any episodes of violence, explicit sex, or anything much in the way of plot. The sentiment overwhelmed Rousseau's readers in the eighteenth century—thousands of them, not merely Jean Ranson. By studying their responses, we can put his case in perspective and get a broader view of the gap that separates the readers of the Old Regime from the readers of today.

Although we have very few statistics on book sales under the Old Regime, it is clear that *La Nouvelle Héloïse* was perhaps the biggest best-seller of the century. The demand for copies outran the supply so badly that booksellers rented it out by the day and even by the hour, charging twelve sous for sixty minutes with one volume, according to L.-S. Mercier. At least seventy editions were published before 1800—probably more than for any other novel in the previous history of publishing. True, the most sophisticated men of letters, sticklers for correctness like Voltaire and Grimm, found the style overblown and the subject distasteful. But ordinary readers from all ranks of society were swept off their feet. They wept, they suffocated, they raved, they looked deep into their lives and resolved to live better, then they poured their hearts out in more tears—and in letters to Rousseau, who collected their testimonials in a huge bundle, which has survived for the inspection of posterity.[60]

In going through Rousseau's *Nouvelle Héloïse* mail, one is struck everywhere by the sound of sobbing: "tears," "sighs," and "torment" from the young publisher C.-J. Panckoucke; "delicious tears" and "ecstasy" from the Genevan J.-L. Buisson; "tears" and "delicious outpourings of the heart" from A.-J. Loyseau de Mauléon; "such delicious tears" from Charlotte Bourette of Paris that the mere thought of them set her to weeping more; so many "sweet tears" for J.-J.-P. Fromaget that "at every page my soul melted." The abbé Cahagne read the same passages aloud to friends at least ten times, each time with bursts of tears all around:

"One must suffocate, one must abandon the book, one must weep, one must write to you that one is choking with emotion and weeping." The novel drove J.-F. Bastide to his bed and nearly drove him mad, or so he believed, while it produced the opposite effect on Daniel Roguin, who sobbed so violently that he cured himself of a severe cold. The baron de La Sarraz declared that the only way to read the book was behind locked doors, so that one could weep at one's ease, without being interrupted by the servants. J.-V. Capperonnier de Gauffecourt read only a few pages at a time because his health was too weak to withstand the emotion. But his friend, the abbé Jacques Pernetti, congratulated himself on being robust enough to get through all six volumes without stopping, despite the pounding of his heart. The marquise de Polignac made it to Julie's deathbed scene in volume six but then broke down: "I dare not tell you the effect it made on me. No, I was past weeping. A sharp pain convulsed me. My heart was crushed. Julie dying was no longer an unknown person. I believed I was her sister, her friend, her Claire. My seizure became so strong that if I had not put the book away I would have been as ill as all those who attended that virtuous woman in her last moments." Lower down on the social scale, Charlotte de La Taille cried her heart out at the death of Julie and did not regain her composure for eight days. Sensing that the end was near for the heroine, Louis François, a retired army officer, found it impossible to continue, though he had wept his way without a halt through the earlier volumes:

> You have driven me crazy about her. Imagine then the tears that her death must have wrung from me. Can you believe it? I spent three days without daring to read the last letter, from M. de Wolmar to Saint-Preux. I knew how gripping every detail of it would be. But I could not bear the idea of Julie dead or dying. Still, I finally had to overcome my aversion. Never have I wept such delicious tears. That reading created such a powerful effect on me that I believe I would have gladly died during that supreme moment.

Readers from all ranks of society and all corners of the Continent reacted in the same way. As a normally restrained Swiss reviewer put it: "One must die of pleasure after reading this book, . . . or rather one must live in order to read it again and again."[61]

La Nouvelle Héloïse did not produce the first epidemic of emotion in the history of literature. Richardson had already set off waves of sobbing in England, and Lessing had done the same in Germany. Rousseau differed from them in that he inspired his readers with an overwhelming desire to make contact with the lives behind the printed page—the lives of his characters and his own. Thus after confessing to a confidante that she had wept her heart out over Rousseau's lovers, Mme de Polignac explained to a friend that she had felt an irresistible need to see Rousseau himself:

> You know that as long as he only appeared to me to be a philosopher, a man of wit, I never considered attempting to get to know him. But Julie's lover, the man who loved her as she deserved to be loved, oh! that is not the same thing. My first impulse was to order my horses harnessed so that I could go to Montmorency and see him, no matter what the cost, and tell him how much his tenderness places him above other men in my eyes, to persuade him to let me see the portrait of Julie, to kiss it, to kneel before it, and to worship that divine woman who never ceased to be a model of all the virtues even when she lost her virtue.[62]

Exactly as Rousseau had foreseen in the prefaces, his readers wanted to believe that Julie, Saint-Preux, Claire, and the others had really existed. They saw him as Julie's lover, or at least as someone who must have experienced all the passions of the characters in order to have described them so convincingly. And so they wanted to write to him, to send letters of their own, to assure him that they had felt such emotions in their lives, however obscure, and that their feelings responded to his—in a word, that they understood.

Thus Rousseau's correspondence became the logical extension of his epistolary novel. In sending letters to him, his readers conveyed reassurances that his message had got across, passing beyond the printed page from his soul into theirs. "It seems to me that one cannot exchange thoughts with you without being filled with your spirit," wrote Louis François. ". . . I have hardly lived as virtuously as Julie, but the soul of Saint-Preux had passed completely into mine. And Julie in the grave! After that I could see nothing but a frightful emptiness in nature. Am I wrong then to say that there is no equal to you on earth? Who but the great Rousseau can overwhelm his readers in that way? Who else can wield a pen so force-fully as to make his soul pass into theirs?" The same impulse over-came relatively sober readers, like the Protestant minister Paul-Claude Moultou:

> No, Monsieur, I can no longer keep quiet. You have overwhelmed my soul. It is full to bursting, and it must share its torment with you. . . . Oh Julie! Oh Saint-Preux! Oh Claire! Oh Edouard! What planet do your souls inhabit, and how can I unite mine with yours? They are the offspring of your heart, Monsieur; your mind alone could not have made them as they are. Open that heart to me so that I can contemplate the living models of the characters whose virtues made me weep such sweet tears.[63]

Of course, one must make allowances for the hypersensitive style of the time, but many of the letters have a ring of authen-ticity. A certain Mme Du Verger wrote from an obscure outpost in the provinces because of an invincible desire to know whether Rousseau's characters were real:

> Many people who have read your book and discussed it with me assert that it is only a clever fabrication on your part. I can't believe that. If so, how could a mistaken reading have produced sensations like the ones I felt when I read the book? I implore you, Monsieur, tell me: did Julie really live? Is Saint-Preux still alive? What country on this earth does he inhabit? Claire, sweet Claire, did she follow her dear friend to the grave? M. de Wolmar, milord Edouard, all those persons, are they only imaginary as some want to convince me? If that be the case, what kind of a world do we inhabit, in which virtue is but an idea? Happy mortal, perhaps you alone know it and practice it.

Above all, she wanted to make contact with Rousseau himself: "I would not speak to you so freely, if your way of thinking were not already known to me by your works. Besides, I should say straight away that if you were determined to make conquests, mine would not flatter you."[64]

The suggestion of seduction shows through many of the letters from Jean-Jacques's female admirers. Who better understood love than the lover, or at least the creator, of Julie? Women threw themselves at him, in letters and in pilgrimages to his retreat at Montmorency. Marie-Anne Alissan de La Tour cast herself as Julie, while her friend Marie-Madeleine Bernardoni took the role of Claire, and together they deluged Rousseau with letters so artfully turned that soon he was playing Saint-Preux to them in a correspondence that lasted several years.[65] Rousseau later noted with some satisfaction in his *Confessions* that his novel had overwhelmed society ladies, even though it represented a rejection of *le monde:* "Opinions were divided among men of letters, but in society everyone agreed. Women especially became so intoxicated with the book and with its author that there were few of them, even of the highest rank, whom I could not have had, if I had attempted their conquest." He told the story of one grande dame who began to read the book after supper, while being dressed for a ball. At midnight, still reading, she ordered her horses to be harnessed. At two o'clock her servants reminded her that the carriage was waiting, but she read on. By four, she was still reading feverishly. Her watch had stopped, so she rang to enquire about the time—and then decided to send the horses back to the stable, undress, and spend the rest of the night in rapturous communion with Saint-Preux, Julie, and Jean-Jacques.[66]

Of course, *La Nouvelle Héloïse* is a love story, but it was love of virtue that Rousseau's readers confessed when they tried to explain the emotion that he had aroused in them. "I would like to take hold of you and squeeze you in my arms," wrote Jean-Joseph-Pierre Fromaget, a minor tax official. ". . . I must express my gratitude, Monsieur, for all the pleasure you have given me, for all the sweet tears that Saint-Preux, Julie, Mme D'Etange have made me shed. I gladly would have become each of the characters you created. At each page my soul melted: Oh! is not virtue beautiful!"[67] In trying to make contact with Rousseau by letter, many of his readers were driven by a need to confess to him just as they took him to be confessing to them—indirectly through the letters of *La Nouvelle Héloïse* before the open baring of the soul that was to come in the *Confessions.* They wanted to tell him how they identified with his characters, how they, too, had loved, sinned, suffered, and resolved to be virtuous again in the midst of a wicked and uncomprehending world. They knew his novel was true because they had read its message in their lives.

An anonymous reader overseas explained that he had had to

leave his Julie behind in France. While sobbing through *La Nouvelle Héloïse,* he had seen his life unfurl before him and had felt a powerful urge "to throw my arms around you and to thank you a thousand times for the delicious tears that you wrung out of me." A young woman wrote that she could identify with Rousseau's characters, unlike those in all the other novels she had read, because they did not occupy a specific social station but rather represented a general way of thinking and feeling, one that everyone could apply to their own lives and thus become more virtuous. An austere Genevan, who disapproved of all novels, found himself carried away despite his principles: "I confess that I felt all the feelings expressed in those letters become personified in me while reading them and that I became successively Julie, Wolmar, Bomston, often Claire but rarely Saint-Preux, except in the first part." As soon as he put down the book Panckoucke picked up the pen, driven by a need to tell all—even though he did not have much to tell (his speculations in publishing had only begun and he had not yet dreamt of cornering the market for the works of Voltaire):

> Your divine works, Monsieur, are an all-consuming fire. They have penetrated my soul, fortified my heart, enlightened my mind. For a long time my reason, given over to the deceiving illusions of an impetuous youth, became lost in the search for truth. I sought happiness, and it eluded me. . . . The study of some modern authors had confirmed my meditations, and I was already a thorough scoundrel in my heart without having yet done anything that could make me blush. I needed a god, and a mighty god, to pull me away from that precipice, and you, Monsieur, are the god who has performed the miracle. The reading of your *Héloïse* has completed what your other works had already begun. How many tears did I shed over it! How many sighs and torments! How often did I see my own guilt. Ever since I read your blessed book, I have burned with the love of virtue, and my heart, which I had thought extinguished, beats harder than ever. Feeling has taken over once again: love, pity, virtue, sweet friendship have for ever conquered my soul.[68]

Again and again the readers returned to the same theme. Jean-Jacques had made them see deeper into the meaning of their lives. They may have erred like Julie and Saint-Preux, but they had always loved virtue in their hearts and now they would dedicate themselves to it—not virtue in the abstract, but the homespun variety, which they would work into the fabric of their family lives. M. Rousselot, B.-L. de Lenfant de la Patrière, A.-L. Lalive de Jully read, wept, and resolved to get a grip on their lives. F.-C. Constant de Rebecque learned to love her husband by picturing him as Saint-Preux and herself as Julie. And J.-L. Le Cointe saw his whole family in a new light: "Sincerely committed to a young wife, I have learned from you, and she has, too, that what had seemed to us to be a mere attachment based on the habit of living together is in fact a most tender love. At the age of twenty-eight, I am a father of four children, and I will follow your lessons in order to form them into men—not the kind of men you see everywhere around you, but the kind that we see in you alone."[69]

It would be wrong to dismiss such effusions as fan mail—although the very idea of a writer receiving mail from unknown admirers was a significant novelty, part of the new cult of the writer that Rousseau was helping to create. Naïve and sentimental as the letters may seem today, they testify to the effectiveness of Rousseau's rhetoric two hundred years ago. His "fans" read him in the way that he asked to be read and threw themselves into the role called for in the prefaces. "In truth, Monsieur, I do not think that you can find on earth a reader more worthy of you than I am," wrote A.-J. Loyseau de Mauléon. "There is not a description, not a sentiment, not a reflection, not a principle in your book that does not correspond to my unhappy lot." In describing the way they suspended their critical instinct, identified with the characters, and let waves of emotion wash over themselves, the readers paraphrased or quoted, consciously or not, the instructions that Rousseau had given them in the prefaces. One admirer explained that he had been so moved by Julie's love story that he knew it must be true; only to the heartless sophisticates of *le monde* could it be "a fiction." Another reproduced the moral argument of the prefaces almost exactly, concluding, "I feel myself to be a better person ever since I read your novel, which I hope is not a novel." And a third made the allusion explicit: "Your book produced in me the effects that you had foreseen in your preface."[70]

The flood of tears unloosed by *La Nouvelle Héloïse* in 1761 should not be considered as just another wave of preromantic sentimentality. It was a response to a new rhetorical situation. Reader and writer communed across the printed page, each of them assuming the ideal form envisioned in the text. Jean-Jacques opened up his soul to those who could read him right, and his readers felt their own souls elevated above the imperfections of their ordinary existence. Having made contact with "*l'Ami* Jean-Jacques," they then felt capable of repossessing their lives, as spouses, parents, and citizens, exactly as Ranson was to do a few years later, when he began to read Rousseau.

Ranson was not, therefore, an aberration. The letters that he sent to Ostervald from 1774 to 1785 show the same kind of response that one can find spread out horizontally, so to speak, in the letters received by Rousseau in 1761. The two dimensions complement each other and suggest that Rousseauistic reading was an important phenomenon in prerevolutionary France. How important? One cannot measure it precisely, but one can hold it up against the main governing hypothesis—in fact, the only broad generalization—in the newly emerging field of the history of reading: namely, that a "reading revolution" (*Leserevolution*) took place in Europe toward the end of the eighteenth century.

As developed by Rolf Engelsing and other German scholars, this notion divides the development of reading into two phases.[71] From the Renaissance until 1750 approximately, Europeans read "intensively." They had access to very few books—the Bible, devotional works, an occasional chapbook or an almanac—and they read them over and over again, meditating on them inwardly or sharing them aloud with others in family and social gatherings (the *Spinnstube* and *veillée*). In the second half of the eighteenth century, educated people began to read "extensively." They ran through a great deal of printed matter, especially novels and journals, the favorite genres in the reading clubs (*Lesegesellschaften, cabinets littéraires*) that proliferated everywhere in urban centers. And they read each item only once, for amusement, then raced on to the next.

The distinction between intensive and extensive reading may serve as a way to contrast the behavior of readers five centuries ago with that of readers today, but does it help one to locate a turning point in the late eighteenth century? Not if Ranson's case has any typicality. True, Ranson read a great many novels and journals, and he sometimes read them with friends, in a way that bears some resemblance to the sociability of the German *Lesegesellschaften.* Thus he remarked in a letter to Ostervald of 1774, "Nordingh, who reads various journals with me, asks you to stop sending yours to him because the copy I receive will do for both of us."[72] But reading of this kind did not exclude intensity, and seven years later Ranson wrote that he was cutting down on his subscriptions to journals in order to read still more intensively: "I must say that I am overwhelmed with periodicals, which take away time that I should devote to solid reading; so instead of increasing the number I receive, I am doing all I can to reduce it."[73] Ranson's interest in contemporary novels did not mean that he neglected the classics, or that he read the great figures of French literature rapidly and only once. He wrote that he liked Mercier and the *Tableau de Paris,* "but I cannot forgive him for what he says about Racine, a divine poet, whom I never reread without discovering new charms."[74] One could hardly find a more intensive reader than Ranson, and his reading became more intense as he did more of it. If anything, it illustrates a "reading revolution" in reverse.

That Ranson's way of reading did not run counter to the main trend of his time can be appreciated by the German counterpart of Viard: *Die Kunst Bücher zu Lesen* (Jena, 1799), a manual on reading by Johann Adam Bergk, which should be the embodiment of a *Leserevolution,* if there were one. Instead of dwelling on problems of pronunciation in the manner of Viard, Bergk propounded a full-blown "art of reading." He began with advice on how to approach books physically. You should never read while standing or after having finished a meal. Instead, you should wash your face with cold water and take your book outdoors, where you can read it in the bosom of nature—and aloud, for the sound of the voice facilitates the penetration of ideas. But most important, you should have the right spiritual disposition. Instead of responding passively to the text, you should throw yourself into it, seize its meaning, and apply it to your own life. "We must relate everything we read to our 'I,' reflect on everything from our personal point of view, and never lose sight of the consideration that study makes us freer and more independent, and that it should help us find an outlet for the expression of our heart and mind."[75] Bergk attributed this conception of reading to Jean-Jacques Rousseau. He devoted a crucial chapter to Rousseau and cited on his title page the very lines from *La Nouvelle Héloïse* that meant so much to readers like Ranson: "To read little and meditate a great deal upon our reading, or to talk it over extensively between ourselves, that is the way to thoroughly digest it."[76] This notion is quite compatible with Viard's emphasis on reading as a moral preparation for living. In fact, the reading that was expounded in the textbooks, called for by Rousseau, and experienced by Ranson was essentially the same; but it was not the "extensive" reading of Engelsing's revolution.

It seems to me, in short, that no such revolution took place. But something happened to the way that readers responded to texts in the late eighteenth century. How many readers? How many texts? The quantitative questions will not admit of answers. One can only assert that the quality of reading changed in a broad but immeasurable public toward the end of the Old Regime. Although many writers prepared the way for this change, I would attribute it primarily to the rise of Rousseauism. Rousseau taught his readers to "digest" books so thoroughly that literature became absorbed in life. The Rousseauistic readers fell in love, married, and raised children by steeping themselves in print. They were not, of course, the first to respond dramatically to books. Rousseau's own reading showed the influence of the intense, personal religiosity of his Calvinist heritage. His public probably applied an old style of religious reading to new material, notably the novel, which had previously seemed incompatible with it. And there may be a spark of that spirit in the way readers have reacted to Nietzsche or Camus or even popular psychology today. But to search for parallels to Rousseauistic reading in other ages is to blur its specificity and to blunt its significance. Ranson and his contemporaries belonged to a peculiar species of reader, one that arose in the eighteenth century and that began to die out in the age of Madame Bovary. The Rousseauistic readers of prerevolutionary France threw themselves into texts with a passion that we can barely imagine, that is as alien to us as the lust for plunder among the Norsemen . . . or the fear of demons among the Balinese.

If I had to place this kind of reading in a general pattern, I would locate it between the reading intended to please (*plaire*) in the late seventeenth century and to amuse (*distraire*) in the late nineteenth century. But that schema is also too simplistic. It leaves no room for those who read in order to reach heaven, to understand the laws of nature, to improve their manners, or, eventually, to repair their radios. Reading has assumed too many forms to follow a single course of development. But its Rousseauistic variety should be recognised as a distinct historical phenomenon and should not be confused with reading in the present, for the readers of the Old Regime lived in a mental world that is almost unthinkable today.

The need to think the almost unthinkable and to capture the differences in the ways men have construed the world brings us back to Jean Ranson. I must admit in the end that I do find him exemplary, not because he conforms to any statistical pattern but because he was exactly the "other" addressed in Rousseau's writing. He embodied both the ideal reader envisioned in the text and the real reader who bought the books. And the way he brought those roles together demonstrated the effectiveness of Rousseauistic rhetoric. By stamping his vision of the world on Ranson's daily life, Rousseau showed how he could touch lives everywhere. And by absorbing the texts as Rousseau taught him, Ranson testified to a new relationship between the reader and the printed word. Writer and reader together realized a transformation in a mode of communication that went far beyond literature and that would leave its mark on several generations of revolutionaries and romantics.

APPENDIX: RANSON'S ORDERS FOR BOOKS, 1775–85

The following list covers all the books Ranson ordered from the STN from 1775 to 1785. As he gave only a brief version of the titles, each title, along with other bibliographical information (including the format for works of more than one volume), has been given according to information available in various bibliographies of eighteenth-century literature. It is impossible to know precisely which edition of the books Ranson received, so the dates of the editions given here correspond as closely as possible to the dates of

Ranson's orders. In order to know which editions were available, I have relied primarily on the catalogues of the STN, which were sent regularly to La Rochelle. The STN did a huge wholesale trade in addition to its printing business—the catalogue of 1785 contains 800 titles—and it received books that it did not have in stock from other Swiss publishers. So Ranson could have procured virtually any current book from his supplier in Neuchâtel. But it should be remembered that he bought books from other sources, notably his local bookseller Guillaume Pavie. Thus the following list has a bias in favor of Swiss publications, and it provides only a general indication of Ranson's current reading, not an exact inventory of his library.

The original spelling of the titles has been retained, along with the place of publication given on the title pages. I was not able to identify three of the books.

I. Religion (12 titles)
Holy Scripture, devotional works

La Sainte Bible, qui contient le vieux & le nouveau Testament, revue & corrigée sur le texte hébreu & grec, par les pasteurs & professeurs de l'église de Genève, avec les arguments & les réflexions sur les chapitres de l'Ecriture-sainte, & des notes, par J. F. Ostervald (Neuchâtel, 1779), 2 vols. in-folio.

Les psaumes de David, mis en vers françois, avec les cantiques pour les principales solemnités (Vévey, 1778).

Abrégé de l'histoire-sainte & du catéchisme d'Ostervald (Neuchâtel, 1784).

Recueil de prières, précédé d'un traité de la prière, avec l'explication et la paraphrase de l'Oraison dominicale (Celle, 1762), by J.-E. Roques.

La nourriture de l'ame, ou recueil de prières pour tous les jours de la semaine, pour les principales fêtes de l'année & sur différens sujets intéressans (Neuchâtel, 1785), by J. F. Ostervald.

Morale évangélique, ou discours sur le sermon de N.S.J.C. sur la montagne (Neuchâtel, 1776), 7 vols. in-8°, by J.-E. Bertrand.

Sermons

Année évangélique, ou sermons pour tous les dimanches & fêtes de l'année (Lausanne, 1780), 7 vols. in-8°, by J.-F. Durand.

Sermons sur les dogmes fondamentaux de la religion naturelle (Neuchâtel, 1783), by H.-D. Chaillet.

Sermons sur différens textes de l'Ecriture-sainte (Neuchâtel, 1779), 2 vols. in-8°, by J.-E. Bertrand.

Sermons de Jean Perdriau [not identified].

Sermons sur divers textes de l'Ecriture-sainte (Genève, 1780), 2 vols. in-8°, by J. E. Romilly.

II. History, travel, geography (4 titles)

Histoire philosophique et politique des établissemens et du commerce des Européens dans les deux Indes (Genève, 1780), 4 vols. in-4°, by G.-T. Raynal.

Voyage en Sicile et à Malte, traduit de l'anglois de M. Brydone, par M. Démeunier (Londres, 1776), 2 vols. in-8°, by Patrick Brydone.

Voyage historique & littéraire dans la Suisse occidentale (Neuchâtel, 1781), 2 vols. in-8°, by J.-R. Sinner.

Description des montagnes & des vallées qui font partie de la principauté de Neuchâtel & Valengin (Neuchâtel, 1766), by F.-S. Ostervald.

[*Abrégé élémentaire de l'histoire universelle* et *Cours de géographie élémentaire:* see under Children's books.]

III. Belles-lettres (14 titles)

Works

Oeuvres de Molière (Rouen, 1779), 8 vols. in-12.

Oeuvres de M. La Harpe (Paris, 1778), 6 vols. in-8°.

Oeuvres de Crébillon père (Paris, 1774), 3 vols. in-12.

Oeuvres complètes d'Alexis Piron (Neuchâtel, 1777), 7 vols. in-8°.

Oeuvres de J.-J. Rousseau (Neuchâtel, 1775), 11 vols. in-8°.

Oeuvres de J.-J. Rousseau (Genève, 1782), 31 vols. in-12.

Oeuvres posthumes de J.-J. Rousseau, ou recueil de pièces manuscrites pour servir de supplément aux éditions publiées pendant sa vie (Neuchâtel et Genève, 1782–83), 12 vols. in-8°.

Novels

Histoire de François Wills ou le triomphe de la bienfaisance (Neuchâtel, 1774), by S. J. Pratt.

Le paysan perverti, ou les dangers de la ville, histoire récente mise au jour d'après les véritables lettres des personnages (La Haye, 1776), 4 vols. in-12, by N.-E. Restif de la Bretonne.

Adèle et Théodore ou lettres sur l'éducation, contenant tous les principes relatifs aux trois différens plans d'éducation des princes, des jeunes personnes, & des hommes (Paris, 1782), by S.-F. Ducrest de Saint-Aubin, marquise de Sillery, comtesse de Genlis.

Histoire de l'admirable Don Quichotte de la Manche (Lyon, 1781), 6 vols. in-12, by Miguel de Cervantes y Saavedra.

Other

Théâtre de société (Neuchâtel, 1781), 2 vols. in-8°, by Mme de Genlis.

L'an deux mille quatre cent quarante, rêve s'il en fut jamais (Londres, 1775), by L.-S. Mercier.

Mon bonnet de nuit (Neuchâtel, 1784), 2 vols. in-8°, by L.-S. Mercier.

IV. Medicine (2 titles)

Soins faciles pour la propreté de la bouche & pour la conservation des dents, par M. Bourdet, dentiste, suivi de l'art de soigner les pieds (Lausanne, 1782), by Bernard Bourdet.

Avis, contenant la manière de préparer une remède contre la rage, publié à Berlin par ordre du Roi de Prusse [not identified].

V. Children's books, pedagogy (18 titles)

Amusement

Théâtre d'éducation, à l'usage des jeunes personnes (Paris, 1785), by Mme de Genlis.

Nouveaux contes moraux (Lyon, 1776), 2 vols. in-12, by Marie Leprince de Beaumont.

L'ami des enfants (Lausanne, 1783), 5 vols. in-12, by Arnaud Berquin.

Fables de La Fontaine (Paris, 1779), by Jean de La Fontaine.

Les hochets moraux, ou contes pour la première enfance (Paris, 1784), 2 vols. in-12, by Monget.

Les jeux d'enfans, poème tiré du hollandois (Neuchâtel, 1781), by A.-A.-J. Feutry.

Lectures pour les enfans, ou choix de petits contes également propres à les amuser & à leur faire aimer la vertu (Genève, 1780), anonymous.

Magasin des enfans, par Mad. le Prince de Beaumont, suivi des conversations entre la jeune Emilie & sa mère (Neuchâtel, 1780), 2 vols. in-12, par Marie Leprince de Beaumont.

Conversations d'Emilie, ou entretiens instructifs & amusans d'une mère avec sa fille (Lausanne, 1784), 2 vols. in-12, by L.-F.-P. Tardieu d'Esclavelles, marquise d'Epinay.

Entretiens, drames, et contes moraux à l'usage des enfans (La Haye, 1778), by M.-E. Bouée de Lafite.

Instruction

Annales de la vertu, ou cours d'histoire à l'usage des jeunes personnes (Paris, 1781), 2 vols. in-8°, by Mme de Genlis.

Cours de géographie élémentaire, par demandes & réponses (Neuchâtel, 1783), by F.-S. Ostervald.

Les vrais principes de la lecture, de l'orthographe et de la prononciation françoise, suivis d'un petit traité de la ponctuation, des premiers élémens de la grammaire et de la prosodie françoise et de différentes pièces de lecture propres à donner des notions simples & faciles sur toutes les parties de nos connoissances (Paris, 1763), by N.-A. Viard.

Abrégé élémentaire de l'histoire universelle destiné à l'usage de la jeunesse (s.l., 1771), by Mathurin Veyssière de Lacroze and J.-H.-S. Formey.

Pedagogy, moral education

Legs d'un père à ses filles (Lausanne, 1775), by John Gregory.

Dissertation sur l'éducation physique des enfants, (Paris, 1762), by J. Ballexserd.

Education morale, ou réponse à cette question, comment doit-on gouverner l'esprit et le coeur d'un enfant, pour le faire parvenir un jour à l'état d'homme heureux et utile (1770), by J.-A. Comparet.

Instructions d'un père à ses enfans sur le principe de la vertu & du bonheur (Genève, 1783), by Abraham Trembley.

VI. Other (9 titles)

Encyclopédie, ou dictionnaire raisonné des sciences, des arts & des métiers (Genève et Neuchâtel, 1778–79), 36 vols. of text and 3 vols. of plates in-4°.

Le socrate rustique, ou description de la conduite économique et morale d'un paysan philosophe (Lausanne, 1777), by Hans Caspar Hirzel.

Le messager boiteux (Berne, 1777).

Mémoires secrets pour servir à l'histoire de la république des lettres en France depuis 1762 jusqu'à nos jours (Londres, 1777–83), 21 vols. in-12, attributed to Louis Petit de Bachaumont and others.

Relation ou notice des derniers jours de M. J.-J. Rousseau, circonstances de sa mort et quels sont les ouvrages posthumes qu'on peut attendre de lui (Londres, 1778), by A.-G. Le Bègue de Presles and J.-H. Magellan.

Discours sur l'économie politique (Geneva, 1785), by Jean-Jacques Rousseau.

Lettres de feu M. de Haller contre M. de Voltaire (Berne, 1778), by Albrecht von Haller.

Tableau de Paris (Neuchâtel, 1783), 8 vols. in-8°, by L.-S. Mercier.

Portraits des rois de France (Neuchâtel, 1784), 4 vols. in-8°, by L.-S. Mercier.

CONCLUSION

HAVING MADE this quick trial run through eighteenth-century culture, can we draw any conclusions about the history of *mentalités?* The genre remains obscure, although the French have tried to surround it with prolegomena and discourses on method. The most revealing of their programmatic statements is an essay by Pierre Chaunu: "Un Nouveau Champ pour l'histoire sérielle: Le Quantitatif au troisième niveau" ("A New Field for Statistical History: Quantification at the Third Level.") Chaunu makes explicit a set of assumptions that can be found almost everywhere in recent French historiography, that unites Marxists and revisionists, that determines the structure of the best doctoral theses, and that is inscribed in the title of France's most influential historical journal, *Annales: Économies, sociétés, civilisations*—namely, that one can distinguish levels in the past; that the third level (culture) somehow derives from the first two (economics and demography, and social structure); and that third-level phenomena can be understood in the same way as those on the deeper levels (by means of statistical analysis, the play of structure and conjuncture, and considerations of long-term change rather than of events). This historiographical tradition, usually identified loosely as the "*Annales* school," has contributed enormously to our understanding of the past—more, I should think, than any other trend in history writing since the beginning of this century. But all three of its assumptions strike me as dubious, and I would especially question the third.[1]

The French attempt to measure attitudes by counting—counting masses for the dead, pictures of Purgatory, titles of books, speeches in academies, furniture in inventories, crimes in police records, invocations to the Virgin Mary in wills, and pounds of candle wax burned to patron saints in churches. The numbers can be fascinating, especially when they are compiled with the masterly hand of a Michel Vovelle or a Daniel Roche. But they are nothing more than symptoms produced by the historian himself, and they can be interpreted in wildly different ways. Vovelle sees dechristianization in the drop in the graphs of masses said for souls in Purgatory; Philippe Ariès sees a tendency toward a more inward and intense form of spirituality. To the secular left (Vovelle, Roche, Roger Chartier), the statistical curves generally indicate *embourgeoisement* of world view; to the religious right (Ariès, Chaunu, Bernard Plongeron), they reveal new patterns of family affection and charity. The only point of agreement seems to be the dictum of Ernest Labrousse: "Everything derives from the curve." Labrousse's work represents the supreme "discourse on method" of modern French historiography, according to Chaunu; but it misrepresents cultural phenomena. Unlike the price series of economics, the vital statistics of demography, and the (more problematic) professional categories in social history, cultural objects are not manufactured by the historian but by the people he studies. They give off meaning. They need to be read, not counted. Despite its strong start fifteen years ago, the history of *mentalités* seems to be running out of momentum in France. If so, the explanation may lie in an overcommitment to the quantification of culture and an undervaluation of the symbolic element in social intercourse.[2]

The French formula, with its implicit references to Marxism and structuralism, never had much appeal to the tribes identified as "Anglo-Saxon" in France. But cultural history has its problems within our own tradition. How many of our books begin by sketching the social background of the subject and end by filling in the culture? This tendency runs through the entire series on *The*

Rise of Modern Europe edited by William Langer, the most eminent American historian of his generation, and especially through the volume written for the series by Langer himself. It makes sense to us as a mode of exposition, but it does so because of an unspoken assumption that if we can get the social setting right the cultural content will somehow follow. We structure our work in a way that implies that cultural systems derive from social orders. Perhaps they do, but how? The question must be confronted, yet it is rarely recognized. And if we fail to face up to it, we may fall into a naïve kind of functionalism. Keith Thomas begins his magisterial *Religion and the Decline of Magic* with a chapter on the harsh and uncertain conditions of life in the sixteenth and seventeenth centuries, when witchcraft flourished, and ends it with a chapter on the improved conditions in the eighteenth century, when it died out. He seems to imply that social conditions determined popular beliefs. But when confronted with so bold and bald a proposition, he backed down—and wisely so, for it would have committed him to a simple, stimulus-and-response view of attitude formation and it would not even have made sense of the chronology. Life in English villages did not improve dramatically between 1650 and 1750. Indeed, attitudes often changed during periods of relative stability and remained relatively stable during times of upheaval, as Lawrence Stone discovered in his study of English family life. Philippe Ariès found the same tendency in France, and even Michel Vovelle confessed to an inability to correlate religious attitudes with social change at the end of his massive *Piété baroque et déchristianisation*.[3]

I mention these historians, not in order to snipe at them but because they are the best in the profession; yet whenever they try to join social and cultural history, they run into the same kind of problem. Perhaps a more successful juncture could be made by orienting cultural history in a new direction: toward anthropology. Of course, that suggestion is not really new. Keith Thomas made it long ago, and before him E. E. Evans-Pritchard urged anthropologists to turn toward history. Several anthropological books by historians and historical books by anthropologists have shown that the two disciplines are destined to converge.[4]

But how? The way to a thoroughly anthropological history remains unclear, and I doubt that historians can find one by taking bits and pieces from the neighboring discipline, or even by borrowing a full-fledged methodology. Anthropologists have no common method, no all-embracing theory. If merely asked for a definition of culture, they are liable to explode in clan warfare. But despite their disagreements, they share a general orientation. In their different ways among their different tribes, they usually try to see things from the native's point of view, to understand what he means, and to seek out the social dimensions of meaning. They work from the assumption that symbols are shared, like the air we breathe or, to adopt their favorite metaphor, the language we speak.

At the risk of putting words in the mouths of my own native informants, I think it fair to say that the preoccupation with language among anthropologists includes a concern for expressivity and style as well as lexicology and syntax, and that this concern applies to societies as well as individuals. Each of us speaks in his own manner, but we share the same grammar—all the more so as we are usually unconscious of it. Grammatical slips, or deviations from the idiom, can be detected by everyone, even the illiterate—unless the "errors" belong to a popular dialect, in which case they are not erroneous—because some things are generally considered to be wrong and some things cannot be said. We can move from one language to another, but in doing so we accept new constraints and make new mistakes. We also adopt a different tone, enjoying the *je ne sais quoi* of *Sprachgefühl*. The untranslatability of such terms suggests that it is not extravagant to entertain the notion of tone and style in cultures—the sort of thing one senses in comparing expressions like "bloody-minded" and *grogneur* or cross-linguistic borrowings like *le fair-play anglais* and "French finesse" or cross-cultural insults like "French leave" and *capote anglaise*. Anthropologists may have overworked the concept of culture-as-language, but it provides a tonic to historians. For if culture is idiomatic, it is retrievable. And if enough of its texts have survived, it can be excavated from the archives. We can stop straining to see how the documents "reflect" their social surroundings, because they were imbedded in a symbolic world that was social and cultural at the same time.

But how can we put together symbolic worlds that collapsed centuries ago? This book is an attempt to do just that. Only the reader can pronounce on its success. But as I have been so free with my criticism of others, I should confess some of my own methodological shortcomings. I worry especially about two: my failure to resolve the problem of proof and the problem of representativeness. The first part of this book, and the first chapter in particular, is distressingly imprecise in its deployment of evidence (a word that I prefer to proof). Folklore may be a legitimate science, but it operates best in the present, where the tellers of tales may be heard, recorded, filmed, and interviewed. We can never form more than an approximate idea of how tales were told in the past. We do not even know exactly when and where they were told or what their texts were. The evidence is so vague that some would give up the whole enterprise, but I think it would be a greater mistake to reject the use of folklore than to venture an inadequate interpretation of it. The imperfect recordings of folktales are nearly all that is left of the oral traditions of the Old Regime, and they are the richest source at our disposal if we want to make contact with the mental world of peasants in the past. At the risk of arousing a Rankean backlash, I would even argue that this kind of cultural history should not be subjected to the same standards of evidence that rule in the history of international relations or politics. World views cannot be pinned down with "proof." They are bound to be fuzzy around the edges, and they will slip through the fingers if one grabs at them as if they were pages from the *Congressional Record.*

In avoiding the danger of a misplaced positivism, we should not fall into the opposite error of thinking that anything is permitted in anthropological history. We can get cultures wrong just as we can make mistakes in speech. World views are not empty of evidence, so we should be able to work our way through to them, not by taking intuitive leaps into airy climates of opinion but by poring over sources. In the case of historical folklore, we can study all the versions of a tale in one tradition and compare them systematically with tales in other traditions. We may not be able to get far beyond general considerations of cultural style—and I fear that my generalizations may appear overly impressionistic—but we should make contact with the otherness in other cultures.

My own suggestion about a way of making contact is to search for opacity in texts. As I tried to illustrate in explicating the cat massacre of the rue Saint-Séverin, the most promising moment in research can be the most puzzling. When we run into something that seems unthinkable to us, we may have hit upon a valid point of entry into an alien mentality. And once we have puzzled through to the native's point of view, we should be able to roam about in his symbolic world. To get the joke in the case of something as unfunny as a ritual slaughter of cats is a first step toward "getting" the culture.

However, that procedure raises the second problem: Is there not something arbitrary in the selection of such material and something abusive in drawing general conclusions from it? How can I know that I have struck a chord of sensitivity that runs throughout a culture rather than a note of individual idiosyncrasy—the raving of a peculiarly cruel printer or the obsessions of an unusually garrulous Montpelliérain? I must admit that those objections make me feel uneasy. My first inclination is to forestall criticism by issuing denials: I do not pretend to present a typical peasant, artisan, bourgeois, bureaucrat, *philosophe,* or romantic. The chapters are meant to interconnect but not to interlock like the parts of a systematic treatise. They were written as essays—to essay ideas and try out different directions of cultural interpretation. I have tried to write in an informal manner and to expose my theoretical assumptions, even at the risk of sounding pretentious and of abusing the first person singular, a form I have generally avoided.

That said, I confess that I do not see a clear way of distinguishing idiom from individuality. I can only testify to the importance of working back and forth between texts and contexts. That may not be much of a methodology, but it has advantages. It does not flatten out the idiosyncratic element in history, and it allows for consideration of the common ground of experience. To proceed in a contrary manner, by first establishing the idiom and then explaining the individual expression, does not seem workable. We never meet pure idiom. We interpret texts. But the general grammar of other cultures must be imbedded in the documents they left behind, and we must be able to dig it out. Perhaps other diggers will succeed where I have failed.

But I doubt that any of us will come up with the final answers. The questions keep changing, and history never stops. We are not accorded "bottom lines" or last words; but if there were any, they would belong to Marc Bloch, who knew that when historians venture into the past they seek to make contact with vanished humanity. Whatever their professional baggage, they must follow their noses and trust to their sense of smell: "A good historian resembles the ogre of the legend. Wherever he smells human flesh, he knows that there he will find his prey."[5]

NOTES

Chapter 1

1. This text and those of the other French folktales discussed in this essay come from Paul Delarue and Marie-Louise Tenèze, *Le Conte populaire français* (Paris, 1976), 3 vols., which is the best of the French folktale collections because it provides all the recorded versions of each tale along with background information about how they were gathered from oral sources. Delarue and Tenèze also arrange the tales according to the standard Aarne-Thompson classification scheme, so they can be compared with versions of the same "tale type" in other oral traditions. See Antti Aarne and Stith Thompson, *The Types of the Folktale: A Classification and Bibliography* (2nd rev.; Helsinki, 1973). References hereafter are to the Aarne-Thompson designations, which can be used to locate the texts in Delarue-Tenèze. In this case, for example, the tale belongs to tale type 333, "The Glutton," and thirty-five versions of it appear in *Le Conte populaire français*, I, 373–81. I have chosen the most common version for my translation. For more information on folktales as a historical source, see Stith Thompson, *The Folktale* (Berkeley and Los Angeles, 1977; 1st ed. 1946) and the references in note 7 and 8 to this chapter.

2. Erich Fromm, *The Forgotten Language: An Introduction to the Understanding of Dreams, Fairy Tales and Myths* (New York, 1951), pp. 235–41, quotation from p. 240.

3. On the sources and transmission of "Little Red Riding Hood," see Johannes Bolte and Georg Polívka, *Anmerkungen zu den Kinder- und Hausmärchen der Brüder Grimm*, 5 vols. (Leipzig, 1913–32), I, 234–37 and IV, 431–34 and, for more recent work, Wilhelm Schoof, *Zur Entstehungsgeschichte der Grimmschen Märchen* (Hamburg, 1959), pp. 59–61 and 74–77. My reading of the evidence supports the interpretations of H. V. Velten, "The Influence of Charles Perrault's *Contes de ma mère l'Oie*," *The Germanic Review* V (1930), 4–18 and Paul Delarue, "Les Contes merveilleux de Perrault et la tradition populaire," *Bulletin folklorique d'Ile-de-France*, new series, (July-Oct., 1951), 221–28 and 251–60. The Grimms also published a second version of the tale, which ends like the tale known as "The Three Little

Pigs" in English (tale type 124). They got it from Dorothea Wild, the future wife of Wilhelm Grimm. She in turn learned it from her housemaid, "die alte Marie," whom Schoof has identified as Marie Müller, the widow of a blacksmith killed in the American Revolutionary War: Schoof, *Zur Entstehungsgeschichte,* pp. 59–61. Although the Grimms took pains to make accurate transcriptions of the tales told to them, they rewrote the texts considerably as they proceeded from edition to edition. For their rewriting of "Little Red Riding Hood," see Bolte and Polívka, *Anmerkungen,* IV, 455.

4. Bruno Bettelheim, *The Uses of Enchantment: The Meaning and Importance of Fairy Tales* (New York, 1977), pp. 166–83.

5. Bettelheim's interpretation of folktales can be reduced to four false propositions: that the tales have usually been intended for children (ibid., p. 15), that they must always have a happy ending (ibid., p. 37), that they are "timeless" (ibid., p. 97), and that they can be applied, in the versions familiar to modern Americans, to "any society" (ibid., p. 5). In criticizing the psychoanalytic reading of folktales, I do not mean to imply that the tales contain no subconscious or irrational elements. I mean to take issue with the anachronistic and reductionistic use of Freudian ideas. For further examples, see the interpretations of "The Frog King" (a phallic fantasy), "Aladdin" (a masturbation fantasy), "Jack and the Beanstalk" (an oedipal fantasy, although there is some confusion as to who is castrated, the father or the son, when Jack chops down the beanstalk), and other tales in Ernest Jones, "Psychoanalysis and Folklore" and William H. Desmonde, "Jack and the Beanstalk" in *The Study of Folklore,* ed. Alan Dundes (Englewood Cliffs, 1965), pp. 88–102 and 107–9 and Sigmund Freud and D. E. Oppenheim, *Dreams in Folklore* (New York, 1958).

6. For examples of work that combines sensitivity to linguistics, narrative modes, and cultural context, see Melville Herskovits and Frances Herskovits, *Dahomean Narrative: a Cross-cultural Analysis* (Evanston, Ill., 1958); Linda Dégh, *Folktales and Society: Story-telling in a Hungarian Peasant Community* (Bloomington, Ind., 1969); *The Social Use of Metaphor: Essays on the Anthropology of Rhetoric,* ed. J. David Sapir and J. Christopher Crocker (Philadelphia, 1977); and Keith H. Basso, *Portraits of "the Whiteman": Linguistic Play and Cultural Symbols among the Western Apache* (New York, 1979). An exemplary study of narrative in an oral tradition that has died out is Dell H. Hymes, "The 'Wife' Who 'Goes Out' Like a Man: Reinterpretation of a Clackamas Chinook Myth," in *Structural Analysis of Oral Tradition,* ed. Pierre Maranda and Elli Köngäs Maranda (Philadelphia, 1971).

7. See Aarne and Thompson, *Types of the Folktale;* Thompson, *Folktale;* and Vladimir Propp, *Morphology of the Folktale,* trans. Laurence Scott (Austin, 1968). Aarne and Thompson used the "historical-geographical" or "Finnish" method, developed by Kaarle Krohn, to produce a world-wide survey and classification of folktales. Other scholars working in the same vein have done monographs on individual tales or cycles of tales. See, for example, Marian R. Cox, *Cinderella: Three Hundred and Forty-five Variants* (London, 1893) and Kurt Ranke, *Die Zwei Brüder: eine Studie zur Vergleichenden Märchenforschung,* FF (Folklore Fellows) Communications No. 114 (Helsinki, 1934). The most important general study of European folktales is still the *Anmerkungen* of Bolte and Polívka. More recent work, especially in the United States, tends to emphasize the linguistic and ethnographic aspects of folktales, to relate them to other forms of folklore, and to interpret them as performances rather than as written texts. See Dundes, *Study of Folklore;* Alan Dundes, *Interpreting Folklore* (Bloomington, Ind., 1980); Richard M. Dorson, *Folklore: Selected Essays* (Bloomington, Ind., 1972); and *Toward New Perspectives in Folklore,* ed. Américo Paredes and Richard Bauman (Austin, 1972).

8. This information comes from Paul Delarue's introduction to *Le Conte populaire français,* I, 7–99, which is the best general account of folklore research in France and which also contains a thorough bibliography. The most important collections of French folktales, aside from that of Delarue and Tenèze, are Emmanuel Cosquin, *Contes populaires de Lorraine* (Paris, 1886), 2 vols.; Paul Sébillot, *Contes populaires de la Haute Bretagne* (Paris, 1880–82), 3 vols.; and J. F. Bladé, *Contes populaires de la Gascogne* (Paris, 1886), 3 vols. Texts and studies of tales

have also appeared in journals devoted to French folklore, notably *Arts et traditions populaires, Mélusine,* and *Bulletin folklorique d'Ile-de-France.* I have drawn on all these sources but have relied primarily on Delarue and Tenèze, *Le Conte populaire français.*

9. Delarue, "Les contes merveilleux de Perrault."

10. William Thoms launched the term "folklore" in 1846, two decades before Edward Tylor introduced a similar term, "culture," among English-speaking anthropologists. See Thoms, "Folklore" and William R. Bascom, "Folklore and Anthropology" in Dundes, *Study of Folklore,* pp. 4–6 and 25–33.

11. Noël du Fail, *Propos rustiques de Maistre Leon Ladulfi Champenois,* chap. 5, in *Conteurs français du XVIe siècle,* ed. Pierre Jourda (Paris, 1956), pp. 620–21.

12. French folklore could be subjected to a structuralist or formalist analysis of the sort used by Claude Lévi-Strauss and Vladimir Propp. I have tried out those methods on several tales but abandoned them for the looser study of structure that is presented in the last part of this essay. For an example of structuralist analysis applied successfully to tales that could only be known through written texts long after they were recorded, see Hymes, "The 'Wife' Who 'Goes Out' Like a Man."

13. Albert B. Lord, *The Singer of Tales* (Cambridge, Mass., 1960).

14. Propp, *Morphology of the Folktale.*

15. Lowie's remark is quoted in Richard Dorson, "The Debate over the Trustworthiness of Oral Traditional History" in Dorson, *Folklore: Selected Essays,* p. 202.

16. On the different issues of historicity and continuity in oral narratives, see Dorson, "The Debate over the Trustworthiness of Oral Traditional History"; Robert Lowie, "Some Cases of Repeated Reproduction" in Dundes, *Study of Folklore,* pp. 259–64; Jan Vansina, *Oral Tradition: A Study in Historical Methodology* (Chicago, 1965); and Herbert T. Hoover, "Oral History in the United States," in *The Past Before Us: Contemporary Historical Writing in the United States,* ed. Michael Kammen (Ithaca and London, 1980), pp. 391–407.

17. Frank Hamilton Cushing, *Zuni Folk Tales* (New York and London, 1901), pp. 411–22. Although Cushing was one of the first researchers to master the Zuni language and record Zuni tales, his translations should be read with some reservations as to their accuracy; they contain an admixture of Victorian religiosity. See Dennis Tedlock, "On the Translation of Style in Oral Narrative," in *Toward New Perspectives in Folklore,* ed. Américo Paredes and Richard Bauman, pp. 115–18.

18. Jack Goody, *The Domestication of the Savage Mind* (Cambridge, 1977). See also the studies published by Goody as *Literacy in Traditional Societies* (Cambridge, 1968). Although he claims not to hold a "great divide" view of history, Goody distinguishes all societies that have acquired writing from all those that have not. Most folklorists and anthropologists reject such an either-or, before-and-after dichotomy, and attribute considerable stability to oral traditions, even after the spread of literacy. See, for example, Thompson, *The Folktale,* p. 437; Francis Lee Utley, "Folk Literature: An Operational Definition," in Dundes, *Study of Folklore,* p. 15; and Alan Dundes, "The Transmission of Folklore," ibid., p. 217.

19. Raymond D. Jameson, *Three Lectures on Chinese Folklore* (Peking, 1932).

20. This remark occurs in Perrault's version, which contains a sophisticated reworking of the dialogue in the peasant versions. See Delarue and Tenèze, *Le Conte populaire français,* I, 306–24.

21. "Jean de l'Ours," tale type 301B.

22. See "Le Conte de Parle," tale type 328 and "La Belle Eulalie," tale type 313.

23. "Pitchin-Pitchot," tale type 327C.

24. Among the other general works that treat the Old Regime as a peculiar social order that existed in France between the Renaissance and the Revolution, see Pierre Goubert, *L'Ancien Régime* (Paris, 1969 and 1973), 2 vols. and Roland Mousnier, *Les Institutions de la France sous la monarchie absolue, 1598–1789* (Paris, 1974). These books contain adequate bibliographical guides to the vast literature on French social history during this period.

25. Le Roy Ladurie, "L'Histoire immobile," *Annales: Economies, sociétés, civilisations,*

XXIX (1974), 673–92. See also Fernand Braudel's remarks on "une histoire quasi immobile" in the preface to *La Méditerranée et le monde méditerranéen à l'époque de Philippe II,* reprinted in Braudel, *Ecrits sur l'histoire* (Paris, 1969), p. 11. The notion of an "unmoving" early modern France owed a great deal to the Malthusian interpretation of social history developed by Jean Meuvret in the 1940s and 1950s. See especially his influential article, "Les Crises de subsistances et la démographie de la France d'Ancien Régime," *Population,* II (1947), 643–47. Historical demographers have now begun to undercut that view. See, for example, Jacques Dupâquier, "Révolution française et révolution démographique" in *Vom Ancien Régime zur Französischen Revolution: Forschungen and Perspektiven,* ed. Ernst Hinrichs, Eberhard Schmitt, and Rudolf Vierhaus (Göttingen, 1978), pp. 233–60.

26. For examples of the vast literature on the peasantry and the rural and urban poor, see Pierre Goubert, *Beauvais et le Beauvaisis de 1600 à 1730: Contribution à l'histoire sociale de la France du XVIIe siècle* (Paris, 1960) and Olwen H. Hufton, *The Poor of Eighteenth-Century France, 1750–1789* (Oxford, 1974).

27. For surveys of demographic history, see Dupâquier, "Révolution française et révolution démographique"; Pierre Guillaume and Jean-Pierre Poussou, *Démographie historique* (Paris, 1970); and Pierre Goubert, "Le Poids du monde rural" in *Histoire économique et sociale de la France,* ed. Ernest Labrousse and Fernand Braudel (Paris, 1970), pp. 3–158.

28. Delarue and Tenèze, *Le Conte populaire français,* II, 143.

29. Ibid., II, 145.

30. Ibid., I, 279.

31. Ibid., I, 289.

32. Quotations from ibid., I, 353, 357, 358, and 360.

33. Ibid., II, 398.

34. Ibid., II, 394.

35. Ibid., II, 269.

36. Ibid., I, 275.

37. Ibid., II, 480; II, 53; II, 182; and I, 270.

38. It might be objected that these two frameworks exhaust the possibilities. But stories could be organized around other dualities: city-country, north-south, land-sea, present-past. The opposition of the village and the open road seems especially appropriate for tales told by peasants under the Old Regime.

39. Delarue and Tenèze, *Le Conte populaire français,* II, 216.

40. "Jean de Bordeaux," tale type 506A; "L'Amour des trois oranges," tale type 408; "Courbasset," tale type 425A.

41. Delarue and Tenèze, *Le Conte populaire français,* II, 569.

42. Thus the beginning of "Les Trois Fils adroits," tale type 654 (ibid., II, 562): "A poor man had three sons. When they were grown he told them that he had no work to give them and that they had to leave in order to learn some work and support themselves."

43. See "Maille-chêne," tale type 650; "Le Vieux Militaire," tale type 475; "Le Rusé voleur," tale type 653; and "La Mort dans une bouteille," tale type 331.

44. Quotations from Delarue and Tenèze, *Le Conte populaire français,* II, 415.

45. This is where the argument has been left in the few attempts made thus far to bring folklore and social history together. See, for example, Lutz Röhrich, *Märchen und Wirklichkeit: Eine Volkskundliche Untersuchung* (Wiesbaden, 1956); Charles Phythian-Adams, *Local History and Folklore: A New Framework* (London, 1975); Eugen Weber, "The Reality of Folktales," *Journal of the History of Ideas,* XLII (1981), 93–113; and Peter Taylor and Hermann Rebel, "Hessian Peasant Women, Their Families, and the Draft: A Social-Historical Interpretation of Four Tales from the Grimm Collection," *Journal of Family History,* VI (1981), pp. 347–78.

46. Iona Opie and Peter Opie examine the origins and historicity of English nursery rhymes in their authoritative survey of all the texts, *The Oxford Dictionary of Nursery Rhymes* (London, 1975). It provides the basis for the following discussion.

47. The first volume of *Tommy Thumb's Pretty Song Book* is missing from the British Library copy, the only one in existence. A sequel, *The Famous Tommy Thumb's Little Story-Book*, begins with the tale of Tom Thumb and ends with a selection of nursery rhymes. Other collections do not generally refer to Tom Thumb, except indirectly, as in "I had a little husband" and "Dance, thumbkin, dance." The name of Mother Goose was attached to the rhymes through *Mother Goose's Melody, or Sonnets for the Cradle,* which was first published in the 1760s and reprinted many times thereafter. See Opie and Opie, *Oxford Dictionary of Nursery Rhymes,* 32–35.

48. Katharine M. Briggs, *A Dictionary of British Folk-Tales in the English Language,* 4 vols. (London, 1970–71), I, 531. This collection, which is comparable to the Delarue-Tenèze collection of French folktales, is the main source for the following discussion. I have also relied heavily on Bolte and Polívka, *Anmerkungen.*

49. Briggs, *Dictionary of British Folk-Tales,* I, 331.

50. The quotations come from the version in Delarue and Tenèze, *Le Conte populaire français,* I, 330–34 and are given in order to illustrate the kind of dialogue that characterizes the French tales. It should go without saying that one cannot know exactly what words were used by eighteenth-century raconteurs.

51. The English version of the tale is in Briggs, *Dictionary of British Folk-Tales,* I, 391–93; the French is in Delarue and Tenèze, *Le Conte populaire français,* I, 110–12. No comparable collection of Italian folktales exists, although there are some good works on certain regions of Italy like Giuseppe Pitrè, *Novelle popolare toscane* (Florence, 1885). The best-known Italian anthology, *Fiabe italiane* by Italo Calvino (Turin, 1956), is now available in a translation by George Martin, *Italian Folktales* (New York, 1980). Calvino cannot be faulted for ignorance of academic folklore studies, but he sometimes modifies the tales for literary purposes. Still, he indicates the modifications in his notes, and it must be acknowledged that the Grimms themselves kept touching up their texts. Wherever possible, I have gone back to the great seventeeth-century collection of tales by Giambattista Basile. I am unable to read Basile's flowery Neapolitan dialect, however, and have had to rely on the translations by Benedetto Croce, *Il pentamerone ossia la fiaba delle fiabe,* 2 vols. (Bari, 1925) and by N. M. Penzer, *The Pentamerone of Giambattista Basile,* 2 vols. (London, 1932). Although the English version is actually a retranslation from Croce's Italian, it contains some excellent "Folklore addenda." In this case, the text of the tale comes from Calvino, *Italian Folktales,* pp. 284–88.

52. The Grimms' tales are numbered according to a standard order and therefore can be located in any edition. I have used Bolte and Polívka, *Anmerkungen* for variations and background information, but for reasons of convenience refer to the most accessible English translation, by Margaret Hunt and James Stern, *The Complete Grimms' Fairy Tales* (New York, 1972). The Italian version of this tale type is in Calvino, *Italian Folktales,* pp. 3–4.

53. Calvino, *Italian Folktales,* pp. 75–76.

54. Calvino, *Italian Folktales,* pp. 26–30.

55. Hunt and Stern, *Complete Grimms' Fairy Tales,* p. 217.

56. Briggs, *Dictionary of British Folk-Tales,* I, 446–47.

57. Hunt and Stern, *Complete Grimms' Fairy Tales,* p. 209.

58. Delarue and Tenèze, *Le Conte populaire français,* II, 456.

59. See, for example, "La Tige de fève," tale type 555; and "De Fischer un sine Fru," Grimm 19.

60. Delarue and Tenèze, *Le Conte populaire français,* I, 181.

61. Twenty of the thirty-nine versions of the tale recorded in France mention the dance in the thorns. The villain is the priest in thirteen of them. Only once, in a tale from Lorraine, is he a Jew.

62. "Il faut hurler avec les loups," A. J. Panckoucke, *Dictionnaire des proverbes françois, et des façons de parler comiques, burlesques et familières* (Paris, 1749), p. 194.

63. See Paul Radin, *The Trickster: A Study in American Indian Mythology* (New York, 1956) and Lawrence Levine, *Black Culture and Black Consciousness: Afro-American Folk*

Thought from Slavery to Freedom (New York, 1977).

64. Delarue and Tenèze, *Le Conte populaire français*, I, 374.

65. See Jan De Vries, *Die Märchen von klugen Rätsellösern und das kluge Mädchen* (Helsinki, 1928) and Albert Wesselski, *Der Knabenkönig und das kluge Mädchen* (Prague, 1929).

66. Delarue and Tenèze, *Le Conte populaire français*, I, 110. For an example of a tale that pits peasant against seigneur in a manner that suggests something akin to class war, see "René et son seigneur" in Cosquin, *Contes populaires de Lorraine*, I, 108–11. It has no aura of magic or make-believe. The seigneur is not disguised as a giant; and he is fleeced and then murdered by a peasant hero who uses nothing but cunning and dupery.

67. Delarue and Tenèze, *Le Conte populaire français*, I, 331.

68. Ibid., I, 346.

69. The following proverbs have been chosen from the *Dictionnaire des proverbes françois* of 1749 and from the entry for "Proverbe" in the *Nouveau petit Larousse* of 1968 in order to illustrate the continuity and the peculiarly French style of proverbialism over the last two centuries. Of course many proverbs go back to the Middle Ages and have been collected by connoisseurs since the Renaissance. See Natalie Z. Davis, "Proverbial Wisdom and Popular Errors" in Davis, *Society and Culture in Early Modern France* (Stanford, 1975).

70. See Marc Soriano, *Les Contes de Perrault: Culture savante et traditions populaires* (Paris, 1968) and Soriano, *Le Dossier Perrault* (Paris, 1972).

71. Problems of interpreting the social basis and the transmission of culture in early modern France have been debated extensively in the recent outpouring of studies in the history of popular culture. My own views are much closer to those advanced by Peter Burke in his excellent survey of the literature, *Popular Culture in Early Modern Europe* (London and New York, 1978) than they are to those of Robert Muchembled in his general synthesis, *Culture populaire et culture des élites dans la France moderne, XVe–XVIIe siècles* (Paris, 1968).

72. This notion of cultural style derives from the interpretive strain in cultural anthropology. See, for example, Edward Sapir, "Culture, Genuine and Spurious," in Sapir, *Culture, Language and Personality* (Berkeley, 1964).

Chapter 2

1. Nicolas Contat, *Anecdotes typographiques où l'on voit la description des coutumes, moeurs et usages singuliers des compagnons imprimeurs,* ed. Giles Barber (Oxford, 1980). The original manuscript is dated 1762. Barber provides a thorough description of its background and of Contat's career in his introduction. The account of the cat massacre occurs on pp. 48–56.

2. Contat, *Anecdotes typographiques,* p. 53.

3. Ibid., pp. 52 and 53.

4. See, for example, Albert Soboul, *La France à la veille de la Révolution* (Paris, 1966), p. 140; and Edward Shorter, "The History of Work in the West: An Overview" in *Work and Community in the West,* ed. Edward Shorter (New York, 1973).

5. The following discussion is derived from Henri-Jean Martin, *Livre, pouvoirs et société à Paris au XVIIe siècle (1598–1701)* (Geneva, 1969); and Paul Chauvet, *Les Ouvriers du livre en France, des origines à la Révolution de 1789* (Paris, 1959). The statistics come from investigations by the authorities of the Old Regime as reported by Martin (II, 699–700) and Chauvet (pp. 126 and 154).

6. For a more detailed discussion of this material, see Robert Darnton, "Work and Culture in an Eighteenth-Century Printing Shop," an Englehard lecture at the Library of Congress to be published by the Library of Congress.

7. Contat, *Anecdotes typographiques,* pp. 68–73.

8. Christ to STN, Jan. 8, 1773, papers of the Société typographique de Neuchâtel, Bibliothèque de la Ville de Neuchâtel, Switzerland, hereafter cited as STN.

Notes

9. STN to Joseph Duplain, July 2, 1777.

10. STN to Louis Vernange, June 26, 1777.

11. Joseph Duplain to STN, Dec. 10, 1778.

12. Contat, *Anecdotes typographiques*, pp. 30–31.

13. Ibid., p. 52.

14. For a recent overview of the vast literature on folklore and French history and bibliographic references, see Nicole Belmont, *Mythes et croyances dans l'ancienne France* (Paris, 1973). The following discussion is based primarily on the material collected in Eugène Rolland, *Faune populaire de la France* (Paris, 1881), IV; Paul Sébillot, *Le Folk-lore de France* (Paris, 1904–7), 4 vols., especially III, 72–155 and IV, 90–98; and to a lesser extent Arnold Van Gennep, *Manuel de folklore français contemporain* (Paris, 1937–58), 9 vols.

15. In Germany and Switzerland, *Katzenmusik* sometimes included mock trials and executions. The etymology of the term is not clear. See E. Hoffmann-Krayer and Hans Bächtold-Stäubli, *Handwörterbuch des deutschen Aberglaubens* (Berlin and Leipzig, 1931–32), IV, 1125–32 and Paul Grebe et al., *Duden Etymologie: Herkunftswörterbuch der deutschen Sprache* (Mannheim, 1963), p. 317.

16. Information on the cat burning in Saint Chamond comes from a letter kindly sent to me by Elinor Accampo of Colorado College. The Metz ceremony is described in A. Benoist, "Traditions et anciennes coutumes du pays messin," *Revue des traditions populaires*, XV (1900), 14.

17. Contat, *Anecdotes typographiques*, pp. 30 and 66–67; and Chauvet, *Les Ouvriers du livre*, pp. 7–12.

18. Contat, *Anecdotes typographiques*, pp. 65–67.

19. Ibid., pp. 37–41, quotation from pp. 39–40.

20. A good example of the genre, *La Misère des apprentis imprimeurs* (1710) is printed as an appendix to Contat, *Anecdotes typographiques*, pp. 101–10. For other examples, see A. C. Cailleau, *Les Misères de ce monde, ou complaintes facétieuses sur les apprentissages des différents arts et métiers de la ville et faubourgs de Paris* (Paris, 1783).

21. The classic study of this process is Arnold Van Gennep, *Les Rites de passage* (Paris, 1908). It has been extended by subsequent ethnographic research, notably that of Victor Turner: *The Forest of Symbols: Aspects of Ndembu Ritual* (Ithaca, N. Y., 1967) and *The Ritual Process* (Chicago, 1969). Jerome's experience fits the Van Gennep-Turner model very well, except in a few respects. He was not considered sacred and dangerous, although the chapel could fine journeymen for drinking with him. He did not live outside adult society, although he left his home for a makeshift room at the edge of the master's household. And he was not exposed to secret *sacra*, although he had to acquire an esoteric lingo and to assimilate a craft ethos after a great deal of tribulation climaxed by a communal meal. Joseph Moxon, Thomas Gent, and Benjamin Franklin mention similar practices in England. In Germany the initiation rite was much more elaborate and had structural similarities to the rites of tribes in Africa, New Guinea, and North America. The apprentice wore a filthy headdress adorned with goat's horns and a fox's tail, indicating that he had reverted to an animal state. As a *Cornut* or *Mittelding*, part man, part beast, he underwent ritual tortures, including the filing of his fingertips. At the final ceremony, the head of the shop knocked off the hat and slapped him in the face. He then emerged newborn—sometimes newly named and even baptized—as a full-fledged journeyman. Such at least was the practice described in German typographical manuals, notably Christian Gottlob Täubel, *Praktisches Handbuch der Buchdruckerkunst für Anfänger* (Leipzig, 1791); Wilhelm Gottlieb Kircher, *Anweisung in der Buchdruckerkunst so viel davon das Drucken betrifft* (Brunswick, 1793); and Johann Christoph Hildebrand, *Handbuch für Buchdrucker-Lehrlinge* (Eisenach, 1835). The rite was related to an ancient popular play, the *Depositio Cornuti typographici*, which was printed by Jacob Redinger in his *Neu aufgesetztes Format Büchlein* (Frankfurt-am-Main, 1679).

22. Contat, *Anecdotes typographiques*, pp. 65–66.

23. The text does not give Jerome's last name, but it stresses the name change and the

acquisition of the "Monsieur": "It is only after the end of the apprenticeship that one is called Monsieur; this quality belongs only to journeymen and not to apprentices" (p. 41). In the wage book of the STN, the journeymen always appear with their "Monsieur," even when they were called by nicknames, such as "Monsieur Bonnemain."

24. The black cat in Manet's *Olympia* represents a common motif, the animal "familiar" of a nude. On Baudelaire's cats, see Roman Jakobson and Claude Lévi-Strauss, "*Les Chats* de Charles Baudelaire," *L'Homme,* II (1962), 5–21; and Michel Riffaterre, "Describing Poetic Structures: Two Approaches to Baudelaire's *Les Chats,*" in *Structuralism,* ed. Jacques Ehrmann (New Haven, 1966).

25. Mary Douglas, *Purity and Danger: An Analysis of Concepts of Pollution and Taboo* (London, 1966); and E. R. Leach, "Anthropological Aspects of Language: Animal Categories and Verbal Abuse," in *New Directions in the Study of Language,* ed. E. H. Lenneberg, (Cambridge, Mass., 1964).

26. Cervantes and Zola adapted traditional cat lore to the themes of their novels. In *Don Quixote* (part II, chap. 46), a sack full of howling cats interrupts the hero's serenade to Altisidora. Taking them for devils, he tries to mow them down with his sword, only to be bested by one of them in single combat. In *Germinal* (part V, chap. 6), the symbolism works in the opposite way. A mob of workers pursues Maigrat, their class enemy, as if he were a cat trying to escape across the rooftops. Screaming "Get the cat! Get the cat!" they castrate his body "like a tomcat" after he falls from the roof. For an example of cat killing as a satire on French legalism, see Friar John's plan to massacre the Furry Lawcats in Rabelais' *Gargantua and Pantagruel,* book V, chap. 15.

27. Mikhail Bakhtin, *Rabelais and His World,* trans. Helene Iswolsky (Cambridge, Mass., 1968). The most important literary version of cat lore to appear in Contat's time was *Les Chats* (Rotterdam, 1728) by François Augustin Paradis de Moncrif. Although it was a mock treatise aimed at a sophisticated audience, it drew on a vast array of popular superstitions and proverbs, many of which appeared in the collections of folklorists a century and a half later.

28. C. S. L. Davies, *Peace, Print and Protestantism* (St. Albans, Herts, 1977). The other references come from the sources cited in note 14. Among the many dictionaries of proverbs and slang, see André-Joseph Panckoucke, *Dictionnaire des proverbes françois et des façons de parler comiques, burlesques, et familières* (Paris, 1748) and Gaston Esnault, *Dictionnaire historique des argots français* (Paris, 1965).

29. Rolland, *Faune populaire,* p. 118. See note 14 for the other sources on which this account is based.

30. Emile Chautard, *La Vie étrange de l'argot* (Paris, 1931), pp. 367–68. The following expressions come from Panckoucke, *Dictionnaire des proverbes françois;* Esnault, *Dictionnaire historique des argots français;* and *Dictionnaire de l'Académie française* (Paris, 1762), which contains a surprising amount of polite cat lore. The impolite lore was transmitted in large measure by children's games and rhymes, some of them dating from the sixteenth century: Claude Gaignebet, *Le Folklore obscène des enfants* (Paris, 1980), p. 260.

31. Sébillot, *Le Folk-lore de France,* III, 93–94.

32. Panckoucke, *Dictionnaire des proverbes françois,* p. 66.

33. This and the following quotations come from Contat's account of the cat massacre, *Anecdotes typographiques,* pp. 48–56.

34. According to Giles Barber (ibid., pp. 7 and 60), the actual Jacques Vincent for whom Contat worked began his own apprenticeship in 1690; so he probably was born about 1675. His wife was born in 1684. Thus when Contat entered the shop, the master was about 62, the mistress about 53, and the bawdy young priest in his twenties. That pattern was common enough in the printing industry, where old masters often left their businesses to younger wives, who in turn took up with still younger journeymen. It was a classic pattern for charivaris, which often mocked disparities in age among newlyweds as well as humiliating cuckolds.

35. Pierre Caron, *Les Massacres de septembre* (Paris, 1935).

Chapter 3

1. The manuscript was published by Joseph Berthelé as "Montpellier en 1768 d'après un manuscrit anonyme inédit" (cited henceforth as *Description,* from the title given to it by its author) in *Archives de la ville de Montpellier* (Montpellier, 1909), IV. On the genre of urban "descriptions," see Hugues Neveux, "Les Discours sur la ville" in *La Ville classique: de la Renaissance aux révolutions,* ed. Roger Chartier, Guy Chaussinand-Nogaret, Hugues Neveux, and Emmanuel Le Roy Ladurie (Paris, 1981), which is volume III in the *Histoire de la France urbaine* currently being published under the direction of Georges Duby. In the case of Montpellier, our author—unfortunately, this awkward term is the best I can find for him— was able to draw on two earlier works: Pierre Gariel, *Idée de la ville de Montpelier [sic], recherchée et présentée aux honestes gens* (Montpellier, 1665); and Charles d'Aigrefeuille, *Histoire de la ville de Montpellier depuis son origine jusqu'à notre temps* (Montpellier, 1737–39), 2 vols. Although he cited them at several points, his text differs from theirs considerably. In its general form, it is much closer to the contemporary *Almanach historique et chronologique de la ville de Montpellier* (Montpellier, 1759) by Dominique Donat, a local lawyer. In an "Avertissement" to the *Almanach,* Donat proposed following it with a general book about Montpellier; so he might well have been the author of the *Description.* But all attempts to find more solid evidence about the identity of the author have failed.

2. *Description,* p. 9. Later sections of the text contain suggestions for improving local institutions, which are written in a style that suggests an enlightened administrator rather than an eighteenth-century Baedeker; so it seems unlikely that the *Description* was intended to be merely a guidebook.

3. Charles Dickens, *Bleak House* (London, 1912), p. 1.

4. This phrase occurs both in Fernand Braudel and Ernest Labrousse, *Histoire économique et sociale de la France* (Paris, 1970), II, 716; and in Robert Mandrou, *La France aux XVIIe et XVIIIe siècles* (Paris, 1970), p. 178. For a similar version of this standard theme, see a third textbook that appeared in the same year: Albert Soboul, *La Civilisation et la Révoltution française* (Paris, 1970), chaps. 17 and 18, and the remarks on "le take-off" on pp. 342–43. "Le take-off" also appears in Pierre Chaunu, *La Civilisation de l'Europe des Lumières* (Paris, 1971), pp. 28–29, but in a less dogmatic formulation. It would be an interesting exercise to trace the transmission of formulas from textbook to textbook and across the ideological barriers that divide the authors.

5. On the rise of "histoire totale" in France, see Jacques Le Goff, "L'Histoire nouvelle" in Jacques Le Goff, Roger Chartier, and Jacques Revel, *La Nouvelle histoire* (Paris, 1978). For examples of the orthodox view of economic-social-cultural change in eighteenth-century France, see the concluding sections by Labrousse in *Histoire économique et sociale de la France,* pp. 693–740; and by Soboul in *La Civilisation et la Révolution française,* pp. 459–480. For other views, see Roland Mousnier, *Les Institutions de la France sous la monarchie absolue 1598–1789,* 2 vols. (Paris, 1974–80); and Régine Robin, *La Société française en 1789: Sémur en Auxois* (Paris, 1970).

6. Despite a few attempts to sketch a general picture of the eighteenth-century bourgeoisie, the literature on the subject remains surprisingly underdeveloped. Elinor Barber, *The Bourgeoisie in 18th Century France* (Princeton, 1955) is superficial, and the best single study is still Bernhard Groethuysen, *Origines de l'esprit bourgeois en France* (Paris, 1956), though it mainly concerns intellectual history. For the monographic work by social historians, see especially Ernest Labrousse, "Voies nouvelles vers une histoire de la bourgeoisie occidentale aux XVIIIe et XIXe siècles (1700–1850)," *X° Congresso internazionale di Scienze Storiche: Roma, Relazioni* (Florence, 1955), IV, 365–96; Adeline Daumard, "Une référence pour l'étude des sociétés urbaines aux XVIIIe et XIXe siècles: Projet de code socio-professionnel," *Revue d'histoire moderne et contemporaine,* X (July–Sept., 1963), 184–210; Roland Mousnier, "Problèmes de méthode dans l'étude des structures sociales des XVIe, XVIIe et XVIIIe

siècles" in *Spiegel der Geschichte: Festgabe für M. Braubach* (Münster, 1964), pp. 550–64; *L'Histoire sociale: sources et méthodes: Colloque de l'Ecole Normale Supérieure de Saint-Cloud (15–16 mai 1965),* a collective work published by the Presses Universitaires de France (Paris, 1967); Adeline Daumard and François Furet, *Structures et relations sociales à Paris au XVIIIe siècle* (Paris, 1961); Daniel Roche and Michel Vovelle, "Bourgeois, rentiers, propriétaires: éléments pour la définition d'une catégorie sociale à la fin du XVIIIe siècle," in *Actes du Quatre-Vingt-Quatrième Congrès National des Sociétés Savantes (Dijon, 1959), Section d'Histoire Moderne et Contemporaine* (Paris, 1960), pp. 419–52; Maurice Garden, *Lyon et les Lyonnais au XVIIIe siècle* (Paris, 1970); and Jean-Claude Perrot, *Genèse d'une ville moderne: Caen au XVIIIe siècle* (Paris and The Hague, 1975), 2 vols. For different reassessments of the nobility, see Guy Chaussinand-Nogaret, *La noblesse au XVIIIe siècle: De la Féodalité aux Lumières* (Paris, 1976) and Patrice Higonnet, *Class, Ideology, and the Rights of Nobles During the French Revolution* (Oxford, 1981).

7. The series of volumes on individual cities published by Privat already covers Le Mans, Toulouse, Brest, Lyon, Rouen, Angers, Nantes, Marseille, Nice, Toulon, Grenoble, Bordeaux, and Nancy; and the *Histoire de la France urbaine* provides an excellent synthesis of this burgeoning literature. Even Lille, which has usually been considered a prime site of urban industrialization, now looks more archaic in its economy—a center for the putting-out industry in the surrounding countryside and of "protoindustrialization": see Pierre Deyon et al., *Aux origines de la révolution industrielle, industrie rurale et fabriques,* a special issue of *Revue du Nord* for January–March 1979. Michel Morineau has argued the case for nongrowth in several articles and in *Les Faux-Semblants d'un démarrage économique: Agriculture et démographie en France au XVIIIe siècle* (Paris, 1971).

8. Daniel Roche, *Le Siècle des Lumières en province: Académies et académiciens provinciaux, 1680–1789* (Paris and The Hague, 1978); Robert Darnton, *The Business of Enlightenment: A Publishing History of the* Encyclopédie, *1775–1800* (Cambridge, Mass., 1979); John Lough, *Paris Theatre Audiences in the Seventeenth and Eighteenth Centuries* (London, 1957); and as an example of reductionist sociology in the interpretation of literature, Lucien Goldmann, "La Pensée des Lumières," *Annales: Economies, sociétés, civilisations,* XX (1967), 752–70.

9. These examples are quoted from the *Dictionnaire universel françois et latin, vulgairement appelé Dictionnaire de Trévoux* (Paris, 1771), II, 11–12; but similar illustrations of contemporary usage can be found in other eighteenth-century dictionaries, notably the entries under "bourgeois" in *Dictionnaire de l'Académie françoise* (Paris, 1762); *Dictionnaire universel contenant généralement tous les mots françois, tant vieux que modernes, et les termes des sciences et des arts* (The Hague, 1727), by Antoine Furetière; *Dictionnaire universel de commerce, d'histoire naturelle, et des arts et métiers* (Copenhagen, 1759), by Jacques Savary des Bruslons, continued by Philemon-Louis Savary; and *Encyclopédie ou dictionnaire raisonné des sciences, des arts et des métiers* (Paris, 1751–72), edited by Diderot and d'Alembert. The dictionaries note certain technical usages: the bourgeois who were exempt from seigneurial law courts in Champagne and Burgundy; the bourgeois who owned commercial ships; and the bourgeois who employed labor. The latter, as defined in the *Dictionnaire de Trévoux,* corresponds closely to the bourgeois of Contat's printing shop: "Workers call the man for whom they work *le bourgeois.* [For example], 'One must serve *le bourgeois*'; 'Masons, artisans always try to fool *le bourgeois.*'" Nuances of social distinctions also show through the definitions. The *Encyclopédie* stresses the connection between "bourgeois" and "citizen" in terms that suggest Rousseau, whereas the *Dictionnaire de l'Académie françoise* notes the pejorative usage of the word: "Bourgeois is also said in a scornful manner as a reproach to a man who is not a gentleman or who has no familiarity with the ways of high society. 'He is merely a bourgeois.' 'That smells of the bourgeois.'" Savary places the bourgeois squarely between the nobility and the common people, but in a favorable light: "Bourgeois. It is generally applied to a citizen who inhabits a city. More particularly, it denotes those citizens who are not counted among the clergy nor the nobility; and more particularly still those who, although not occupying the highest positions in the courts or other distinguished offices, nonetheless are far above the artisans and the common

people, owing to their wealth, their honorable profession, or their commerce. It is in this sense that one says of a man one wants to praise that he is a good bourgeois." Finally, the dictionaries show how the word evoked a style of life. Thus the *Dictionnaire de Trévoux:* "A bourgeois house is a house built simply and without magnificence but in a comfortable and liveable fashion. It is opposed equally to a palace or mansion and to a cabin or cottage of the sort inhabited by peasants and artisans. . . . One also says in ordinary conversation, a bourgeois soup, meaning a good soup. . . . A bourgeois wine [is] . . . wine that has not been doctored, that one keeps in one's cellar, as opposed to cabaret wine."

10. The following discussion is based on Louis Thomas, *Montpellier ville marchande: Histoire économique et sociale de Montpellier des origines à 1870* (Montpellier, 1936); Albert Fabre, *Histoire de Montpellier depuis son origine jusqu'à la fin de la Révolution* (Montpellier, 1897); and Philippe Wolff, ed., *Histoire du Languedoc* (Toulouse, 1967), as well as the sources cited in note 1.

11. *Description,* p. 35.

12. Ibid., p. 35.

13. Ibid., p. 29.

14. Ibid., p. 52.

15. Ibid., p. 18.

16. Louis Dumont, *Homo hierarchicus: Essai sur le système des castes* (Paris, 1966).

17. *Description,* p. 157.

18. Ibid., p. 67.

19. Ibid., p. 67.

20. Ibid., p. 67.

21. Ibid., pp. 35 and 99.

22. Ibid., p. 99.

23. Ibid., p. 98.

24. Ibid., p. 70.

25. Ibid., p. 156.

26. Ibid., p. 38.

27. Ibid., p. 68.

28. Ibid., p. 110.

29. Ibid., p. 158.

30. Ibid., p. 110.

31. Ibid., p. 158.

32. Ibid., p. 151.

33. Ibid., p. 151.

34. Ibid., p. 154.

35. Ibid., p. 155.

36. Ibid., p. 154.

37. Ibid., p. 68.

38. Ibid., p. 54.

39. Ibid., p. 58.

40. Ibid., pp. 57–58.

41. Ibid., p. 69.

42. Ibid., p. 68.

43. Ibid., p. 150.

44. Ibid., p. 149.

45. Ibid., p. 54.

46. See Roche, *Le Siècle des Lumières en province* for a thorough discussion of this theme.

47. *Description,* p. 59.

48. Ibid., p. 27.

49. Ibid., p. 21.

50. Ibid., p. 150.

Chapter 4

An earlier version of Chapter 4 entitled "Policing Writers in Paris circa 1750" appeared in Vol. 5 of *Studies in the Eighteenth Century* Papers presented at the Fifth David Nichol Smith Memorial Seminar, Canberra 1980 edited by J. P. Hardy and J. C. Eade (Oxford: 1983 pp. 143–155)

1. This study is based on the manuscript reports of Joseph d'Hémery in the Bibliothèque Nationale of Paris, nouv. acq. fr. 10781–10783. All quotations come from that source and can be identified easily in the manuscript, because the reports are arranged alphabetically according to the names of the authors under investigation. I plan to publish the full texts of the reports in a volume to be edited in collaboration with Robert Shackleton and eventually to use them for a book on the rise of the intellectual in France. Although they have never been studied as a whole, the reports have been consulted for a few biographical works, notably *Jeunesse de Diderot 1713-1753* (Paris, 1939) by Franco Venturi, which quotes most of the report on Diderot (p. 379).

2. Jacques Hébrail and Joseph de La Porte, *La France littéraire* (Paris, 1756). The authors explained the character and purpose of their work in an *avertissement*, which contained a general appeal for bibliographical information to be sent in by anyone, and especially by unknown writers. The new information appeared in the form of *additions* in the edition of 1756, and *suppléments* were published in 1760, 1762, 1764, and 1784. In the edition of 1762, p. v, the authors estimated that somewhat more than 1,800 *auteurs* were then alive in France. Allowing for the growth in the population, in the prestige of authorship, and in book production, it seems likely that about 1,500 Frenchmen had published a book or pamphlet in 1750.

3. On the much-debated questions concerning generations, cohorts, and other age groups, see Clifton Cherpack, "The Literary Periodization of Eighteenth-Century France," *Publications of the Modern Language Association of America*, LXXXIV (1969), 321–28 and Alan B. Spitzer, "The Historical Problem of Generations," *The American Historical Review*, LXXVIII (1973), 1353–83.

4. On the Saint Malo-Geneva line as a demarcation of socio-cultural history, see Roger Chartier, "Les Deux France: Histoire d'une géographie," *Cahiers d'histoire*, XXIV (1979), 393–415. For a discussion of the Paris-province question, see Robert Escarpit, *Sociologie de la littérature* (Paris, 1968), 41–44. Of course, as Paris is located in the north, one might expect a map of the birthplaces of authors living in Paris to underrepresent the south. It also seems unreasonable to expect a close correlation between the birthplaces of authors and crude indicators of literacy such as those discussed in François Furet and Jacques Ozouf, *Lire et écrire: L'Alphabétisation des Français de Calvin à Jules Ferry* (Paris, 1977), 2 vols.

5. See the article on Favart in J.-F. and L.-G. Michaud, eds., *Biographie universelle* (Paris, 1811–52), XIII, 440–42; as well as the more scholarly studies of Georges Desnoireterres, *Epicuriens et lettrês* (Paris, 1879); and Auguste Font, *Favart, l'Opéra-Comique et la comédie-vaudeville aux XVIIe et XVIIIe siècles* (Paris, 1894).

6. In almost half the cases, the *embastillement* came after the completion of d'Hémery's report. Despite their vigilance concerning suspicious characters, the police did not orient their surveillance toward the criminal element in the republic of letters but rather attempted to do a general survey of all the writers they could find.

7. The attempts of officials to increase the power of the state by systematic study of its resources goes back to Machiavelli and the development of "reason of state" as a principle of government. Although this tendency has usually been treated as an aspect of political theory, it also belongs to the history of bureaucracy and to the spread of "rationalization" (rather than Englightenment), as Max Weber understood it. For a recent survey of the literature on the intellectual history side of the question, see Michael Stolleis, "*Arcana imperii* und *Ratio*

status: Bemerkungen zur politischen Theorie des frühen 17. Jahrhunderts," *Veröffentlichung der Joachim-Jungius-Gesellschaft der Wissenschaften*, no. 39 (Göttingen, 1980), 5–34.

8. Thus the report on Jean-François de Bastide: "He is a Provençal, is witty but not talented, and fucks Madame de Valence, the mistress of M. Vanoé, the ambassador of Holland."

9. See Robert Mandrou, *De la Culture populaire aux XVIIe et XVIIIe siècles: La Bibliothèque bleue de Troyes* (Paris, 1964).

10. For more information on all these intrigues, see the works cited in note 5.

11. The character of Laurès's poetry, which is now deservedly forgotten, can be appreciated from a glance at his *Epître à M. le comte de Bernis* (Paris, 1752) and his *Epître à Madame la marquise de Pompadour*, no place or date of publication.

12. See d'Alembert, *Essai sur la société des gens de lettres et des grands, sur la réputation, sur les mécènes et sur les récompenses littéraires*, in d'Alembert's *Mélanges de littérature, d'histoire et de philosophie* (Amsterdam, 1773; lst ed., 1752).

13. This theme appears most prominently in d'Alembert's *Essai sur la société des gens de lettres*, Voltaire's *Lettres philosophiques* of 1734, the anonymous tract *Le Philosophe* of 1743, and the article PHILOSOPHE in vol. XIII of the *Encyclopédie*. For further details, see the following chapter.

14. The verse comes from *Journal et mémoires du marquis d'Argenson*, E.J.B. Rathery, ed. (Paris, 1863), p. 402. D'Hémery mentioned this song and many similar ones but did not transcribe them in his reports.

15. I have used the term "intellectual" without defining it because I have tried to establish its boundaries by reconstructing the contemporary context of "authors." I should explain, however, that I do not think that intellectuals and authors are the same thing and that I derive my concept of the intellectual from sociologists like Karl Mannheim, Edward Shils, and Pierre Bourdieu. See especially Bourdieu, *Questions de sociologie* (Paris, 1980).

Chapter 5

Chapter 5 was originally presented as a lecture at the Herzog August Bibliothek Wolfenbüttel in May 1981.

1. John Lough, *The 'Encyclopédie'* (New York, 1971), p. 61.

2. Michel Foucault, *The Order of Things: An Archeology of the Human Sciences* (New York, 1973), p. xv.

3. See Roger Shattuck, *The Forbidden Experiment: The Story of the Wild Boy of Aveyron* (New York, 1980).

4. For fuller accounts of this argument, see E. R. Leach, "Anthropological Aspects of Language: Animal Categories and Verbal Abuse" in *New Directions in the Study of Language,* ed. E. H. Lenneberg (Cambridge, Mass., 1964); Mary Douglas, *Purity and Danger: An Analysis of Concepts of Pollution and Taboo* (London, 1966); R. N. H. Bulmer, "Why Is the Cassowary Not a Bird? A Problem of Zoological Taxonomy Among the Karam of the New Guinea Highlands," *Man,* II (1967), 5–25; and S. J. Tambiah, "Animals Are Good to Think and to Prohibit," *Ethnology,* VIII (1969), 423–59.

5. On "method" and the early schemes for ordering the arts and sciences, see Walter Ong, *Ramus, Method, and the Decay of Dialogue: From the Art of Discourse to the Art of Reason* (Cambridge, Mass., 1958); Neal W. Gilbert, *Renaissance Concepts of Method* (New York, 1960); Paul Oskar Kristeller, "The Modern System of the Arts," in Kristeller, *Renaissance Thought II: Papers on Humanism and the Arts* (New York, 1965), 163–227; Frances Yates, *The Art of Memory* (London, 1966); Leroy E. Loemker, *Struggle for Synthesis: The Seventeenth*

Century Background of Leibniz's Synthesis of Order and Freedom (Cambridge, Mass., 1972); and Paolo Rossi, *Philosophy, Technology and the Arts in the Early Modern Era* (New York, 1970). On encyclopedias before Diderot's *Encyclopédie*, see Robert Collison, *Encyclopaedias: Their History throughout the Ages* (New York, 1964); and Frank A. Kafker, ed., *Notable Encyclopedias of the Seventeenth and Eighteenth Centuries: Nine Predecessors of the Encyclopédie, Studies on Voltaire and the Eighteenth Century,* CXCIV (Oxford, 1981). For a recent but rather superficial overview of systems for classifying knowledge, see Fritz Machlup, *Knowledge: The Branches of Learning* (Princeton, 1981). I am indebted to Anthony Grafton for bibliographical guidance and criticism in my attempts to make sense of these subjects.

6. *Discours préliminaire* in *Encyclopédie, ou Dictionnaire raisonné des sciences, des arts et des métiers, par une société de gens de lettres* (Paris, 1751–72), I, i. All subsequent references to the *Discours préliminaire* come from the first edition of the *Encyclopédie*.

7. *Prospectus de l'Encyclopédie* in Denis Diderot, *Oeuvres complètes* (Paris, 1969), II, 281. On the notion of an encyclopedia as a circle or great chain of knowledge, see also Diderot's key article, ENCYCLOPÉDIE in *Encyclopédie,* V, reprinted in Diderot, *Oeuvres complètes,* II, 365–463.

8. *Discours préliminaire,* p. xv.

9. *Prospectus,* p. 285–86.

10. *Prospectus,* p. 285.

11. Ephraim Chambers, *Cyclopaedia: or an Universal Dictionary of Arts and Sciences,* 5th ed. (London, 1741), I, p. ii.

12. Ibid., p. iii.

13. *Discours préliminaire,* p. xxiv.

14. See the articles in the *Mémoires de Trévoux,* Jan. and Feb., 1751, reprinted in Diderot, *Oeuvres complètes,* II, 325–32 and 352–55.

15. Francis Bacon, *The Advancement of Learning,* ed. W. A. Wright (Oxford, 1876), p. 268.

16. Ibid., p. 99.

17. Ibid., p. 86.

18. *Discours préliminaire,* p. xvii.

19. Bacon, *Advancement of Learning,* p. 86.

20. Ibid., p. 85.

21. *Discours préliminaire,* p. xlvii.

22. *Lettre de M. Diderot au R. P. Berthier, jésuite* in Diderot, *Oeuvres complètes,* II, 334.

23. *Discours préliminaire,* p. li.

24. *Encyclopédie,* I, 498.

25. Bacon, *Advancement of Learning,* pp. 109–10. Bacon acknowledged the force of inductive reasoning about God, but he considered it dangerous: "Out of the contemplation of nature, or ground of human knowledges, to induce any verity or persuasion concerning the points of faith, is in my judgement not safe" (p. 109).

26. *Discours préliminaire,* p. xvii.

27. Ibid., p. xlviii. For Locke's version of this argument, see *An Essay Concerning Human Understanding,* ed. A. S. Pringle-Pattison (Oxford, 1960), book II, chap. 23, 154–74.

28. *Discours préliminaire,* p. iii.

29. Ibid., p. iv.

30. Ibid., p. iv.

31. Ibid., p. iii.

32. Ibid., p. ix.

33. Ibid., p. xiv.

34. Ibid., p. ix.

35. Ibid., p. xiv.

36. Ibid., p. xvii.

37. See also d'Alembert's "Avertissement" to the third volume of the *Encyclopédie* (III,

iv): "In this work, one will not find . . . the conquerors who have devasted the earth, but rather the immortal geniuses who have enlightened it. Nor [will one find] a crowd of sovereigns who should have been proscribed from history. Even the names of princes and great personages have no right to a place in the *Encyclopédie*, except by virtue of the good they have done for science, because the *Encyclopédie* owes everything to talent and nothing to titles. It is the history of the human spirit, not of the vanity of mankind."

38. *Discours préliminaire*, p. xxvi.

39. Ibid., p. xxvi.

40. Ibid., p. xxvii.

41. Ibid., p. xxvi.

42. D'Alembert, *Essai sur la société des gens de lettres et des grands, sur la réputation, sur les Mécènes, et sur les récompenses littéraires* in *Mélanges de littérature, d'histoire et de philosophie* (Amsterdam, 1773; 1st ed., 1752), p. 330.

43. *Encyclopédie*, VII, 599.

44. On the metamorphoses of this essay, which Voltaire also reprinted in *Les Lois de Minos* (1773), see Herbert Dieckmann, *Le Philosophe: Texts and Interpretation* (Saint Louis, 1948).

45. For documentation of this theme, which still needs further exploration, see Ira Wade, *"The Philosophe" in the French Drama of the Eighteenth Century* (Princeton, 1926).

46. For a preliminary survey of *philosophe* and *Encyclopédiste* as terms in vogue during the eighteenth century, see Ferdinand Brunot, *Histoire de la langue française des origines à nos jours* (Paris, 1966), VI, part 1, 3–27.

47. D'Alembert also stressed this in the "Avertissement" (*Encyclopédie*, III, iv): "It is thus principally by its philosophical spirit that we shall attempt to make this dictionary stand out."

Chapter 6

1. This essay is an attempt to combine traditional history, based on archival research, with textual interpretation of the kind developed by literary critics such as Wolfgang Iser, Hans Robert Jauss, Wayne Booth, Stanley Fish, Walter Ong, Jonathan Culler, Louis Marin, and others. For a survey of the work in this field and a thorough bibliography, see Susan R. Suleiman and Inge Crosman, eds., *The Reader in the Text: Essays on Audience and Interpretation* (Princeton, 1980). As examples of work concerning Rousseau, see: Robert J. Ellrich, *Rousseau and His Reader: The Rhetorical Situation of the Major Works* (Chapel Hill, 1969); Harald Weinrich, "Muss es Romanlektüre geben? Anmerkungen zu Rousseau und zu den Lesern der *Nouvelle Héloïse,*" in *Leser und Lesen im 18. Jahrhundert,* ed. Rainer Gruenter (Heidelberg, 1977), pp. 28–32; Roger Bauer, "Einführung in einige Texte von Jean-Jacques Rousseau," in *Leser und Lesen,* pp. 33–39; and Hans Robert Jauss, *Ästhetische Erfahrung und literarische Hermeneutik* (Frankfurt am Main, 1982), pp. 585–653.

2. I owe this information to A. L. Becker, who has observed many Balinese funerals as a linguist and ethnographer.

3. References to Ranson's dossier, in the Bibliothèque de la ville de Neuchâtel, ms. 1204, will be indicated hereafter by the abbreviation STN. Some excerpts from it will be published by R. A. Leigh in volumes XL and XLI of the *Correspondance complète de Jean-Jacques Rousseau.* The information on Ranson from La Rochelle comes from his marriage contracts of June 24, 1777, and Nov. 29, 1788, Archives départementales de la Charente-Maritime, Minutes Crassous 3 E 776 and Minutes Roy 3 E 89, which were most obligingly sent to me in photocopy by Mlle O. de Saint-Affrique.

4. Ranson made his own estimate of his wealth in his marriage contract of Nov. 29,

1788. In a letter to the STN of March 16, 1779, he remarked that the war had damaged the trade in La Rochelle severely, although it had not hurt his own business. The livre tournois cannot be converted meaningfully into modern currencies; but as an example of its value in the eighteenth century, a skilled artisan often made about five hundred livres in a year.

5. For a survey of the literature on eighteenth-century libraries and reading habits in general, see Robert Darnton, "Reading, Writing, and Publishing in Eighteenth-Century France: A Case Study in the Sociology of Literature," *Daedalus* (Winter 1971), 214–56. The most recent study is Michel Marion, *Recherches sur les bibliothèques privées à Paris au milieu de XVIIIe siècle (1750–1759)* (Paris, 1978).

6. Ranson to STN, April 29, 1775.

7. Ranson to STN, Sept. 27, 1780.

8. Ranson to STN, Oct. 17, 1775.

9. Ranson to STN, March 8, 1777.

10. Ranson to STN, Dec. 27, 1774.

11. Ranson to STN, Aug. 30, 1785.

12. Ranson to STN, June 10, 1777.

13. Pavie to STN, March 4, 1772.

14. For example, "False religions. One calls heretics all those who do not believe everything that the Catholic religion commands us to believe. Such are Lutherans, Calvinists, and many others": N.-A. Viard, *Les vrais principes de la lecture . . .* (Paris, 1763), p. 76.

15. Ranson to STN, Aug. 9, 1775.

16. Ranson to STN, Oct. 17, 1775.

17. Viard, *Les vrais principes de la lecture,* p. i.

18. Ibid., p. xi.

19. Ibid., p. 26.

20. Ibid., p. x.

21. J.-J. Rousseau, *Emile ou de l'éducation* in *Oeuvres complètes,* Bibliothèque de la Pléiade (Paris, 1969), IV, 358.

22. J.-J. Rousseau, *Les Confessions de J.-J. Rousseau* in *Oeuvres complètes* (Paris, 1959), I, 8.

23. Ibid., pp. 8–9.

24. J.-J. Rousseau, *Julie, ou La Nouvelle Héloïse* in *Oeuvres complètes* (Paris, 1961), II, 57–58.

25. Ibid., II, 56–57.

26. Rousseau, *Confessions,* I, 111–12.

27. Rousseau, *La Nouvelle Héloïse,* II, 5.

28. Ibid., II, 12.

29. Ibid., II, 5.

30. Ibid., II, 5.

31. Ibid., II, 6.

32. Rousseau wore his title "citizen of Geneva" defiantly on the title pages of the works that he wrote during this period, notably his open letters to d'Alembert and to Christophe de Beaumont. The latter offered a provocative contrast between the simple Swiss republican and the powerful archbishop of Paris: *Jean-Jacques Rousseau, citoyen de Genève, à Christophe de Beaumont, archevêque de Paris, duc de S. Cloud, pair de France, commandeur de l'ordre du Saint-Esprit, proviseur de Sorbonne, etc.* Rousseau left "citizen of Geneva" off the title page of *La Nouvelle Héloïse* because he did not want to "profane" the name of his fatherland in associating it with a novel: *La Nouvelle Héloïse,* II, 27. In the eighteenth century novels were often considered either morally suspect or a low form of literature, and novelists usually did not put their names on the title pages of their books. In fact, people rarely used first names in their everyday activities, except perhaps among the peasantry. By identifying himself as "Jean-Jacques," Rousseau invited his readers to enter into an unusual, intimate relationship.

33. Rousseau, *La Nouvelle Héloïse,* II, 18–19.

34. On the split with Diderot and the circumstances in which Rousseau wrote *La Nou-*

velle Héloïse, see the critical study by Bernard Guyon in *Oeuvres complètes,* II, xviii–lxx.

35. Rousseau, *La Nouvelle Héloïse,* II, 16.
36. Ibid., II, 16.
37. Ibid., II, 15.
38. Ibid., II, 11.
39. Ibid., II, 29.
40. Ibid., II, 26–27.
41. Ibid., II, 27.
42. Rousseau, *Emile,* IV, 357.
43. Ranson to STN, Aug. 9, 1775.
44. Ranson to STN, Jan. 25, 1777.
45. Ranson to STN, March 8, 1777.
46. Ranson to STN, June 10, 1777.
47. Ranson to STN, July 12, 1777.
48. Ranson to STN, Sept. 27, 1777.
49. Ranson to STN, Nov. 29, 1777.
50. Ranson to STN, May 16, 1778.
51. Ranson to STN, Aug. 1, 1778.
52. Ranson to STN, Sept. 12, 1778.
53. The Ransons had named their daughter Elisabeth for Ranson's mother. The information on the children's births and the family names comes primarily from the contract for Ranson's second marriage, dated Nov. 29, 1788. His first wife, Madeleine Raboteau, had died sometime within the previous three years, and Ranson married her cousin, Jeanne Françoise Raboteau.
54. Ranson to STN, Dec. 27, 1778.
55. Ranson to STN, March 16, 1779.
56. See Philippe Ariès, *L'Enfant et la vie familiale sous l'Ancien Régime* (Paris, 1960).
57. Rousseau, *La Nouvelle Héloïse,* II, 23.
58. Ranson to STN, Sept. 16, 1780.
59. The last letter in Ranson's dossier is dated August 30, 1785. Ranson almost certainly continued to write to Ostervald after that date, but the letters are not to be found in the STN papers because Ostervald withdrew from the direction of the STN's affairs in 1784/85. Thus one cannot follow Ranson's career and family life to the death of his first wife, his remarriage, and through the Revolution. As mentioned above, he played a minor and moderate role in local revolutionary politics, and he died on August 5, 1823, at the age of seventy-five, having outlived his second wife.
60. For a general view of the response to *La Nouvelle Héloïse,* which includes a brief study of the mail received by Rousseau, see Daniel Mornet, *La Nouvelle Héloïse* (Paris, 1925), I, 247–67. Mornet's findings have been extended in the more systematic and sociological analysis by Daniel Roche, "Les primitifs du Rousseauisme: une analyse sociologique et quantitative de la correspondance de J.-J. Rousseau," *Annales: Economies, sociétés, civilisations* (Jan.–Feb., 1971), xxvi, pp. 151–72. The texts of the letters received by Rousseau can now be read in the splendid edition of Rousseau's correspondence by R. A. Leigh: *Correspondance complète de Jean Jacques Rousseau* (Geneva, 1969), vols. VIII–X.
61. The quotations and other references, in the order of their appearance, come from Rousseau's *Correspondance complète:* C.-J. Panckoucke to Rousseau, Feb., 1761, VIII, 77–78; J.-L. Buisson to Rousseau, Feb. 11, 1761, VIII, 88; A. -J. Loyseau de Mauléon to Rousseau, Feb. 18, 1761, VIII, 130; Charlotte Bourette to Rousseau, Feb. 21, 1761, VIII, 148; J.-J.-P. Fromaget to Rousseau, June 5, 1761, IX, 3; abbé Cahagne to Rousseau, Feb. 27, 1761, VIII, 187 and 191; J.-F. Bastide to Rousseau, Feb. 12, 1761, VIII, 91–92; Daniel Roguin to Rousseau, Feb. 27, 1761, VIII, 181; A.-P. de Gingins, baron de La Sarraz to Rousseau, March (?), 1761, VIII, 263; Jacques Pernetti and Jean-Vincent Capperonnier de Gauffecourt to Rousseau, Feb. 26, 1761, VIII, 178; D.-M.-Z.-A. Mazarini-Mancini, marquise de Polig-

nac to M. -M. de Brémond d'Ars, marquise de Verdelin, Feb. 3, 1761, VIII, 56; Charlotte de La Taille to Rousseau, March 10, 1761, VIII, 239–40; Louis François to Rousseau, March 24, 1761, VIII, 278–79; and the issue of the *Journal helvétique* of February, 1761, quoted in VIII, 73.

62. D.-M.-Z.-A. Mazarini-Mancini, marquise de Polignac to M.-M. de Brémond d'Ars, marquise de Verdelin, Feb. 3, 1761, in *Correspondance complète,* VIII, 56–57.

63. Louis François to Rousseau, March 24, 1761, in *Correspondance complète,* VIII, 278–79; and Paul-Claude Moultou to Rousseau, March 7, 1761, VIII, 225–26.

64. Mme Du Verger to Rousseau, Jan. 22, 1762, in *Correspondance complète,* X, 47.

65. See *Correspondance complète,* IX, 132–55, for the beginning of this correspondence.

66. Rousseau, *Confessions,* I, 545–47.

67. Fromaget to Rousseau, June 5, 1761, in *Correspondance complète,* IX, 3.

68. An anonymous reader to Rousseau, April 6, 1761, in *Correspondance complète,* VIII, 296; letter from an anonymous young woman, March, 1761 (?), VIII, 258–59; Pierre de La Roche to Rousseau, Oct. 16, 1761, IX, 168; and C. -J. Panckoucke to Rousseau, Feb., 1761, VIII, 77–78.

69. M. Rousselot to Rousseau, March 15, 1761, in *Correspondance complète,* VIII, 252; B.-L. de Lenfant de la Patrière, baron de Bormes to Rousseau, March 27, 1761, VIII, 280–81; A.-A. Lalive de Jully to Rousseau, Jan. 31, 1761, VIII, 43; F.-C. Constant de Rebecque to F.-M.-S. Constant de Rebecque, Feb. 9, 1761 (?), VIII, 72; and J.-L. Le Cointe to Rousseau, April 5, 1761, VIII, 292–93.

70. A.-J. Loyseau de Mauléon to Rousseau, Feb. 18, 1761, in *Correspondance complète,* VIII, 131; an anonymous reader to Rousseau, April 6, 1761, VIII, 296; an anonymous reader to Rousseau, March, 1761, VIII, 256–57; and an anonymous reader to Rousseau, March, 1761, VIII, 257–58. All of these phrases, and expressions in other letters received by Rousseau, adhered closely to the phrasing of the prefaces.

71. Rolf Engelsing, *Der Bürger als Leser: Lesergeschichte in Deutschland 1500–1800* (Stuttgart, 1974). For critical discussions of Engelsing's thesis, see Reinhart Siegert, *Aufklärung und Volkslektüre exemplarisch dargestellt an Rudolph Zacharias Becker und seinem "Noth- und Hülfsbüchlein" mit einer Bibliographie zum Gesamtthema* (Frankfurt am Main, 1978); and Martin Welke, "Gemeinsame Lektüre und frühe Formen von Gruppenbildungen im 17. und 18. Jahrhundert: Zeitungslesen in Deutschland," in *Lesegesellschaften und bürgerliche Emanzipation: Ein europäischer Vergleich,* ed. Otto Dann (Munich, 1981).

72. Ranson to STN, Dec. 27, 1774.

73. Ranson to STN, May 8, 1781.

74. Ranson to STN, June 12, 1785.

75. Johann Adam Bergk, *Die Kunst Bücher zu Lesen* (Jena, 1799), 411.

76. For example, on p. 302 of ibid. Bergk emphasized, "Rousseau with his blazing, creative imagination and with his penetrating understanding overwhelms us in his grip and affords us a pleasure that pierces to the innermost recesses of our heart. He tears the veil away from the secrets of nature, and his descriptions like a mighty torrent sweep us off our feet."

Conclusion

1. Pierre Chaunu, "Un Nouveau Champ pour l'histoire sérielle: Le Quantitatif au troisième niveau" in Pierre Chaunu, *Histoire quantitative, histoire sérielle* (Paris, 1978), pp. 216–30. By *sérielle* Chaunu means something more specific than statistical or quantitative, but the word does not translate well as "serial". Also, Chaunu does not discuss the way phenomena

Notes

from the first two levels affect those on the third. For an explicit account of that theme, see Fernand Braudel and Ernest Labrousse, *Histoire économique et sociale de la France* (Paris, 1970), II, 693–740; and Albert Soboul, *La Civilisation et la Révolution française* (Paris, 1970), pp. 459–80. For discussions of the history of *mentalités* as a genre, see the essays by Lucien Febvre reprinted in *Combats pour l'histoire* (Paris, 1965), pp. 207–39; Georges Duby, "Histoire des mentalités" in *L'Histoire et ses méthodes (Encyclopédie de la Pléiade,* Paris, 1961), pp. 937–66; Alphonse Dupront, "Problèmes et méthodes d'une histoire de la psychologie collective," *Annales: Economies, sociétés, civilisations,* XVI (1961), 3–11; Louis Trénard, "Histoire des mentalités collectives: Les Livres, bilans et perspectives," *Revue d'histoire moderne et contemporaine,* XV (1968), 691–703; Robert Mandrou, "Histoire sociale et histoire des mentalités," *La Nouvelle Critique* (1972), pp. 3–11; Jacques Le Goff, "Les Mentalités: Une Histoire ambiguë," in *Faire de l'histoire,* ed. Jacques Le Goff and Pierre Nora (Paris, 1974), III, 76–94; Philippe Ariès, "L'Histoire des mentalités," in *La Nouvelle Histoire,* ed. Jacques Le Goff, Roger Chartier, and Jacques Revel (Paris, 1978), pp. 402–22; and Michel Vovelle, "Histoire des mentalités—Histoire des résistances de ou les prisons de la longue durée," *History of European Ideas* II (1981), 1–18. *La Nouvelle Histoire* provides a survey of the historiographical trends that are identified with the *"Annales* school." For examples of excellent doctoral theses that are constructed according to the same model, see F. G. Dreyfus, *Sociétés et mentalités à Mayence dans la seconde moitié du dix-huitième siècle* (Paris, 1968): part I, "Economie," part II, "Structure sociale," part III, "Mentalités et culture"; Maurice Garden, *Lyon et les Lyonnais au XVIIIe siècle* (Paris, 1970): part I, "Démographie," part II, "Société," part III, "Structures mentales et comportements collectifs"; and François Lebrun, *Les Hommes et la mort en Anjou aux 17e et 18e siècles* (Paris, 1971): part I, "Structures économiques et socio-géographiques," part II, "Structure démographique," part III, "Mentalités."

2. Ernest Labrousse, *La Crise de l'économie française à la fin de l'Ancien Régime et au début de la Révolution* (Paris, 1944), I, xxix; Pierre Chaunu, "Dynamique conjoncturelle et histoire sérielle: Point de vue d'historien," in Chaunu, *Histoire quantitative, histoire sérielle,* p. 17. I have attempted to survey the French literature in a series of articles in *The New York Review of Books,* some of which have been republished as "The History of *Mentalités:* Recent Writings on Revolution, Criminality, and Death in France," in *Structure, Consciousness, and History,* ed. Richard H. Brown and Stanford M. Lyman (Cambridge, 1978), pp. 106–36. It should be added that some historians connected with the *Annales,* notably Jacques Le Goff and Jean-Claude Schmitt, are now turning away from the quantitative analysis of culture and toward anthropology. See Roger Chartier, "Intellectual or socio-cultural history? The French trajectories," in *Modern European Intellectual History: Reappraisals and New Perspectives,* ed. Dominick La Capra and Steven L. Kaplan (Ithaca, 1982), pp. 13–46; and André Burguière, "The Fate of the History of *Mentalités* in the *Annales,*" *Comparative Studies in Society and History,* XXIV (1982), 424–37. However, this anthropology generally remains restricted within the structuralist system of Claude Lévi-Strauss or the functionalism derived from Emile Durkheim. It has not been affected by the symbolic strain in American anthropology, which developed under the influence of Edward B. Tylor and Franz Boas, nor by the Weberian strain, which has flowered in the work of Clifford Geertz. While Americans tend to ignore systems of relations, the French generally neglect systems of meaning.

3. William Langer, *Political and Social Upheaval, 1832–1852* (New York, 1969); Keith Thomas, *Religion and the Decline of Magic* (New York, 1971); Hildred Geertz and Keith Thomas, "An Anthropology of Religion and Magic," *Journal of Interdisciplinary History,* VI (1975), 71–109; Lawrence Stone, *The Family, Sex and Marriage in England, 1500–1800* (New York, 1977); Philippe Ariès, *L'Homme devant la mort* (Paris, 1977); and Michel Vovelle, *Piété baroque et déchristianisation en Provence au XVIIIe siècle: Les Attitudes devant la mort d'après les clauses des testaments* (Paris, 1973).

4. Keith Thomas, "History and Anthropology," *Past and Present,* no. 24 (1963), 3–24; E. E. Evans-Pritchard, "Anthropology and History," in E. E. Evans-Pritchard, *Essays in Social Anthropology* (London, 1962). It would be vain to list all the works in anthropology and

history where the two disciplines come together. The reader interested in pursuing the subject can consult the works of Clifford Geertz, Victor Turner, Renato Rosaldo, Shelly Errington, Louis Dumont, Marshall Sahlins, B. S. Cohn, James Fernandez, Jacques Le Goff, Emmanuel Le Roy Ladurie, Jean-Claude Schmitt, Natalie Davis, William Sewell, Lawrence Levine, Greg Dening, and Rhys Isaac, to name only a few of the most talented authors.

5. Marc Bloch, *Apologie pour l'histoire ou métier d'historien* (Paris, 1974; an edition of a text written in 1941 and 1942), p. 35.

INDEX

Aarne, Antti, 12, 16, 20, 21, 265*n*1, 266*n*7

Abrégé de l'histoire de France (Hénault), 166

Académie des dames, L' (pornographic text), 96

Académie Française, 157, 158, 164, 167, 170, 174

Académie de Musique (Montpellier), 115, 134, 138

Académie Royale des Sciences (Montpellier), 115

Académie des Sciences (Paris), 138

Accampo, Elinor, 271*n*16

Advancement of Learning, The (Bacon), 209

Aigrefeuille, Charles de, 140, 273*n*1

Aix-la-Chapelle, Peace of, 168

"Aladdin," 266*n*5

Alembert, Jean le Rond d', 170, 172, 193–209, 274*n*9, 277*n*13, 278*n*37, 279*n*47, 280*n*32; police reports on, 150, 158, 181; Rousseau's break with, 230

Alloués (underqualified printers), 80, 82

American Revolution, 39

Animals: classification of, 192–93; ontological position of, 89; torture of, as popular amusement, 89; *see also* Cats

Annales (periodical), 237

Annales: Economies, sociétés, civilisations (journal), 257

Année littéraire, L', 174, 237

Anseaume, Louis, 172

Anthropological history, 3–4, 6, 259–61

Anticlericalism, 52

Anti-Semitism, 52

Apprentices: during carnival, 83; living conditions of, 75–76, 79; razzing of, 87–88

Aquinas, Thomas, 195, 205, 206

Archiconfrérie du Saint-Sacrement, 118

Aretino, 96

Argens, marquis d', 177–78, 189

Argenson, comte d', 167, 177, 183, 188

Ariès, Philippe, 258, 259, 283*n*1

Artisans: as authors, 153–54; idealization of, by historians, 79; of Montpellier, 125–27, 130–36, 141; *see also* Printing shops

Aristotle, 193, 205, 206

Arts, Encyclopedist view of, 199

Atheism, 181–85

"At the Siege of Belle Isle," 39

Augustins, 117, 121

Aulnoy, Marie Catherine d', 11, 62

Auteur laquais, L' (Wagnon), 153

Authors, *see* Writers

About the Author

ROBERT DARNTON is Professor of History
at Princeton University and a MacArthur Prize
Fellow. His book, *The Literary Underground
of the Old Regime* was nominated for an American
Book Award in 1983.